Women Writing the West Indies, 1804–1939

This pioneering study of previously unknown or marginal West Indian writing by women, queries the accepted wisdom that women's voices were absent from the narrative record until the late twentieth century. It demonstrates that while only a few texts by non-white women have survived, an eclectic body of work by white women – expatriate, resident and creole – does exist. Surveying a sample of fascinating material from novels, stories and homilies, memoirs, letters, travel journals and autobiographies, the book focuses on who these women were, and what kind of narratives they produced. It also asks whether these can be subsumed under a single classificatory label, "West Indian women's writing," and how the narratives construct the region, for those at home and those at the centre, during a particularly important period in the formulation of West Indian and English identities.

The first section considers how early texts demonstrate multiple narrative positions, and the interdependence of black and white female roles and identities which confound simplified reductions. The central section focuses on women's construction of "the West Indies" and how the region and its people emerge in terms of disparate, even contradictory tropes. The book concludes with an overview of theoretical debates on colonial discourse, and suggests the advantages and pitfalls of several "mainstream" postcolonial approaches.

The scope and depth of this book make it essential reading for students and academics within the fields of colonial, postcolonial, feminist and Caribbean literary history.

Evelyn O'Callaghan is a senior lecturer in English at the University of the West Indies, Barbados. She recently edited an early Antiguan novel, *With Silent Tread* by Frieda Cassin (2002).

Postcolonial Literatures

Edited in collaboration with the Centre for Colonial and Postcolonial Studies, University of Kent at Canterbury.

This series aims to present a wide range of scholarly and innovative research into postcolonial literatures by specialists in the field. Volumes will concentrate on writers and writing originating in previously (or presently) colonised areas, and will include material from non-anglophone as well as anglophone colonies and literatures. The series will also include collections of important essays from older journals, and re-issues of classic texts on postcolonial subjects. Routledge is pleased to invite proposals for new books in the series. Interested authors should contact either Lyn Innes and Rod Edmond at the Centre for Colonial and Post-colonial Studies, University of Kent at Canterbury, or Joe Whiting, Commissioning Editor for Routledge Research.

The series comprises two strands:

Routledge Research in Postcolonial Literatures is a forum for innovative new research intended for a high-level specialist readership, and the titles will be available in hardback only. Titles include

1. Magical Realism in West African Fiction
Brenda Cooper, University of Cape Town

2. The Postcolonial Jane Austen
Edited by You–me Park, George Washington University and Rajeswari Sunder Rajan, University of Oxford

3. Contemporary Caribbean Women's Poetry
Making style
Denise deCaires Narain, University of Sussex

4. Animism and Politics in African Literature
Caroline Rooney, University of Kent at Canterbury

5. Caribbean–English Passages
Intertextuality in a Postcolonial tradition
Tobias Döring, Freie Universität, Berlin

6. Islands in History and Representation
Edited by Rod Edmond, University of Kent at Canterbury and Vanessa Smith, University of Sydney

7. Civility, Literature, and Culture in British India
Discipline and identity in the colonial context
Anindyo Roy, Colby College, USA

8. Women Writing the West Indies, 1804–1939
"A hot place, belonging to Us"
Evelyn O'Callaghan, University of the West Indies, Barbados

9. Postcolonial Pacific Writing
Representations of the body
Michelle Keown, University of Stirling

10. Writing Woman, Writing Place
Contemporary Australian and South African fiction
Sue Kossew, University of New South Wales

Readings in Postcolonial Literatures aims to address the needs of students and teachers, and the titles will be published in hardback and paperback. Titles include:

1. Selected Essays of Wilson Harris
Edited by Andrew Bundy

Women Writing the West Indies, 1804–1939

"A hot place, belonging to Us"

Evelyn O'Callaghan

Routledge
Taylor & Francis Group

LONDON AND NEW YORK

First published 2004
by Routledge
11 New Fetter Lane, London EC4P 4EE

Simultaneously published in the USA and Canada
by Routledge
29 West 35th Street, New York, NY 10001

Routledge is an imprint of the Taylor & Francis Group

Typeset in Baskerville by RefineCatch Limited, Bungay, Suffolk
Printed and bound in Great Britain by MPG Books Ltd, Bodmin

British Library Cataloguing in Publication Data
A catalogue record for this book is available from the British Library

Library of Congress Cataloging in Publication Data
A catalog record for this book has been requested
ISBN 0–415–28883–5

For my father Patrick, a great traveler, who *would* have been able to read this one; and for Philip, who will.

Contents

Acknowledgments

I wish to acknowledge Alan Moss of the University of the West Indies (Cave Hill) main library for his help and advice in acquiring rare material, and thanks also to library staff at the Institute of Jamaica in Kingston, the Bodleian and Rhodes House libraries in Oxford, the British Library and the Royal Commonwealth Library in London, and the Library of Congress in Washington. I am particularly grateful to colleagues at the University of the West Indies: Professor Edward Baugh, who supervised my doctoral research; Jane Bryce and Richard Clarke who were always available with advice, encouragement and helpful suggestions; Professor Hilary Beckles for arguing history; and Professor Mark McWatt for his calming influence. Denise deCaires Narain was extremely helpful in the final editing stages. I also want to thank Professor Lyn Innes for suggesting someone might actually *want* to read a book like this, and Alison Donnell, Olive Senior, Sandra Pouchet Paquet, Stephen Slemon and Helen Tiffin for feedback at various stages of the project. My debt to my family goes beyond words.

A conference paper comprising a section of Chapter 2 appears in Bruce Bennett et al. (eds.) *Resistance and Reconciliation: Writings in the Commonwealth: Essays from the Twelfth ACLALS Conference* (Canberra: ALCALS in association with the School of Language, Literature and Communication, University of New South Wales at ADFA, 2003); an earlier version of part of Chapter 3 is to be published as an essay in Glenn Hooper (ed.) *Landscape and Empire, 1800–2000* (Aldershot: Ashgate Press, forthcoming).

Quotations from *Lady Nugent's Journal* of her Residence in Jamaica from 1801–1805, are taken from the Institute of Jamaica edition (1966). *Lady Nugent's Journal* is now published by the University of West Indies Press, quotations appear here with permission.

Every effort has been made to contact the copyright holders for their permission to reprint material in this book. The publishers would be grateful to hear from any copyright holder who is not here acknowledged and will undertake to rectify any errors or omissions in future editions of this book.

Introduction

The "absence" of early West Indian writing by women

WE DON'T KNOW **WHAT** MIRANDA/Antoinette/Miss Ann IS FEEL-
ING AT ANY STAGE OF THE SLAVE/PLANTATION CONTINUUM
because Prospero never wrote about her & it is only now in the 1990s that
she's beginning to write about herself . . .

(Brathwaite 1995: 73; emphasis in original)

In the quotation above, the poet E. Kamau Brathwaite employs a telling literary
short-hand to say something about white women in the eighteenth- and nineteenth-century West Indies.[1] Firstly, he notes that they came in three familiar
models. There is Miranda, Shakespeare's beautiful, virginal symbol of desirable
English/European womanhood. Miranda is a younger version of Miss Ann,
whose respectful title evokes the plantation mistress, the pious but firm lady of the
Great House. Then there is Antoinette, the disturbed white creole of Jean Rhys's
Wide Sargasso Sea (1968) who, associated as she is with black culture, occupies a
more indeterminate space in colonial mythology. Secondly, Brathwaite claims that
their lives and experiences formed no part of the narrative record. White men did
not write them into the official discourse of colonial rule, because they had no
official part in the project; and they could not or did not write about themselves
until centuries later (the 1990s). I want to start with this apparent absence of white
women's narrative voices from West Indian literary history, and proceed by
questioning what such "silence" might in fact articulate.

This book began as a quest to establish whether any *non-white* women's writings
had survived from before the twentieth century. I found only a handful. The
generally agreed chronological line begins with the short histories of Methodism
by (free colored) Elizabeth Hart Thwaites and Anne Hart Gilbert (first circulated
1804),[2] continues with Mary Prince's slave narrative (1831)[3] and ends with (free
colored) Mary Seacole's autobiographical *Wonderful Adventures* (first published
1857).[4] There is then a gap of some seventy years until 1931, when the Jamaican
Una Marson published a short story called "Sojourn" in *The Cosmopolitan*, a
magazine she edited.[5] Why so few? This rate of publication must be seen in the
context of a history of colonial deprivation which decreed very limited access of

women generally, and non-white women in particular, to education and even to basic literacy. During slavery, white men took some measure of responsibility for their mixed-race progeny and, especially in Jamaica and St Kitts, provided them with private primary schooling and occasionally sent them abroad for further studies; but the vast majority of such cases were free colored boys.[6] There is evidence of a few educated free blacks, again mostly male.[7] And missionaries (particularly the Moravians, Presbyterians and Baptists) tirelessly canvassed planters to allow slaves access to instruction.

Generally speaking, however, educational opportunities for most slaves in the British West Indian colonies was negligible. However well intentioned the missionaries, limited finances, lack of buildings and qualified teachers, and the limited time given slaves for attendance, mitigated against their efforts. An inventory of those in a position to write *any* kind of document in the pre-emancipation period and for some time afterwards, would include most elite white, some poor white, several free colored and a few black males. There *were* some literate black women in the Anglophone Caribbean during the slavery period,[8] largely thanks to missionary education, and it is significant that the texts of the Hart sisters and Mary Prince are produced in collaboration with liberal metropolitan missionary institutions. But in 1857, Bishop Mitchinson reported that there was hardly any provision made for the education of girls in Barbados,[9] and the ratio of girls' schools to boys' schools as well as of female to male "scholars" enrolled in mixed schools in the island in 1850, indicates woefully inadequate educational opportunities for young women.

And even if the few educated non-white women harbored literary aspirations, all outlets were controlled by the British authorities and catered to the "English" tastes cultivated by the plantocracy. There *were* several periodicals, literary magazines and newspapers in the West Indies in the nineteenth century, and embryonic local publishing facilities, but access to these was extremely restricted. Indeed, in 1821 a white schoolmistress, Eliza Fenwick, wrote from Barbados bemoaning the fact that there was no circulating library in the island and that while there were a few book societies, "One, called the Literary Association, refuse all members till their number is reduced; & the other I was deter'd from offering myself to being told one of their earliest rules was an exclusion of all *School Keepers*" (1927: 216; emphasis in original). The 1864 *Catalogue of Books* of the Colonial Literary and Reading Society in Jamaica advertised an entry fee of ten shillings and sixpence, with an annual subscription of thirty shillings, an impossible sum for the vast majority. Like the early twentieth-century literary and debating societies in the island, the focus was entirely on traditional British literature and catered to "genteel" and leisured readers.[10]

But while the records show few texts by non-white women during the nineteenth and early twentieth centuries, this does not mean that there was *no* women's writing from the West Indies. Far from it. Brenda Berrian's *Bibliography of Women Writers from the Caribbean* (1989) cites Prince and Seacole, and goes on to list texts by white women: Pamela Smith's collection of folklore (1899), Mary Lockett's novel *Christopher* (1902), and Clarine Stephenson's poem (in the 1909 edition of the *Jamaican Times*) and novel *Undine* (1911). Digging deeper, I encountered even earlier texts, and I have no doubt this study outlines only the tip of the iceberg. So how has the claim that West Indian writing by women is a late twentieth-century phenomenon (as articulated by Brathwaite) become an orthodoxy? For instance, Erika Smilowitz (1984: 19) claims that apart from Lady Nugent's journal and a few abolitionist novels written about the region by English women in the eighteenth century, "the West Indies have . . . been a remarkably barren region as far as women writers are concerned." What I want to concentrate on here is the anomaly of supposed "barrenness" alongside the existence of scores of early texts.

Later critical studies have tended to reinforce this impression of a void. Carole Boyce Davies and Elaine Savory Fido, for example, introduce their important collection of essays on *Caribbean Women and Literature* (1990: 1) with this statement: "[t]he concept of voicelessness necessarily informs any discussion of Caribbean women and literature." By voicelessness they

> mean the historical absence of the woman writer's text; the absence of a specifically female position on major issues such as slavery, colonialism, decolonization, women's rights and more direct social and cultural issues. By voicelessness we also mean silence: the inability to express a position in the language of the "master" as well as the textual construction of the woman as silent.
>
> (ibid.)

Like Smilowitz, the assumption here is that "the woman writer's text" is missing. Boyce Davies and Savory Fido do acknowledge that "[t]here has been a long history of women writing in the Caribbean" (1990: 2), referring to Francophone texts which "appeared before the end of the nineteenth century, perhaps even earlier" (Wilson 1987: v). Further, they point to Marjorie Engber's bibliography[11] as containing references to "many unknown women writers" (Boyce Davies and Savory Fido 1990: 2) but nothing more is said about these "unknowns." So despite the apparently "barren" terrain, quite a few (unknown) women *were* indeed writing in the Caribbean from at least the nineteenth century. What this suggests, perhaps, is a matter of distinction between Caribbean women writers and women writing in/about the region, with critical ears attuned to some voices but deaf to others; after all, as Davies and Fido assert, voicelessness "also denotes articulation that goes unheard." And even among Caribbean women writers, there have been periods when some have been excised from the literary record; for example, Campbell (1982) asks why the eminent critic Sylvia Wynter names Ada Quayle as the first West Indian woman novelist, to the exclusion of Elma Napier, Jean Rhys and Phyllis Shand Allfrey, all of whom produced novels much earlier?[12]

Critical selectivity with regard to women's writing is not, of course, peculiar to the Caribbean. As feminist scholarship has demonstrated, female-authored texts are generally not so much missing from national archives, as ignored. "The majority of eighteenth-century novels were actually written by women," Ian Watt observes dryly, "but this had long remained a purely quantitative assertion of dominance" (1977: 339). Until recently, the existence of hundreds of writers and thousands of texts was simply forgotten. Introducing *The Feminist Companion to Literature in English*, Blain et al. (1990) detail the difficulties they faced in accessing early women's writing in English, writing which has been "un- and under-represented in our literary culture" (vii) and, until very recently, generally treated with critical condescension. Determining the "absence" (or not) of early women's writing then, involves asking who are the arbiters of value at a particular time, and what ethnocentric or gendered discourses inform their judgements. Are women's novels devalued because of their "female" concerns (the home) and features (sentimental)? Are their writings excluded because of the low status of the literary vehicle they choose (the journal, for example, or the travel narrative)? Can poor literary quality be overlooked if a narrative addresses certain kinds of matter, or brings new perspectives to bear on it? How does an author's class, race and nationality impact on the reception of her work? Are early narratives now devalued because of their assumed political (retrogressive) stances, or indeed because they are badly written by our standards? Are they now valorized because of their apparently coded *progressive* stance, even if they are at the same time of dubious literary merit by our standards?

Donnell (1998: 2–3) considers that the ideological underpinnings of West Indian canon-formation in the 1970s promoted readings of earlier texts "as being in harmony with, as shaping and being shaped by a developmental history of decolonisation and emergent nationalism." This teleology, she argues, is evident in the selective attention paid to a certain core of authors:

> The canonical pathway forged by these repeated names encourages us to witness the fading allegiance to colonial culture in the works of H.G. DeLisser and Thomas MacDermot and to locate the early voices of a nationalist tradition in those of CLR James and Claude McKay. Together then these nominated few navigate a fairly smooth, if highly selective and all-male, crossing from colony to nation – a crossing in which literature and history make a happy couple . . . the exclusion or selection of pre-1950 writers becomes a means by which to side-step works which were, and perhaps remain, out of step with the prevailing politics of reading, a way to ignore those texts which never made the crossing successfully.

Let us consider this notion of the "prevailing politics of reading" in relation to what is meant by a "woman writer's text" in the West Indies. What exactly qualifies? A sample of critical studies since the 1990s suggests that race is the determining factor: that is, the West Indian woman writer's text is one written by/ about black women. So Selwyn Cudjoe introduces *Caribbean Women Writers* (1990) with an implicit understanding that such writers, with few exceptions, are non-white if not black. Cudjoe's overview attempts to identify a *tradition* of women's writing from the West Indies, and his is the usual trajectory from Prince and

Seacole, through a void when it seems nothing was written by women until well into the twentieth century. Again, "there appears to be a significant gap in the recorded novelistic writings of Caribbean women after the later half of the nineteenth and the early part of the twentieth centuries"(15). Yet the texts I have identified are virtually all published in the very period Cudjoe defines as a "gap," so presumably none are by "Caribbean women." More recently, Kathleen Renk (1999: 12) differentiates between "postindependence" and "earlier colonialist and nationalist writers," although acknowledging that the later group "were also assisted by the work of many earlier women writers, for example, Mary Seacole, Pamela Smith, Henrietta Jenkin, Sylvia Wynter and Merle Hodge." This lumping together of women who wrote between 1857 and 1970 is unhelpful, and there is no attempt to specify *how* the nineteenth century authors "assisted" the late twentieth-century practitioners; in fact, of the list above only Hodge's text appears in Renk's chapter notes or bibliography. Given that the book's focus is "specific textual and discursive connections between contemporary Anglophone Caribbean women's narratives and Victorian literature" (1999: 2), it is odd that the earlier writers merit so little attention.

Isabel Hoving's examination of Caribbean migrant women's writing (2001: 2–3) reiterates that Caribbean women's writing begins in the 1970s, although acknowledging earlier "silenced" voices such as Prince's slave narrative; after this "slow and sparse beginning" the literary terrain is once again painted as barren until the writing "finds a clear, exhilarating direction in the 1930s" with the dawning of an "Afrocentric focus" (4). Aligning her historical overview with Cudjoe's, she clearly perceives "a female literary tradition" in the Caribbean, which appears to be a black working-class tradition: "[f]or women have been writing, just as they were – at least as much as the men – part of the degrading slave labor, the struggles against oppression, and the struggles for independence" (3). Another study, this time devoted to contemporary Caribbean women's poetry, explains that "[t]here *was* a considerable body of writing generated within the West Indies . . . but this writing was generally dismissed as *not truly West Indian*, partly because many of these writers were English, but also because of the unquestioning mimicry of colonial forms and the inscription of colonial ideology which characterized this writing" (deCaries Narain 2002: 4; emphasis in original). Her close study of the early twentieth-century poetry of Allfrey[13] (white Dominican) and Marson (black Jamaican) queries the so-called "belatedness of Caribbean women's 'arrival' on the literary scene" (vii), in an attempt to "extend the notion of who qualifies as a literary precursor and to interrogate the grounds upon which such categories are constructed" (1). Although several critics do allude, if vaguely, to earlier texts (by women like Smith, Jenkin, Allfrey) few discuss them, and there are clearly divergent views of the history of women's writing in the region. Did Anglophone writers begin to publish at the turn of the twentieth century, in the 1930s, or the 1970s?

There are also divergent views about what constitutes a West Indian woman writer. The tendency for anthologies and critical studies of Caribbean women's writing to feature cover illustrations of exclusively black women, and more specifically black working-class women, sets up an expectation with regard to the writing itself (deCaires Narain and O'Callaghan 1994: 625). These may be governed by marketing strategies which inevitably reflect publishers' preconceptions about race and class in the Caribbean, or indeed by simple demographics. But are these sufficient grounds for maintaining simplistic binary oppositions regarding the "authenticity" of any one group of writers? Certainly, the early white women writers, by virtue of their race and the status this generally conferred, represent an "outsider's" perspective on the black majority, and the voices of non-whites are often silenced in their accounts. However, this is not to argue for a simplistic equation of West Indian with "non-white." And yet this does seem to be the implicit view. For instance, Ramchand's pioneering study of the West Indian novel (1972: 225) includes narratives by white creoles, seeing their texts as "socially relevant" in the articulation of the "terrified consciousness" of elites in the decolonizing process. Given the "demanding context of Black nationalism," he acknowledged this inclusion to be unpopular: in the 1950s and 1960s, West Indian critics were naturally concerned with redressing the balance of centuries of colonial exploitation and racism, and with the promotion of the voice of the oppressed. Ramchand (1988: 95) seems to have been persuaded by this view, as he subsequently argues that West Indian literature is a twentieth-century phenomenon and, as for the earlier body of narratives, when it:

> was not the production of planters and planter-types, government officials, visitors, missionaries and other birds of passage writing from alien perspectives, it was the writing of a small group or class either pursuing its own narrow interests or committed to the idea of Europe as home and center.

Similar thinking informs the downplaying of critical studies of colonial discourse[14] on the grounds that deconstructing imperial representations is at the expense of the real work of privileging counter-discursive "native" productions (Brydon and Tiffin 1993: 26). Gareth Griffiths (1987: 13) dismisses such "first texts produced in a postcolonial society" as the proper subject of theoretical investigation: they represent only "the viewpoint of the colonizing centre" because the writers – "gentrified settlers, administrators . . . travelers, sightseers" – appear "to have been born hand in hand with the Imperial enterprise."[15]

   Neither Ramchand nor Griffiths disqualify these narratives because of the race of their authors, but because of their colonialist vision. But for another (vitally important) theorist of Caribbean literature, Edward Kamau Brathwaite, race has been the crucial factor in the debate. "There are of course, 'white people' in the West Indies," he admits (1963: 16), "but these are regarded either as too far apart to count or too inextricably mixed into the whole problem to be considered as separate." While noting changes over time in Brathwaite's prolific critical output, Edward Baugh (1981: 113) concedes that he has fairly consistently posited "the folk" or "the broadly ex-African base" as the matrix of Caribbean culture.[16] Logically, then, white writers (those who have been "inextricably mixed" are presumably no longer a separate entity) are thus peripheral to a West Indian literary tradition. This does appear to be the conclusion of Brathwaite's treatise on the integration of other groups into the Afro-Caribbean "norm and model":

> White creoles in the English and French West Indies have separated themselves by too wide a gulf, and have contributed too little culturally, as a *group*, to give credence to the notion that they can, given the present structure, meaningfully identify or be identified with the spiritual world on this side of the Sargasso Sea.
> (Brathwaite 1974: 38; emphasis in original)

One can debate what changes have taken place in "the present structure" since the 1970s to account for the recent literary production of "white" West Indian writers like Robert Antoni, Michelle Cliff, Lawrence Scott, Anthony Winkler and Jane King-Hippolyte, or indeed to ask whether such writers constitute "a *group*," but the focus on race as a criterion for inclusion in West Indian literature now seems to be in need of revision.[17] With reference to the earlier writers, Brathwaite's argument as I understand it is that the historical and ideological nature of colonialism raised insurmountable barriers between white West Indians (writers included) and the racial and cultural mainstream, so that the texts of the former could not constitute a truthful "recognition of the realities of the situation": white writers' texts, in other words, were irrelevant to the experience and perceptions of the non-white majority.

Implicit in this argument is a transparent model of the literary text, as well as the notion that white writers can only write about "white experience" of the region which is irrelevant to "black experience." More recently Brathwaite (1995) revisits the discussion and contextualizes his earlier assertions.[18] Yet his essay seems to end up reiterating a racially based concept of "relevance," a position increasingly interrogated by contemporary (black and white) critics and theorists. At a certain period in the consolidation of a nascent literary tradition and national identity, such a strategy may have been politically necessary; now, I suggest, we must take account of such developments as the interrogation of nationalism and the ideological overdetermination of fictive texts which it imposed. More subtle and flexible critical responses are required in the context of West Indian literature which has come of age and no longer needs to buttress identity by rigidly suppressing diversity. Indeed, there are now so many "kinds" of West Indians (and West Indian writing), both within and outside the region, that it is timely to revise and rework such a limited definition. More productively, we might embrace Brathwaite's spirit of inclusiveness, as discussed in his theory of creolization as *creative* as well as imitative acculturation. It is Brathwaite, after all, who opposes the view of Caribbean culture as a static plural entity in favor of a vision of productive friction. In art, he feels, the goal is a "meaningful federation of cultures." "[T]here will be no 'one West Indian voice' in West Indian literature," he concludes, "because there *is* no 'one West Indian voice'" (1969: 270; emphasis in original). West Indian societies have, since the beginning, been (uneasily) composed of several races and presumably any definition of the literary culture of such societies will have to take this into account.[19]

The "transparent text" model also underlies the assumption that once the woman writer's text makes it into print, we can access "a specifically female position." But consider the case of Mary Prince's narrative, for example, hailed as the first instance of the West Indian woman's voice. Prince's *History* presents itself as an autobiographical "slave narrative"; but her account, as noted, has been through two sets of mediation by the time it appears in print. Prince's narrative is dictated, her editor Thomas Pringle tells us, to "a lady who happened to be at the time residing in my family as a visitor" (1987: 185) and is further "pruned" by himself, "to exclude redundances and gross grammatical errors, so as to render it clearly intelligible." Of course all texts undergo editorial shaping, and the very nature of the slave narrative as a genre with its own internal rules as to structure and content suggests a significant ordering and selection process which renders the term "autobiography" – that is, self-authored – somewhat problematic in the case of Prince's *History*. Hence Ferguson, editing the text much later, speculates as to the involvement of Pringle and the amanuensis in the articulation of Prince's life, and the "contending agendas of such a multi-tiered narrative" (1992: 282–3). Like Ferguson, Patricia Morton (1996: 17) points out that abolitionists, male and female, considered it necessary to portray "slave women as either helpless victims of white male sexual lust and/or as paragons of female sexual virtue." How much, then, is the "Mary Prince" encountered in the text a construct of Pringle and his avowedly abolitionist circle? And as Gillian Whitlock points out, if Pringle "desired Prince to speak as an authentic subject for abolitionist rhetoric, so Ferguson in her edition desires to … exhume the independent, authentic subject pursued by late twentieth-century feminism" (2000: 32). Do such considerations not to some extent compromise readings which unproblematically render her voice as representative of black West Indian womanhood? In fact, as Whitlock asks (33), how useful are terms like self and author, authenticity and experience for an understanding of "the negotiations which took place around this hybrid text"?

My intention is to suggest a more flexible critical framework – *not* a new set of definitive parameters – for conceptualizing West Indian women's writing. It appears that the compulsion to categorize in an overly restricted schema contributes to the invisibility, the "absence," the "voicelessness," of many of the early narratives. There is a need to question models of literary history which insist on rigid periodization, estimate texts according to their conformity with a "colonialist" or "black nationalist" focus, or impose prescriptive notions of "the" Caribbean woman's voice. This study offers no convenient grid for placing over an eclectic body of writing; rather, it offers an introductory survey of unknown or little-known works, and suggests some of the multiple possible readings of these gendered accounts of a vanished world.

The early narratives: problems of "categorization"

I begin my survey in 1804, the year of the Hart sisters' "Histories." It is also the year before *Lady Nugent's Journal* was completed (it was subsequently printed for private circulation in 1839, and only published in 1907). I end with Alice Durie's *One Brown Gal* in 1939,[20] the year World War II began. This, I feel, is a fitting cut-off point for an overview of early narratives as it marks the period of consolidation of anti-colonial, pro-independence agitation in the West Indies out of which was born "modern" West Indian literature as we currently conceive of it.[21] Where relevant to particular themes or issues, I do mention slightly later texts, particularly those set during the period in question. The corpus of writing discussed in this study is largely the production of elite or middle-class white women born or resident in the West Indies which, in light of some of the critical assumptions raised above, makes it difficult to assign the blanket term "West Indian women's texts." In addition, the works are so utterly diverse – in terms of genre – as to defy categorization. Again, in terms of "quality," they vary from frankly educational, barely concealed efforts to sketch the West Indies for a foreign readership, to fine evocations of place and people that still resonate for contemporary West Indian readers. In terms of ideology, many are offensively racist and colonialist; others are sensitive to cultural and racial difference; some can be considered proto-feminist, while many reinforce patriarchal constructs. Within this group of narratives, linked here by their West Indian subject matter, one can identify subsets. Some, according to Brereton (1993: 2–3), are by British women "resident in, or visiting, the Caribbean, with family and social connections to the islands' white elite"; others – by Mary Prince, Mary Seacole and Yseult Bridges – are by "Caribbean women, representing the range of ethnic and class diversity found in the nineteenth century Caribbean." Both these groups, residents and creoles, are distinguished from women who were "simply tourists."

I want to stress from the outset the exploratory nature of my project: the diversity of the writers, and of their generic choices, literary craftsmanship and ideological orientations, makes difficult any totalizing statements about the works "as a group." Similarly, the writing does not fit easily within existing paradigms of West Indian literary development such as those sketched by Brathwaite (1978: 185):

> [W]e must recognize that our literature began on the slave plantation with imitation Euro-writing by Europeans and white creoles on the one hand, and the often unremembered sound-poems, stories and religious litanies of the slaves on the other; that after slavery (c.1838–1938) we entered into a slough of colonial despond when very little creative work was produced among the literate and the existent folk culture was attacked/submerged . . . The anti-colonial consciousness of the period from 1900 produced our first authentic novels.

What I do want to argue is that attention to the early accounts by women adds to the body of literary representations of the region in unforeseen and illuminating ways. These narratives form part of the feminist and postcolonial projects of recuperating lost or silenced voices, and comparing their insights and formal strategies with later writing by women of the region, may help to deflect us from categorizing Caribbean women's writing in a narrowly prescriptive manner.

Accordingly, the term I have chosen to describe the selection of texts examined here, "narratives of the West Indies by women," is imposed by the material's resistance to neat authorial or generic categories. The texts themselves include a wide spectrum of narratives: novels of all kinds, travelogues, letters, memoirs, journals, autobiographies, stories, collections of folklore, educational or moral sketches, and so on. Many texts also permeate boundaries between these narrative "types." For instance, Percy Adams acknowledges the distinction between "novel" and "travel account" while noting similarities – particularly in texts from the early period – in language, tone, philosophy, "even to literary conventions and motives for composition" (1983: 278). Autobiographical theory also points up the slippery nature of the form as a literary creation of self. Journals and collections of letters, generally considered intimate and autobiographical, are severely self-censored when written for publication: this is clear in the comparison of the journals of Nugent and Carmichael. Which, if either, is really "autobiographical"? And how is one to refer to *The Youthful Female Missionary* (1839), representing itself as a "memoir" of Mary Ann Hutchins by her father, yet compiled almost entirely of her correspondence with him? If Mary Prince's voice is mediated by other (not entirely acknowledged) voices, Hutchins's memoir, which advertises the shaping hand of her father, consists almost entirely of her *own* articulation. Then there is Ethel Maud Symmonett's *Jamaica: Queen of the Carib Sea* (1895), ostensibly a novel but reading like a promotional "tour guide" of the island. Textual motivation is also relevant: given that Mrs Tonna's novel *The System* (1827), Hutchins's memoir and Mary Prince's autobiography are primarily contributions to the anti-slavery cause, while Carmichael's *Domestic Manners* (published in 1833) is a pro-planter defense of the institution, should the ideological/political concerns of a text (rather than the genre) be the chief factor in classifying it?

Various types of "narrative" are yoked into service as educational socio-histories, anti-slavery propaganda, or promotional tourist guides. Novels seem thinly disguised autobiographies or regional histories; "autobiographies" are so sensational as to appear fictions; collections of letters are structured like stories; political histories masquerade as travelogues; so-called fictions are vehicles for cataloguing native folklore and "superstitions." The texts elude categorization and call into question the usefulness of traditional generic boundaries in approaching the material.[22] It is, perhaps, possible to argue that this generic instability reflects women writers' struggle to situate themselves within discourses from which, in the nineteenth century, they were to some extent excluded. For example, to adopt a position *as a woman* within imperial discourse was fraught with difficulties,[23] as was presuming to contribute to "West Indian letters" within a male-dominated literary tradition. The writers in question, by virtue of their gender, would find it difficult to claim a hard and fast site within any one discursive or generic vehicle.

The need to problematize categories applies also to the writers themselves. As noted, some can be termed "West Indian natives" while others plainly cannot, while in the case of long-term residents, rigid criteria of nationality are unhelpful.

Ideally, I would have liked to limit my scope to the work of creole women writers – those born in the region. But the ambiguities of this approach become apparent when considering for example, Lucy Lane Clifford (*c.* 1855–1929). Granddaughter of Branford Lane, one-time speaker in the Barbados House of Assembly (Blain et al. 1990: 216) and daughter of John Lane, a well-known West Indian planter (according to Schlueter 1988), she was a prolific writer with at least fifteen novels, several plays and story collections to her credit. An innovative and exciting writer too, with progressive feminist views on marriage, who blends the macabre with the mundane in many of her stories. But – from my survey – there is nothing about the West Indies in her work. No evidence of influence by West Indian culture, language or landscape. No mention of race or colonialism. One can speculate whether such deliberate evasion/submergence of local material in literary efforts was perhaps a facet of white creole/planter culture at the time, while expatriate writers felt freer to employ "the exotic" local in their endeavors. Such speculation is complicated further, however, by considering other contemporary creole writers who did incorporate, even privilege the local in their work. Lady Mary Anne Barker[24] for example, Jamaican-born daughter of W.G. Stewart, Colonial Secretary of the island, was like Clifford packed off to England at an early age and lived abroad thereafter; but *Stories About:-* (Barker 1873) does evoke a Jamaican childhood and in her writing about the colonies "she describes with sympathy the position of women settlers and servants"(Blain et al. 1990: 61). While it is important not to conflate white creoles with native Englishwomen, nor to gloss over crucial points of differentiation in their ideologies of "home," it is nevertheless futile to expect an invariantly distinctive "West Indian voice" or perspective.

In any case, the example of Clifford contrasts markedly with that of Mrs Augusta Zelia Fraser ("Alice Spinner"), an Englishwoman who accompanied her husband to Jamaica in 1892. Her residence there informs her two keenly observed novelistic representations (of race and gender as well as the creole consciousness) which are plainly relevant here. Most of the creole writers, often the product of English schooling and very much influenced by imperial ideology, are "West Indian" in a very different sense than is currently understood; the West Indies existed very much as a part of a broader entity, the British Empire. None the less, their engagement with island society and landscape reflect a sense, however ambivalent, of attachment to the region. Therefore, I have included both native women writers and expatriates (who resided in the region for a time) as well as a few professional writers who simply visited the West Indies to gather "material" (Gertrude Atherton, for example). I also mention others for whom the Caribbean was an important trope and focus in their texts. What links these narratives together, then, is "the West Indies" in their works.

Of course the region had long been intimately "known" in Europe and North America through a corpus of traveler's tales, histories and anti-slavery texts. Carlyle, James Anthony Froude, Trollope: all these authoritative and supposedly "eye witness" commentators need to be read with an awareness "that the invention of the Caribbean as a European enterprise required little knowledge of the region and, in fact, depended upon a willed ignorance, an always already constructed narrative of the Other within and by metropolitan discourses" (Gregg 1995: 11). Given the wealth of books, reports, surveys of and treatises on the region, an Englishwoman who wished to compose a pious abolitionist tale without leaving home might draw on the likes of Lucy Townsend's *Scrapbook on Negro Slaves* (1825) which includes colonial documents, pamphlets, newspaper clippings from the *Jamaica Royal Gazette* and much else.[25] Certainly, several narratives draw extensively on earlier "histories" of the West Indies; such intertextuality can be observed in the writing of Winifred James, Minna Caroline Smith and Ella Wheeler Wilcox, all of whom acknowledge Nugent's journal. One can argue that these narratives overlay one set of observations on an earlier set, enriching the fiction of imperial history. Again, what links the writers under discussion here is less their geographical provenance than an investigation into the ways they inserted themselves, as female subjects, into the "text" of the West Indies.

The "West Indies" as trope

My first two chapters deal with textual aspects of white women's lives during the period, and the last two suggest some ways of reading texts by/about white women; in the two central chapters my focus is mainly on the actual term – the "West Indies" – and on how that trope functions in a variety of nineteenth- and early twentieth-century female-authored texts. Certainly, several texts share in colonial constructions of "the West Indies" simply as periphery, but in specific ways their focus differs from that of the master(s) narrative. Marginal within the contemporary power structures, women wrote themselves in the texts, and in that they recuperated themselves as subjects, their narratives offer new perspectives on the colonial enterprise and indeed, revealing choices of genre and form. I want to highlight, then, how gender informs what – and how – the stories tell us about the West Indies.[26]

For example, it is apparent from the number of texts written and published that women writers in the nineteenth century desired a West Indian topos – but why? Perhaps this had to do with money.[27] After all, the West Indies was where the money came from, where fortunes were made; hence the fascination with how exactly it was produced, especially in an economic system that women might see as an alternative to that which constrained them in the Mother Country. The plantation system in particular suggested a self-contained, almost domestic arrangement with which women might identify. And it produced commodities women were familiar with on a day-to-day basis, such as tea and sugar. Certainly in Jane Austen's *Northanger Abbey*, it is implicit that the characters live on money coming from a "space outside" and from the labor of natives, much as British capitalism depended on the work of women in/at home. This shadowy space outside becomes a site of possibility (and danger) outside orthodox European rules and mores,[28] and I want to explore this ambivalent construction in specific texts.

Again, given the disparate proportion of marriageable women to available men in the mid-Victorian period, prospects were bleak for women who could not achieve the ideal of marriage and family. The "problem" of the unmarried woman[29] without the support of a husband was epitomized in the figure of the governess, who "constituted the border between the normative (working) man and the normative (non-working) woman" (Poovey 1988: 14). Middle-class and educated, yet in a low-status and poorly paid job, she was part of a family yet lacked its compensations and walked a thin line between respectability and the fate of the "fallen woman." So in story after story among the early narratives, the West Indies is conceived of as a place of escape and potential fulfilment, where the governess/teacher who escapes her dilemma in England seeks love and security.

"The West Indies" reveals itself in the texts as a shifting ground of projections and representations. In a similar manner, this study intends the defamiliarization of "the mistress," a subject position unproblematically associated in West Indian literature with the white woman. My intention is to investigate the *variety* of subject positions represented, and of the complex power relations described. Catherine Hall (1993) has charged that history as a discipline has tended to maintain an unproblematized notion of white identity within discussions of empire. Given that the textual construction of the colonized is inseparably bound up with that of the colonizer, and that as far as the female colonizer is concerned, the term itself is problematic – Robin Visel, for instance, posits (1988: 39) that "the white settler woman can best be described as half-colonized" – I want to read the early texts, like Hall, for a more nuanced understanding of race and ethnicity in reconstructing white men and women of the past. As Hall intends it, such an approach may lead to imagining white and black identities which are not necessarily rooted in a sense of imperial power and superiority.

In the absence of a definitive literary map on which to conveniently place this body of writing/writers, I offer instead a survey within a theoretical framework (discussed below), of gendered textual constructions of the place and its people; further research can usefully augment this study by comparisons with male-authored accounts. I have tried to attend to constraints imposed by the historical context: what questions could be asked at the time? What issues could be raised? Women who entered the public forum in/through narratives in the nineteenth century operated of necessity within a context of debate and discussion on such issues as slavery, marriage, women's rights, viable economic systems and the like. Thus the debates of the period made possible both the questions women posed in their texts and how the writers could represent themselves. An obvious, but sometimes overlooked point to be borne in mind when reading early works is that, as Jane Haggis observes, "no European writer, however critical of the status quo, could avoid, at that time, expressing a hierarchy which positioned themselves 'above' . . . those others 'below' . . . It was the discourse providing the culturally available means of ordering and representing their thought" (1998: 63). Acknowledging this limitation, I focus on the most common motifs that emerge in these early depictions of the West Indies, querying why these might have been important to writers and readers then, as well as now. After about 1865, the writing offers a somewhat more recognizable picture of the West Indies as we currently conceive it through historical sources; prior to this, the images in many texts tend to belong to the terrain of the romance. But even in the early twentieth century, it is clear that white writers were unable to transcend certain stereotypical representations of the territory. However, it is precisely in the illumination of such ambivalent, even contradictory representations of the West Indies and West Indian subjects, that the value of this work resides. My strategy, then, is to try to push back the boundaries of what constitutes West Indian literary history and to move beyond limited readings of what "they" said about "us."

Theoretical considerations

If the texts defy easy classification, it is counterproductive to employ theoretical approaches which limit themselves to categorical boundaries and tend to homogenization in the interest of certain ideological or formal constraints. As the texts themselves often resist neat labels, so too should readings. Nevertheless, as noted, I envisage this study as contributing in part to the postcolonial/feminist project of "recuperating lost and silenced voices" and analyzing the role of these voices in the construction of the West Indies from a woman-authored perspective.

With a few exceptions, such works have been considered unrewarding subjects for nationalist, postcolonial and, sometimes, feminist enquiry. None the less certain feminist concerns which also seem to me to be crucial to the postcolonial project, inform my reading: the rejection of essentializing generalizations and of fixed and transparent notions of the "self"; the importance of historicizing; the refusal to valorize marginality as, for example, a celebration of victimhood; and the need to recognize shifting – thus often relative – power positions. Differences and contradictions of all kinds proliferate in these narratives. Rather than see this as daunting, I look for a model to the specifically creole nature of Caribbean society, its plurality and syncretism which constantly undermine the monolithic in all forms of cultural production. Thus, in reading these female-authored texts as voicing a *range* of variant female "versions" on socio-historical experience in the region, such texts are not read merely as "other" to those of the male colonial elite or to those of contemporary black women's writing. "Difference" is not interpreted here to reduce works to a literature of opposition – whether by inverting patriarchal devaluations of the feminine or nationalistic devaluations of "irrelevant" elite scribbling – in order to "redress the balance." The interaction of the multiple filaments of class, race and cultural difference, as well as gender difference, is a primary focus in my investigation, as is a close attention to the contested sites of power that underlie such interaction.

Accordingly, I attend to "the primacy of relations of oppression for understanding the conditions of literary and critical production" (Brydon and Tiffin 1993: 24) and try to sketch in the relevant socio-historical factors affecting subject constitution within this discourse. As Midgely observes (1998: 7), most studies of white Western women and imperialism focus on India and Africa between the 1860s and the 1940s, from the "high imperialism" characterized by the British Raj and the "scramble for Africa" to the dawn of decolonization. Haggis (1998) reminds us of the difficulties of analyzing colonial narratives by white women, without falling prey to the temptation either to romanticize such women as feminist heroines in order to have them conform to current ideals (47), or to recuperate them as victims of the male colonizing adventure, thus excluding them from complicity and positioning them in the interstices of the masculine project, to forge a different, more benevolent relationship with native "sisters" (48). While my focus covers the period, it deals with a different territory; and while I attempt to "recuperate" the texts of white colonial women, my purpose is not to demonstrate their contribution to Empire or to debunk myths about their racial prejudices, but to examine how their work constructs the West Indies and how they insert themselves into their own accounts.

Finally, one can ask in what ways did the colonial space, a *male* space as popularly conceived in the eighteenth and nineteenth centuries, enable women to step, in some measure, into a man's shoes, and at what cost? Once more, the notion of "female identity" in the colony, the outside space, is evasive. To some extent contemporary West Indian women writers are still negotiating this space as they too seek to write the West Indies from their own angle, and to alert a largely foreign market to the fact that the region is not limited to the literary constructs of Lamming and Naipaul, Brathwaite and Walcott. Now, as then, the "imperial center" is both market for and itself partly the subject of (and thus to some extent, defined by) representations of the West Indies. Therefore I conclude this study by suggesting some possible links between the earlier narratives and more recent writing by regional women.

A note on research pitfalls

While I found this research a valuable source of insight into the construction of a vanished West Indies that yet endures in the historical and popular imagination, accessing primary sources was a long and often tedious process, and it would be ungenerous not to point out to interested readers some of the difficulties and false leads that I have encountered. My naive assumption that early writing from the West Indies would be held in regional archives (and my own situation here) led to an exhaustive search in the West India Reference Library at the Institute of Jamaica, the Barbados Archives and the West Indian Collections in the libraries of the University of the West Indies. While there were positive results, some collections, like the West India Reference Library, were catalogued in a manner that led to many dead ends. Under "Women Writers, Jamaica," for example, were included such tangential material as short stories by women serialized in British publications which were reprinted in Jamaican papers and periodicals.[30] Further, consultation of databases, such as those of the Library of Congress and the Online Computer Library Center in the United States, confirmed that virtually all the relevant texts were published in England. To actually access the literature entailed extensive hands-on research at the (copyright holding) British Library in London and the Bodleian Library at Oxford, as well as the library of the Royal Commonwealth Society in London and the Rhodes House Library in Oxford. Such research was slowed by the fragmented nature of collections, archaic cataloguing, missing texts (several works listed in the British Library were irreparably damaged in World War II), and the fragility of those from the earlier period which had survived.

When Farquhar (1981) recounts the lucky discovery of a late nineteenth-century Antiguan text in a dustbin outside the island's public library; and deCaires Narain notes that her investigation of early West Indian poetry by women was similarly hampered by the lack of preservation (1995: 26); when the sole copy of Lockett's *Christopher* which I was able to locate, in the Library of Congress in Washington, was "too fragile" to be copied or reproduced and the pages were visibly disintegrating in my hands, one has to make an urgent case for proper archival attention to this vanishing corpus of texts. Technological innovations have ensured some texts will be reproduced and survive – I read Nancy Prince's *Narrative* (1850) on microfilm, but it is now available in print – but many other "silenced" voices will, unfortunately, become quite literally so. If this study helps to make the case for conservation of such a valuable resource, I will consider the effort worthwhile.

1 Defamiliarizing "the mistress"

Representations of white women in the West Indies

Finding "the" white woman

If the early women's narratives are a diverse lot, the same can be said of white women in the West Indies of the period. This chapter attempts a rapid trawl through historical and literary sources – always admitting the slippage between these – in order to outline what features are generally attributed to this group of women. Naturally, no claim is being made for the correspondence of representations with the actuality of lived experience but, in the absence of other witnesses, it is to these records that we must turn. Which records, though? Many are inconsistent and unreliable, and so of limited use in constructing an identity profile of the white colonial woman in the nineteenth century. Historians themselves admit this. For example,

> In seeking to probe the gender dimension in the history of the Caribbean since European contact, . . . Whether we rely on official records of different kinds, newspapers and periodicals, correspondence and other materials produced by private citizens, missionaries or travelers, or published accounts by residents and visitors, our sources are mostly written by men. We have little recorded testimony by women.
>
> (Brereton 1993: 1)

Male-authored accounts, naturally enough, are not usually concerned with the details of women's lives. Furthermore, as Holst Peterson and Rutherford have pointed out (1986), women had no official place in the drama of imperial conquest; their roles as mothers of heirs and paragons of reassuringly cozy domesticity, were strictly supportive. In different ways, black and white women in the West Indies of the period were chattels, and thus outside the dominant narrative of colonialism in which the main players were men and the main topic was conquest. Colonial women, Anne McClintock maintains, whether shipped out as convicts or domestic servants, serving as officers' wives or working their husband's farms, helping in missionary schools or hospitals, may have believed in and been privileged within empire but they "made none of the direct economic or military decisions of empire and very few reaped its vast profits" (1995: 5). Hence "male theorists of imperialism and postcolonialism have seldom felt moved to explore the gendered dynamics of the subject" (6). Slavery too was "not a joint enterprise; it is not a family enterprise; it is not male and female . . . It is a male enterprise . . . with the wife replaced by housekeeper or mistress" (Brathwaite 1984: 2). And male accounts of a "male enterprise" are not even necessarily reliable. As Gregg notes, imperial narratives by "eyewitness" narrators (who may or may not have even visited the region) are in many cases near fabrications, and literary works based on these "books, reports, surveys, treatises and ruminations written by Western scholars, colonial civil servants, army officers, missionaries, journalists, explorers and travelers" are hardly less suspect (1995: 16). Such sources then, are frequently compromised in terms of useful input on white women's lives in the tropics.

Revisionist Caribbean historical scholarship which questions and displaces the imposed European account, has only recently begun to study women's history. And even then, as Beckles acknowledges (1993: 36), "the primary focus of research . . . is the black woman, with the coloured woman running a competitive second, and the white woman trailing behind at a distance." Howard Johnson, co-editor of *The White Minority on the Caribbean* (1998: ix), explains this focus, noting that the historiography of the Anglophone Caribbean since the 1960s has primarily concentrated on exploring "the historical experiences of the black, and in some territories Indian, majority. This pattern of research and publication is explained by the convergence of historiographical trends and political developments which have affected most territories in the region." Decolonization and the attendant nationalism, as well as "an increased black consciousness" and the search for a "usable past," also had consequences for the writing of history since "[w]ith the sharply increased interest in giving agency to the 'subaltern', the white minority . . . has become peripheralised in historical discourse." Alas, in the essays that constitute the study, white colonial *women* are even more "peripheralised." Verene Shepherd et al. (1995: xii) confirm the belated interest in Caribbean women's history. Thus far, they maintain, the "primary focus of the research has been on the experiences of enslaved black women, with only limited attention to coloured women, white working-class and elite women, and nineteenth-century immigrant women" (xiv). Their collection, it is stressed, intends to "avoid writing a totalising Caribbean women's history" since after all, the region "represents a diversity of ethnic groups" (xv); that said, only one essay is devoted to data on white women.

Granted the relative novelty of serious historiographical reassessment of the place of white women in West Indian history, what are the findings? Even a brief and selective summary of general observations has to be qualified due to complex variations within the region, the result of social developments at different times and in different territories. For example, the seventeenth-century West Indies with its frontier mentality and notably disproportionate number of white men to women, differs considerably from the situation that prevailed a century later when the plantocracy had consolidated itself and, in Barbados anyway, women had established themselves sufficiently for the matriarch of an "old" white family to command a degree of respect. By the nineteenth century there were far more white women in the region and the majority were no longer from the "poor white" indentured laborer class. Yet there were still demographic disparities between the territories. The 1829 census in Barbados suggests that there were 47.1 white males to 52.9 females, while in 1844 the Jamaican figures are 143.2 males to every 100 females (Brathwaite 1984: 2). Within territories too, the distribution of women varied demographically with the highest concentration generally found in towns, so that in the early nineteenth century Lady Nugent could travel through six parishes in rural Jamaica without encountering another white woman. Such variations complicate overviews even for professional historians; none the less, let me attempt to contextualize a reading of the early narratives by looking at the available findings.

What the historians say: the slavery period

In the introduction to *Slave Women in Caribbean Society 1650–1838*, Barbara Bush (1990: xii) quotes from Lucille Mathurin (later Mathurin-Mair) – one of the first West Indian researchers to investigate the place of women in regional history – a neat formula for the hierarchy that obtained in the eighteenth and nineteenth centuries: "the black woman produced, the brown woman served, and the white woman consumed." This formula overlooks the peculiar status of the white female indentured laborer. However, as white female field labor in Barbados had virtually ended in 1700, and the importation of white indentured servants to the region generally had slowed to a trickle by the mid-eighteenth century, even poor white women of humble origins tended to constitute a privileged group in comparison with non-white women. Of course, all women in the West Indies were subject to patriarchal domination, as were their equivalents in England,[1] but as Bush observes, "where the gender united black and white women, race and class divided them" (1990: xii). For all that, both Bush and Brathwaite comment on the extent of interculturation between black and white during slavery. For example, Bush cites Edward Long's opinion that white women in the region "suffered [from] constant intercourse with negroe domestics" whose "drawling, dissonant gibberish" and modes of dress and manners they "insensibly adopted."[2] Bush makes clear that this "contamination" of white women was not peculiar to any class: the plantation mistress enjoyed "constant contact . . . with black domestics" (1990: 25), as did urban white women of modest means who lived by renting out their few slaves, or themselves hiring slaves to service small business enterprises.

Beckles's study of enslaved black women in Barbados (1989) discusses white women only in relation to this focus. Referring to the early period (the mid-seventeenth century), he notes that "white indentured female servants worked in the field gangs alongside the small, but rapidly growing number of enslaved black women" (29). The former were accorded no special treatment in terms of their race until the 1660s, when chattel slavery had been fully developed and slave owners' labor policies became more racially invested. At this point, he continues, as part of "a long-term attempt to elevate white women and degrade black women" (29), white women were prohibited from field work. Thus a visible white female underclass no longer existed to challenge the privileged stereotype of the superior urban/plantation mistress. And the proper place of the mistress was in the domestic sphere; thus for Beckles, the domestic economy "reflected in a powerful way the patriarchal nature of white colonial society" (56). "In comparison to the relative independence of black women," argues Bush (1990: 91), "the white woman in plantation society had a highly subordinate and distinctly unfavorable status, despite the glowing image presented of white womanhood." Elizabeth Fox-Genovese (1988: 47), referring to the plantation South of the same period, concludes that the "figure of the lady, especially the plantation mistress, dominated southern ideals of womanhood." Yet this figure was essentially subordinate: "[e]ffectively, the practical and ideological importance of the household in southern society reinforced gender constraints by ascribing all women to the domination of the male heads of households and to the company of the women of their own households" (39). After all, as Patricia Morton puts it (1996: 7), elite males in the plantation hierarchy had to maintain absolute control over all reproductive females and most crucially, over those who bore their legal heirs. White women, despite their privileged pigmentation, were subject to the rule of fathers and husbands and had no automatic rights to property, to income, or to the custody of their children.[3]

Since white female servants had become rare by the mid-eighteenth century, and were considered unreliable, expensive and morally unsound by the planters, it was considered preferable to train slave women (often mulattoes) for these roles. Such women served as sub-managers in households where the white "mistress" was in residence, and were in full control of the planter's domestic – and often sexual – sphere, where a white wife was absent. Indeed, Beckles continues, "[v]isitors to the colony frequently stated that the number of domestics, in both urban and rural households, was far in excess of the work available, and that this situation should be explained in terms of their social and sexual functions" (1989: 60). Naturally, such domestic arrangements did not always work smoothly. Bush notes that "[m]any Europeans in the West Indies declared women slaves to be more troublesome than men"(1990: 53), and "[f]emale domestic servants were a constant source of irritation, particularly to white women, whose job it was to supervise them" (61). Indeed she cites one observer, John Stewart, arguing that slave women were so "vicious and indolent" that, in managing the household, the white mistress was herself a "a greater slave" (cited in 1990: 61). Beckles's study concurs with this widely held belief, and records the experience of Mrs Fenwick and her travails with the ungovernable domestic slaves she hired during her sojourn in Barbados.[4] Fenwick was not atypical:

> Many white and free-coloured families, and quite often single white women, made a living from the wage earnings of hired female slaves who worked as nannies, nurses, cooks, washerwomen, hucksters, seamstresses, and general labourers. The hiring out of women for sex ran parallel to this market . . .
>
> (Beckles 1989: 143)

He supports the latter claim by reference to an 1815 memoir which mentions a respectable white creole woman who "lets out her negro girls to anyone who will pay for their persons, under the denomination of washerwoman, and becomes very angry if they don't come home in the family way" (143), in order to increase her income by the addition of a new slave child.

The hiring out of slaves was not limited to white women: in the American south, according to Morton (1996: 18), many free colored women lived off the labor of their slaves. In Jamaican towns, "especially Kingston, Port Royal and Montego Bay," notes Lorna Simmonds (1987: 31), "there was a large proportion of free coloured and black female slaveowners," and a corresponding pre-dominance of female slaves. Bush confirms that some white Caribbean women, particularly in urban centers, owned and rented out slaves, although the number of slaves owned was rarely above ten; the large slaveholdings were all male owned. In St Lucia in 1815, Beckles observes, white women owned about 24 percent of slaves, again mostly on properties with less than ten slaves; in Barbados in 1817, they owned 40 percent of the properties with less than ten slaves. The demo-graphic statistics he cites (1993: 70) seem at one point contradictory: overall, "women owned 54 percent of the slaves in the town [Bridgetown]" and "58 percent of slave owners in the capital were female, mostly white, though some were 'coloured' and black"; yet "[t]he majority of slaves in the town were owned by male slave owners." What is clearly meant here is that women, predominantly white women, constituted a little over half of total slave owners in the urban sphere and the majority of their slaves were female, owned in groups of less than ten, while male slave owners in the towns tended to own more male than female slaves, and more slaves overall. On the larger rural estates, of course, where the majority of all slaves were situated, the owners were overwhelmingly white males; Butler (1995: 92–5) calculates that by emancipation, white women owned or controlled only 5 percent of estates in Jamaica and Barbados, including a few large ones.

Beckles (1989: 7) details another statistic, peculiar to Barbados during the slavery period: from 1715, "female predominance in the population was . . . true not only for blacks, but also for whites and free coloureds." Such data has been interpreted in various ways. For example, Beckles notes that in 1814 "William Dickson argued, with much conviction, that the white, female majority tempered the brutish frontier mentality of planters, and civilized the white community in many respects, all of which tended toward the gradual amelioration of the slaves' conditions" (15). However, writing on "White Women and Slavery in the Caribbean" (1993: 80), Beckles casts doubt on the valency of anti-slavery senti-ments among white women in the region, concluding that

> The images that emerged of white women as slave owners in the Caribbean context, then, suggest that they were generally pro-slavery, socially illiberal, and economically exploitative of black women . . . They made valuable con-tributions to the development of the colonial economy and society, not only as the domestic partners of planters, merchants, overseers, and managers, but also as large and small-scale owners of slaves and other forms of property.
>
> (ibid.)

This claim challenges perceptions of white women under slavery as powerless victims of patriarchy, unable to challenge a system that oppressed them as well as black women. Rather, Beckles extrapolates from documentary evidence of slave-holding patterns to posit that despite "the extent to which white women were subordinate to white men within the domestic economy, constitutional provisions, and social culture," the disproportionate female to male ratio in Barbados meant that many unmarried white women were forced to seek their livelihood in fields which "propertied white males considered inadequate, in terms of low rate of returns, or socially dishonourable" (1993: 71),[5] such as acquiring and hiring out a small band of female slaves.

"This evidence," he concludes (73), "can be interpreted to suggest that many black women probably suffered their greatest degree of social exploitation at the hands of white women." Focused on the Barbadian situation (not necessarily typical across the region) Beckles's evidence indicates that while some white women may well have opposed slavery – as did Fenwick – they none the less exploited what little security they could *within* the system, as did the colored and black female slaveowners cited in Morton, Simmonds and Beckles. If that meant buying and renting out a small number of slaves then so be it, however abhorrent individuals might find such an economic strategy. Beckles concedes that "[t]he white female voice was rarely heard" on such matters; since he discovers only a few explicit anti-slavery sentiments, the conclusion is that white women as a group were "generally pro-slavery"(1993: 80). Discussing Nugent's journal,[6] Brathwaite (1984) detects a proto-feminist concern with the betterment of the white and colored Jamaican "ladies"; black women, he drily observes, were not on her visiting rounds. This concern is an interesting insight on his part. Like Ferguson,[7] he links it with Nugent's response to slavery. For Brathwaite, "[t]he whole fact of slavery affected the woman in such a way that she began to conceive of the notion of liberation naturally (liberation for the slave first of all and secondly, at the same time, liberation for herself)" (1984: 13). But Nugent avoids explicit comment on the subject of slavery, which Brathwaite explains as due to the constraints of her official position: ameliorative efforts were restricted to spiritual and physical improvements for the slaves with whom she had contact.[8] Like Beckles, his argument is that in the absence of evidence to the contrary, white women who wrote of the West Indies, regardless of what they thought privately, acquiesced publicly in the matter of black enslavement. Concern for maintaining their own precarious status, he conjectures, precluded articulation of anti-slavery sentiments since "they felt, as part of the establishment, that they could do nothing about it" (1984: 13).

This consensus on the pro-slavery stance of white women in general is modi-fied somewhat by the early narratives I examine, which suggest a variety of positions held by women[9]: indeed, as with Fenwick, it seems a white woman could both censure slavery *and* find herself in the position of buying slaves. Further, as Brereton (1993: 15–16) reminds us, "chronology is important too: upper and middle-class ideas about slavery were transformed in Britain between the 1770s and the 1820s or 1830s." She traces this transformation of attitude across the time span of the texts she discusses. The early travel narrative of Janet Schaw, *Journal of a Lady of Quality* (minimally concerned with the Caribbean), "seems to exemplify the callous indifference [toward the suffering of slaves] of the 1770s," while Nugent's turn of the century account is silent on the institution, "though a degree of sympathy for the slaves might be deduced from her constant use of the term 'poor blackies.' " Fenwick's letters of the early 1820s indicate, for Brereton, that she "is clearly far more uneasy in her mind about the slave system," while Frances Lanaghan[10] who lived in Antigua before and after 1834, condemns slavery unequivocally as an inhumane and indefensible institution in her study (1844). Extending Brereton's survey, we can mention Rachel Wilson Moore, an American touring the West Indies and South America, who expresses horror in her 1867 travelogue that any human being should hold another in thrall. By 1909, when Wilcox published her travel narrative, *Sailing Sunny Seas*, the institution of slavery is straightforwardly condemned as immoral: "wherever slavery exists, cruelty in human nature is developed; since to be a profitable trade, it necessitates buying and selling, and an indifference to family ties and human affections" (1909: 128).

Whatever their attitudes to the institution of slavery, most of these women subscribed to the racial discourse of their day which guaranteed them privilege. Nugent took this rigid color line for granted, only meeting "the coloured ladies" in the privacy of her chamber. Fenwick, on the other hand, was dismayed at the "impassable boundary" which in Barbados meant that "those Creoles whose wealth would introduce them to the first circles in England a white beggar would not speak to here" because of their racial admixture (1927: 169). As Brereton notes (1993: 17), Lanaghan believed it was "at the very least, 'illiberal' to despise people merely because they had darker skins, and she condemned the 'prejudice' of white Antiguans in the 1840s," with "the white ladies" being some of the worst offenders. Given that Lanaghan herself might be seen as one of "the white ladies," the *difference* between various white women's opinions is clear, and this difference is heavily inflected by chronology, the nationality of the writer, her chosen form and intended audience. However, there is no firm evidence of an *inevitable* liberalization of attitudes toward racial distinction among women writers over time, nor a demarcation between the views of Englishwomen and creoles. Brereton's survey (1993: 17–18) illustrates that at the end of the nineteenth century, Bridges (in *Child of the Tropics*) evokes caste lines as rigidly maintained as in eighteenth century Trinidad: the only non-white persons to figure in her recollections are domestics, laborers and employees, and her descriptions of some blacks evinces a deep-seated racism.

Race and gender lines, then, were not always uniform. To illustrate, Brathwaite (1984) discusses an interesting aspect of white female sexuality: the forbidden arena of interracial unions. During a thirty-two-year period (1781–1813) in Jamaica, he finds fourteen instances of white women marrying free colored men. Beckles (1993: 78) also records evidence of sexual relations between black men and white women in seventeenth- and early eighteenth-century Barbados, as in the case of "Peter Perkins, a negro, and Jane Long, a white woman" whose marriage is recorded in the St Michael parish register for December 4, 1685, and whose son shows up in the 1715 census; the same census lists a number of "free born mulattoes who were parented by white women and 'black' and 'coloured' men" (Beckles 1995: 132). Perhaps, Brathwaite muses (1984: 13), "the apartheid system was not as rigid in practice as Edward Long and the racist theorists make us believe." Certainly, attitudes hardened over time. Beckles explains that as slave society matured and white male concern with the number of free non-whites became an issue (a child's status was determined by the mother's condition as slave or free), such unions were vigorously discouraged and/or ceased to appear on the official records. Prior to this, however, interracial anomalies occurred. For example, Brathwaite (1984: 13) mentions the only divorce case brought before a colonial Assembly, in Jamaica in 1739. Elizabeth Manning was the sister of a well-connected man of property, Henry Moore, Lieutenant Governor of Jamaica from 1756–62. Moore's wife, incidentally, was related to that most colonial of West Indian "historians," Edward Long. Elizabeth was married to Edward Manning, a principal merchant of the day, Custos of Kingston and Member of the House of Assembly, where he brought his divorce suit. The correspondent was an equally well-established member of the Jamaican colonial elite, Mr Ballard Beckford. The bombshell was dropped during the hearing. Elizabeth was painted by her husband as a nymphomaniac, and evidence was supplied by a former house-keeper, Mrs O'Hara, who scandalously but convincingly claimed that Mrs Manning on occasion entertained negro men in her chamber at night: "She had heard them in the chamber, kissing and smacking, and she said that she believed the Negro fellow had 'lain with Mrs M'." Naturally, Mrs M. called the house-keeper a liar, but the affair indicates that some respectable white women did not entirely buy into the official line on race relations.

Ultimately, the historians' findings suggest that white women in the nineteenth-century West Indies were not a homogeneous collective. Brathwaite's 1984 analy-sis concentrates on the position of black women in the pre-emancipation period. He notes the low numbers white women in comparison to black, and distinguishes between the elite group of colonial officials' wives and female relatives, and others who had to work for a living, including widowed and single urban women operat-ing small business concerns. His curiosity is piqued by the lack of social history concerning the latter (13):

> More typical of the white woman during this period were the large number of poor, white widows who were doing quite well with their coffee and pimento, and pen keeping and poultry rearing and grass and wood selling. But they were all marginal. They had no say in politics; they had no say in the general economy. It would be very interesting to know, for instance, just what many of those 8,000 white women with that kind of marginal existence in Barbados in 1839 were doing with themselves.

Brodber (1982) has unearthed a rich archive of newspaper clippings from the post-emancipation period, including information about (mostly unmarried) white women who maintained a variety of business ventures. For instance, between 1838 and 1844 the Barbadian press ran advertisements on behalf of the Misses Andrews, Thorpe, Elder and Hamblin for (respectively) services in music tuition, confectionery and pickle-making, house rental and theatrical entertainment (1982: 10). In Jamaican newspapers during the period 1838–1900, Brodber discovers white (and, she suspects, possibly colored) women advertizing for positions as governess or lady's companion; as theatrical entertainers; as organizers of charity bazaars; and as managers of lodging houses and other businesses (22–4). In Trinidad she finds white women working as midwives, druggists and in family businesses. Brereton (1998: 45) observes of colonial Trinidad that

> Very few white women engaged in salaried work in the nineteenth century. A handful of women from 'good' families, unmarried or perhaps widowed and inadequately provided for, ran private kindergartens and schools for elite children, or gave lessons in their own homes, especially music. A few 'lower-order' women were employed as domestics, and some affluent creole families had British or French governesses. By the early decades of the twentieth century, however, it was becoming acceptable for young white girls to work in clerical positions in the private sector, at least before marriage.

And by the early twentieth century, white women were increasingly employed as teachers throughout the West Indies. Yet despite this variety of occupation, the stereotype that has retained currency is that of the white woman as a genteel upper-class lady, mistress of the urban or rural Great House.

What then do we learn from this survey of historical research? Mostly, that the particulars of white female experience have been of tangential interest, except in so far as they contribute to analyses of slavery in general and the condition of slave women in particular. An exception is Brereton's account (1993)[11] which asks the same kinds of questions I pose in this book, and concludes (31) that while

> female-authored texts do not provide a consistently gendered testimony, nor do they always bring a clearly feminine perspective to bear on the Caribbean societies with which they deal . . . they are a rich source of evidence about women's historical experience in the Caribbean which can supplement the mainstream of documents generated by men, and they can help provide a more nuanced view of Caribbean social history.

In the remainder of this chapter, I argue from a selection of such texts that their constructions of white women in the nineteenth century West Indies both conform to *and* complicate the monolithic figure of the "mistress." Attention to differences reveals that the specifics of urban or rural situation color such representations, as does the creole or British provenance of the protagonist/narrator. Further, I stress the vital role in the narratives of creolization, that process of inevitable adaptation undergone by women as well as men in the West Indian space. This is also dealt with in the following chapter, which explores how white women's private and social roles were crucially interconnected with those of black women. In attempting to locate the figure of "the" white woman, I now shift ground: from the deductions of historians to the (equally partial) evidence of literary and autobiographical accounts. Just as the texts in question cannot be slotted into easy categories, so the attributes and values of white colonial woman-hood, and indeed, notions of femininity, assume slippery forms in the narratives' disparate, often contradictory portrayals.

The plantation mistress: "white witch," ministering angel, drudge or pampered degenerate?

The label "woman" is explored by Hazel Carby (1987: 20) in her analysis of ideology underpinning femininity during the period of slavery: her concern is with "two very different but interdependent codes of sexuality . . . for white and black women which coalesce in the figures of the slave and the mistress." Two notions of womanhood coexisted, and the dominant discourse enshrined white females within the "cult of true womanhood," idealizing them as domestic, pious, pure and submissive (23). Beckles (1995: 132–3) observes that with the disappear-ance of working-class white women engaged in the same kind of work as black women, the "resident creole elite patriarchy" in the eighteenth century began to redefine white women according to this restrictive stereotype:

> She was now considered unfit for manual labour on account of her endemic fragility; unsuited to physical exertion in the tropic [*sic*] as a consequence of her possession of a faint heart and a delicate skin; terrified of black male sexuality on account of her chaste, virginal, and jet-white purity; and devoid of lust, gaiety, and passion, having embraced in its fullness the importance of ordered moral discipline and self-denial.

Again, Brodber's *Perceptions of Caribbean Women* from 1838 provides a wealth of examples of this exemplary "Angel in the House," the supportive wife epitomized in the figures of "Excellent Ellen" or "Household Pearl" as popularized in the West Indian media. This construct dominated cultural representations of white womanhood and more importantly, it determined what was considered to be the *norm* of female conduct, especially for middle-class and elite women, regardless of race.

Illustrations of the dominant ideology in practice include distinctions made between black and white women in terms of physical appearance. The ideal (white) female stereotype was timorous, refined and fragile. Arthur (forthcoming: n.p) refers to a letter dated August 2, 1805, written from Antigua to a friend in Britain, in which "Jane B. Kerby" represents herself during a threatened French attack on the island as *precisely* this kind of delicate, fainting female, perfectly reconciled to her subordinate and supportive role:

I cannot attempt to describe our terrors, movings, *removings*, packings and unpackings. I consider myself *now* quite as a heroine, having *commanded myself*... However, I shall always feel as I then did, that men in the moment of honourable danger become so sacred, and so precious, that to distress or annoy them by any foolish selfish feelings is sacrilege: thus I am awed into an appearance of courage, when I am at heart a very woman.

(emphasis in original)

Interestingly, once Jane B.'s feminine credentials ("I am at heart a very woman") are well established, she foregrounds her heroism in the face of the crisis. For of course many women would not or could conform to the ideal. Mary Seacole, for example, a mulatto Jamaican who traveled the world as a single woman, practised medicine, set up and ran several businesses (even on the Crimean battlefields) and publicly and volubly refused racist or sexist derogation, not to mention writing her own life, clearly does not fit the model. Likewise, not all white women subscribed to what Carby terms the "four cardinal virtues" of true womanhood. None the less, the power of the ideology and its societal function remained intact. So Seacole, like Jane B., foregrounds her decorous conduct, becoming dress and soft, womanly heart in order to counteract any impressions of her adventures as unladylike. If the fainting (white) woman was the privileged ideal, then her "other," the (black) working woman, who had to be strong and hardy, was considered unfeminine. As Carby puts it, "[s]trength and ability to bear fatigue, argued to be so distasteful a presence in a white woman, were positive features to be emphasized in the promotion and selling of a black female field hand at a slave auction" (1987: 25). Bush (1990: 15) also elaborates on the logic that postulated black women as the opposite of the European norm and, by extension, "an inferior subspecies of the female sex." Hence urban black working-class women in the 1840s are described thus:

> Many of the negro women ... are so very masculine in their voice, manners and appearance, that it is at times a matter of doubt to say to which sex they belong. This may be attributed to the general system of treatment during slavery ... [which] in time rendered them callous, and in the end, divested them of all those principles of modesty which are so great an ornament to the feminine character, whether in high or low condition of life.
>
> (Lanaghan 1844, vol. 2: 146)

The unintended irony is breathtaking: a "callous" systematic enslavement, administered by a white imperial patriarchy, renders black Jamaican women callous in turn, thus closely resembling their oppressors in their masculine aspect! By contrast, feminine charm, virtue and piety were intrinsic to the "cult of true womanhood" embodied in fictional images of the white ideal (like Brathwaite's Miranda). Under slavery, as Beckles and Carby demonstrate, this ideological construction buttressed the system in which free/slave status passed incontrovertibly from the mother. Accordingly, women's reproductive roles had to be rigidly controlled, in that while white wives gave birth to the inheritors of property, black slave women gave birth to property. Thus, it was crucial to maintain a clear distinction between the two groups of women. This is a focal point in Bush's study (1990); Carby goes on to point out that the two definitions of womanhood were "each dependent on the other for its existence" (1987: 25), and this interdependence informs my reasoning in this chapter and the next.

A virtuous woman in the nineteenth century was, if not a virgin, a respectable matron subject to her husband, and here again the dominant ideology polarizes black and white women. White women were supposedly completely fulfilled in nurturing domesticity and motherhood, and so refined that sexuality was repulsive; black women, who supposedly thought of little else, were by default "fallen" temptresses and therefore subject to institutionalized rape. Naturally, within this scenario,

> the white slave master was not regarded as being responsible for his actions toward his black female slaves. On the contrary, it was the female slave who was held responsible for being a potential, and direct, threat to the conjugal sanctity of the white mistress.
>
> (Carby 1987: 27)

Carby argues the necessity for recognizing that since patriarchy manipulated and ultimately oppressed both black and white women of the period, the dialectical relationship between the sexual construction of slave woman and mistress needs to be addressed. For "[e]xisting outside the definition of true womanhood, black female sexuality was nevertheless used to define what those boundaries were" (30). Indeed, the ideology of "true womanhood" enabled the white mistress to live a contradictory position: subject to patriarchal abuse and exploitation, she was none the less afforded a degree of patriarchal protection and superior status to her "Other," the black slave woman (54). Thus her truly "womanly" tendencies toward delicacy and gentleness and sympathy were, in this context, able to coexist paradoxically with displays of inhumanity toward slave women largely because of the binary oppositions informing the very nature of "womanhood".

If the ideal woman was white, domestic, submissive, virtuous and pious, her embodiment in the Caribbean was the "good" mistress of the West Indian plantation (Brathwaite's Miss Ann). For the mistress in her role as "Angel in the House," a large part of her duties included ministering to the unfortunate blacks. Nugent to some extent represents herself in this light as she visits domestics who are new mothers or ill, organizes entertainments for the servants (1966: 98), distributes clothes and gifts to "the black women" (33) and leftovers from an official feast "to the blackies, which made them all very happy" (43). Her civilizing ministry is particularly evident in her zeal for educating the black domestics in religion. Repeatedly Nugent records this aspect of her duties: "I will begin the new year, at the Penn, by instructing the poor negroes, and if I do but succeed in making them the better understand their duties as Christians, I shall be happy indeed" (49). So too Stella, in Henrietta Jenkin's novel *Cousin Stella; or, Conflict* (1859, vol. 1: 204), rejoins her father in Jamaica "full of projects of keeping papa's house and remodelling the governance of his slaves." A similar self-imposed mission is sketched in *Adelaide Lindsay; a Novel* (1850) by the prolific English writer Mrs Ann Marsh-Caldwell. The first fifty-five pages of the text is set in Jamaica in the 1830s, and opens with a letter from the eponymous heroine detailing her new life. Adelaide subscribes to her father's thesis "that the negro character is *not* of a different nature from that of the white; that it is degenerate only, and therefore susceptible of improvement, moral and intellectual" (9). Therefore she determines like Nugent to play her part in this improvement, planning to teach in the schools her father has established on the estate and act as helpmeet "in indoctrinating your sable pupils" (14).

In 1833 the stereotype of the selfless and dedicated plantation mistress is promoted by Carmichael, "Five Years a Resident in St. Vincent and Trinidad," in her general commentary on these islands over the period 1820–5. Carmichael describes the planters' wives and daughters in St Vincent as leading "arduous" lives of drudgery (1969, vol. 1: 21–3) which leave "them no time for improving the mind" so that (as Nugent also observed) "the ladies are too generally found distinguished for that listlessness, and meagerness of conversation" (vol. 1: 39). By contrast, she finds Trinidadian society more polished, and has "heard that several young ladies, who had been wholly educated in Trinidad, were considered, in point of both the useful and agreeable, quite equal to those who had been in Europe" (vol. 2: 74). This does not tally with the comments of a male observer who lived in Trinidad in the late 1840s, as cited by Brereton (1998: 60): "He considered that most of the Creole women were ignorant and ill-bred, reading nothing but light novels and unable to converse except on local or domestic trivia." In general, Carmichael insists the life of the planter's wife – and by inference her own – is a hard one. Bemoaning the fact that she had not seen more of the region, she explains that "those who endeavour, however imperfectly, to do their duty to their family, and instruct their domestics, will find very little opportunity for excursions of pleasure in the West Indies" (1969, vol. 2: 37).

Like Nugent, Carmichael conceives her duties as mistress to include some religious training of her slaves. But not all religious instruction is approved: her pro-slavery apologia castigates missionaries like the Methodists who, she claims, prohibit dancing among their slave converts but fail to teach the blacks the evils of lying, theft, slander and the like. To add insult to injury, she complains that the missionaries lay all blame for the slaves' poor morals "at the door of the white population" (1969, vol. 1: 234). Again, the clash is apparent between the stern advocate of slavery and planter ascendancy, and the assumption of the role of gentle, patient Christian mistress ministering to the poor slaves, and concerned for their moral training.

The burdensome lot of the urban mistress is testified to by Fenwick who, with her married daughter, ran a school for young (white) ladies in Barbados in the early nineteenth century. The official school day starts at 7.00 a.m. and continues till 4.00 p.m. after which other duties occupy her, until "the exhaustion of my day's labour takes its empire . . . & after inertly enjoying the evening breeze in a

Balcony for an hour or so, [I] lounge to Bed, & hold a war with the Musquitoes till 1\2 past 5 the following morning" (1927: 173). After her son-in-law absconds and her daughter takes ill, Fenwick must also see to the running of the entire household and complains that "no slave that digs the field under a strict driver ever felt more fatigue & lassitude than I do" (191). Hard work and drudgery, then, are the lot of the white mistress in town as well as on the plantation, and this is the case for the *better* class of white women for Fenwick is at pains to point out how much their establishment is *"in fashion"* with the best (and richest) families (167; emphasis in original).

A later novel, *The Golden Violet; The Story of a Lady Novelist* (1936) by Gabrielle Long, features an English lady-novelist, Angelica Cowley, who marries a planter and arrives in post-abolition Jamaica with the anticipation of becoming "a ministering angel amongst grateful savages, as a fair white Queen among bowing slaves" (21). Alas, however, the ministering angel develops a suspiciously unfeminine lust for power as a result of her unlimited control over a subject people. Indeed, Angelica learns to dispense with her role as "Angel in the House" and empower herself *outside* the norms of conventional female morality. Such texts suggest the case is not as simple as Carby's paradigm implies, even within the rigid binary opposition of black and white womanhood. In Angelica, we see traits of another manifestation of the white woman in the West Indies, one who is anything but the ideal feminine norm. This version of the mistress is epitomized in the figure of Annie Palmer, the demonized "white witch of Rosehall" featured in Herbert G. deLisser's eponymous novel, published in 1929.

Set in Jamaica just before emancipation, the novel portrays Annie occupying a position of power unusual for a white woman of her time and place. Having acquired three wealthy husbands and subsequently dispatched them in a variety of unpleasant ways, the widow is the sole owner of Rosehall and other estates, which she governs autocratically. Although a twentieth-century reconstruction, *The White Witch of Rosehall* is important because it represents the mistress as an active plantation manager, and indeed, such women did exist in the nineteenth century. For example, Nugent refers to a Mrs Sympson in Jamaica, a widow who manages the entire estate of "Money Musk," is said to be "an excellent planter, and understands the making of sugar, &c. to perfection" (1966: 58).[12] Annie Palmer might be an excellent planter, but she is also an eroticized sadist, a white British woman contaminated by the heathen practices of blacks in Haiti and Jamaica and by tropical sensuality. Annie takes her pleasure as she wishes and tyrannizes all on the estate through fear: fear of the lash, which she is happy to wield in person, and fear of her supposedly supernatural powers. The *unfeminine* characteristics of the "white witch" are what repeatedly strike the young British hero, as he witnesses her supervising a flogging or actively taking part: "Annie ruled her people by terror, white and black alike. She had witnessed whippings for years and years, and her appetite had grown with what it fed on . . . that first tasting of blood as it were, had awakened a certain lust in her" (deLisser 1958: 80).

Where did deLisser find a model for such a mutation of "Excellent Ellen"? There are certainly precedents in early narratives by women. The horror of

European readers at this depiction of a white woman so inured to slavery that she could go against her "softer" nature and indulge in such brutalization, was exploited in anti-slavery narratives like *The History of Mary Prince*. Mary recalls many instances of cruel treatment at the hands of various mistresses in the West Indies:

> I was licked, and flogged, and pinched by her pitiless fingers in the neck and arms . . . To strip me naked – to hang me by the wrists and lay my flesh open with the cow-skin, was an ordinary punishment for even a slight offence . . . often I have dropped down overcome with sleep and fatigue, till roused from a state of stupor by the whip, and forced to start up my tasks.
>
> (Mary Prince 1987: 194)

Beckles (1993: 76) points up the dismay of European travelers who witnessed such cruel punishments by white mistresses in the West Indies. He cites one observer concluding, after four years' residence in the region, his "conviction that female owners are more cruel than male; their revenge is more durable and their methods of punishment more refined, particularly toward slaves of their own sex." Writing about the plantation mistress of the American south, Weiner (1996: 287) observes that while purity might have been essential to the moral power of white women, this was not case for their husbands and the result was that "these wives generally directed their anger towards black women, transforming them from targets of white men's sexual aggression into shameless seducers." These white women reserved their sympathy, Weiner concludes, for slave women harassed by overseers or other low status white men: for sexual rivals, the mistress became the white witch.

The figure of the vicious mistress predates Mary Prince's account. In the less straitlaced eighteenth century, episodic tales of the sexual peccadillos of white women in the tropics seem to have enjoyed something of a fashion. Maxwell's *The History of Miss Katty N.* (1757) is a case in point. So is *The Jamaica Lady, or, The Life of Bavia* (1963; first published 1720) by "W.P.," another story of an English woman of reduced means who attempts to "make good" in the colonies by being as bad as possible. The novel is set on board a ship leaving Jamaica after the peace of 1713. Among the various scurrilous passengers is the "Jamaica lady," who turns out to be anything but a lady. Her amours and deceptions are exposed in anecdotes related by passengers who are familiar with her history of cheating and licentiousness in Jamaica. Yet another example is *Fortunate Transport* (1755) by "Creole" (sex indeterminate), which purports to be the "true" story of one Polly Haycock, a character in the mould of Daniel Defoe's Moll Flanders. Polly lives by crime and seduction in England until transported to the colonies as indentured servant. There, after great suffering as a result of her status – which includes regularly being stripped, tied to a tree and "whipt till her Back was all over in a Gore of Blood" (33) – Polly finally makes good by virtue of astute marriages and investments. A wealthy woman, she visits England but discovers that she has now "too much of the Spirit of the Planter; that is, a Disposition to use her Servants with great Severity, and scarce any Share of Humanity" (42). This does not go down too well with English servants, needless to say. The narrator makes the point that "all the Creoles in general ... treat free-born *Englishmen* [servants in England] as they do Negroes and Felons in the Plantations, and expect the same Submission from the one as the other" (43; emphasis in original). In *The Jamaica Lady*, a creole woman of "an implacable, revengeful temper" (1963: 94) viciously beats a female slave for sipping the mistress's brandy. Her cruelty leads the ship's captain to comment: "I have heard talk of Furies with whips of steel and hair of serpents, and if it be true that the Devil does employ such instruments, a Negro had better live in Hell than with a Jamaica termagant" (112). Of these three texts only Maxwell's purports to be female-authored, but my point in citing their constructions of white women in the West Indies is how very different these are from the English ideal and how very similar to deLisser's white witch.

The cruelty of the mistress then, is consistently attributed to slavery debasing the natural order of sex-appropriate behavior. Certainly Fenwick, after some time in early nineteenth-century Barbados, reluctantly comes to the conclusion regarding black and colored servants in general, that "[n]othing but the dread of the whip seems capable of rousing them to exertion, & not even that ... can make them honest" (1927: 163). Fenwick herself never actually employs or orders this punishment; but Carmichael, having initially felt a similar distaste for this brutality, eventually comes to sanction corporal punishment of slaves (1969, vol. 1: 327; vol. 2: 6–7). Writing about Jamaica early in the nineteenth century, Nugent generalizes about white creole women that "they appear to me perfect viragos; they never speak but in the most imperious manner to their servants, and are constantly finding fault" (1966: 80). In general, she abhors the cruelty of slave punishments (51, 74) and, unlike most European commentators, she admits of the excessively hard work of the slaves at croptime (62–3). By contrast, she represents their white masters and mistresses leading lives of sloth and sensuality. So far from enjoying an uninterrupted narrative history of decorum and moral rectitude, the figure of the white woman is revealed in several unflattering manifestations. Discussing Bridges's *Victorian Memoirs*, Brereton (1993: 10) observes that "[f]ifty years after the end of slavery, for a white Creole child in Port of Spain" the situation had changed only slightly. Whipping might be taboo, but the narrator's mother "was a domestic tyrant, obsessively critical of her servants' performance (eleven in all, plus sundry less permanent hangers-on), directing their lives with the arrogant self-confidence of a slave-owner's daughter."

The durability of the cruel and degenerate plantation mistress is testified to in a 1957 novel by Ada Quayle, a Jamaican.[13] *The Mistress* is a violent novel of lust, cruelty and betrayal set on an estate in the hills of Jamaica run by a sadistic white mistress and her daughter. In an ironic inversion of normative gender roles, female protagonists are portrayed as intent on proving that "the women was always better than the men in this family" (Quayle 1957: 270) What is actually meant here is that the women are in fact worse than their men: like Annie Palmer, the mistress runs her estate efficiently but with no regard for conventional morals or humane values. Her daughter Laura Pettigrew, the "young mistress," shares her lovers with black and brown women – she is perfectly content to have sex in a field of banana trash – and also shares with the servant women the conviction that women have a right to sexual satisfaction. Coarse in language, sentiment and characterization, the novel is nevertheless of interest in its construction of the white woman as very much creolized. This is signalled in part by her quite distinctively non-English speech, and her distinctly non-British self-identification: "I am a Jamaican," young mistress tells the Parson, "You is a Scot. Keep out of our private business" (45). The mistress figure here represents the degeneration of the white feminine ideal as a result of this creolization. Indeed, when a maid is told that "Buckra people act different," she counters that "The mistress wasn't no better" (69). The notion of white women as transmitters of civilization is brought into question here as the mistress is more identified with "fallen" black women than with models of proper feminine values at "home."

Yet another stereotype recurs in several of the early narratives: that of the idle, pampered white woman, spending her time on dress, on entertainments and excursions, and of course on the vagaries of love. For Nugent, once arrived in the tropics, Europeans of "the upper ranks . . . become indolent and inactive, regardless of every thing but eating, drinking and indulging themselves" (1966: 98). The white "ladies" seem to her a stupid lot (91), happiest when disputing and gossiping (197) or discussing goods with the shopkeepers (179), and maintaining their households "in the Creole style": that is, with numerous black servants "running and lying about" (76). Indeed, the term "creolizing" is coined (117) for extensive periods of idle lounging, apparently something of a fashion among West Indian ladies! Nugent also comments on the amount of time devoted to sartorial considerations: "Did not sit down to breakfast till 9, the ladies being so long making their toilette. They seem to bestow much pains and attention to their dress, and examine me most minutely" (154). These women also seem to her over preoccupied with petty jealousies: "[h]ave several notes, about *white ladies'* disputes and little gossip. Keep clear of it all as well as I can" (196; emphasis in original). Later, back in Europe and reviewing her journal, Nugent is concerned to distance herself from this shallow stereotype (269–70) lest her children read "of all the gaieties and dissipation it records" as evidence that "their little mamma [was] a very dissipated, idle, and thoughtless woman"; thus she hastens to correct this impression by stressing her "good mistress" role, in that "the distressed and poor have never been forgotten, but have always been attended to."

This subtle hierarchy of "real" white womanhood and a more degenerate creole mutation, is entrenched in many texts. For example, Frieda Cassin's novel *With Silent Tread* (1890) records the judgement of a young Englishwoman on a white creole of similar age. The description of poor, vacant Terpsichore is hilarious; but it is significant that the creole is typified specifically by ignorance, conceit, idleness, vanity and complacency.

> The English girl sat on the edge of the bed and watched the West Indian one
> . . . and a sudden wave of pity swept over her for the cramped, imprisoned,

undeveloped life of this girl who knew nothing of the beautiful world of art, of literature, or science in which she might have lived . . . who saw none of the grandeur of nature though cradled in her very lap, whose life was bounded by the price of sugar, the flirtations of her smarter acquaintances, and unhealthy dreams of a romance never to be fulfilled. What woman would this girl become? . . . The conceit without the ignorance might have been bearable; the ignorance without the conceit might have been excused and diminished in time, but the one being hedged in by the other rendered both unassailable

(Cassin 1890: 70–1)

Cassin's observer does note that not all West Indian girls are so colorless; her own cousin is an exception. However, the construction of the creole lady as a "dissipated, idle, and thoughtless woman" was a pervasive one. Quoting from the *Trinidad Gazette* of 1833–4, Arthur (forthcoming: 3–6) includes an amusing series of "letters" in verse from "Miss Margaret——in Town, to Miss Polly——, in Naparima, 30th February 1834."[14] These verses demonstrate media circulation of the privileged (and presumably white) woman as frivolous, if charming. In the first letter, Margaret details the trials of shopping in Port of Spain for her sister's "commissions" and closes with mention of "the *Cricket Ball*, / Where, I hope, to meet my beau, and / Shine the envy of them all." Polly replies that the purchases from "Town" arrived, but in a disgraceful condition:

Yes, Maggie, I'm sure you'd have wept had you seen
The things which you purchased for me with such toil,
Stained – trampl'd on – torn, as if they had been
Stow'd under the salt-fish, mill-grease and lamp-oil.

The rest of the epistle proceeds in the same light vein, concerning prospective husbands and subscriptions to light a church, an aunt and a borrowed necklace. Running this "correspondence" over an extended period suggests the newspaper countenanced representations of elite woman as vacant, idle socialites; it is hard to believe that the historic events of 1834 were unfolding at the same time in the same place.

Lanaghan's *Antigua and the Antiguans* (1844) prefaces comments on the island's white population (*"the pure in blood"*) by carefully distinguishing between creoles and expatriates, and between the upper and (much despised) lower reaches of this group. She is caustic about poor white women ("bottom-foot buckras") who have married up-and-coming male equivalents:

their wives are proceeding with railway speed in the paths of affectation and conceit. From the more useful occupations of washing their own clothes, and mending their own stockings, they now play the part of "my lady," and pass their time in lolling upon a sofa, with an open book before them, ready to take up should "company" arrive; or with wondering ears, listen to their daughters bungling through one of Mozart's waltzes, or stammering over a French fable.[15]

(Lanaghan 1844, vol. 2: 198–9)

Not all the "ladies" of this class "spend their time in this indolent manner": some rear poultry and livestock and cultivate vegetables for sale, and several operate small businesses, but even these are demeaned as money-grubbing, selling goods from a tenement shack to "the negroes upon the neighboring estates, at the very modest profit of about 50 percent!" (vol. 2: 199). Clearly the poor white woman's huckstering proclivities did not desert her as her family moved up the social ladder. Despite such industry, white women of this class are portrayed by Lanaghan as essentially gossips and posers, and their daughters as vain, affected flirts who cultivate haughty manners and a "boasted pretension to superiority" (vol. 2: 200). Another group of white women censured for dressing and acting "equally beyond their sphere in life" are English women brought as servant-girls to Antigua, who then proceed to marry overseers or Irish policemen and immediately pass themselves off as "fine ladies" (vol. 2: 222). Perhaps it is the Irish connection – for the Irish were considered an inferior race – that leads Lanaghan (vol. 2: 200–1) to conflate these vulgar *arrivistes* with stereotypical degenerate creole women of the recent past,

> the days when the young white Creole was left entirely to the care of their black, or low-colored nurses, who imagined they could not better discharge their duty than by giving them their own way. The days when girls of fourteen could find no other amusement than, seated upon the floor, amid their negro attendants, to pass their time in eating "sling" [wet sugar], or sucking sugar-canes, while their listless mothers lay stretched upon their couch, leaving their children to learn their alphabet as best they could.

Not much has improved with regard to the upbringing of white creole girls, she explains. Now, a governess – "some poor damsel, who, to save herself from actual starvation, agrees to wear out her strength, and prostrate her talents" (vol. 2: 197) – is hired for a pittance to teach girls the basics until they are ready for education in England. There, "they are taught to sketch a landscape, complete a butterfly in Poonah painting, play some of the fashionable airs . . . and perhaps embroider a footstool," before being shipped back to the West Indies to "astonish" their proud parents (vol. 2: 201); hardly suitable training for a good mistress's life of drudgery and self-sacrifice.

For those whites of "the higher order" or "of good descent," Lanaghan has surprisingly little to say beyond "that they are fully entitled to the respect they so universally meet with" (vol. 2: 203). Interestingly, she admits creole proprietors to this class, as well as professionals, merchants, clergymen and the like. On their estates, "luxury abounds" (vol. 2: 206–7) and the ladies

> amuse themselves with various feminine and elegant employments; sometimes accompanying their soft voices upon the piano, or on well-strung

harps . . . Others frequent the library, where the works of our best writers may be met with . . . At length comes the hour of luncheon . . . and then the duties of the toilet have to be attended to – a stray ringlet or a captivating dimple taken to task – . . . until the time arrives when a drive in the carriage, or a stroll through some pleasant vale, is practicable. After enjoying these exercises for some time, the dressing-room is once more sought, and beauty receives every assistance that art can give her . . .

At seven, there is dinner with all the trimmings, followed by conversation and music or dancing, and so to bed: the routine is no different from that of their counterparts in an English country house. It is notable that Lanaghan's equally detailed account of the life of ladies from the "coloured gentry" differs very little from that of the elite whites, save that interaction with children is mentioned more often. Brereton (1993: 20) notes that Lanaghan's "picture of the country lady's life is much the same as Bridges's account of the women of the Rostant family on their Santa Cruz (Trinidad) estate in the 1920s." Like Carmichael, Lanaghan's deliberate narrative stance as objective observer (though authenticated by her self-professed knowledge gained from long residence) precludes discussion of her own place as a white woman within the groupings she constructs.

To conclude this overview, I want to refer to a work which is only tangentially relevant to this study, but which serves to illustrate a point. The text is Jeannette Marks's *The Family of the Barrett: A Colonial Romance* (1938), an account of her trip to Jamaica to research the West Indian antecedents of Robert Browning and Elizabeth Barrett Browning. It is clear that in the mix of fictional imagining and citation of "historical facts" the author drew copiously – and uncritically – on early accounts of the island by writers such as Edward Long, Bryan Edwards, Nugent and others, sometimes to the extent of lifting descriptive passages from these works.[16] Indiscriminate borrowing might explain her rendering of the figure of "the mistress" (1938: 187–90) as a kind of amalgam of the observations noted in the examples above:

> The lives of the majority of Creole women were dull and hard and often crude. They lived in the midst of an unvarying round of domestic duties, for the smooth-running of which they were dependent upon their negro slaves . . . If the white mistress at the head domestically of these subservient, sometimes primitive, and always unsubduable retinues of servants was a woman of energy and responsibility, the mistress cared for the servants with a patience and generosity which made her in the midst of overwhelming problems but a "head slave" among slaves. Sometimes the slaves . . . were dangerous, untutored primitives whose training should not have been left to the white women who, nerve-wracked and worn by the conditions of their lives, not infrequently flogged them to the amusement of the children . . . Skill in horsemanship, dancing, music and needlework, in which many of the white Creole women of Jamaica were remarkable, was soon lost in the heavy dreary round of their responsibilities . . . in Jamaica visits that were "visitations"

were the rule and not the exception. These visits relieved the dullness of Jamaican lives . . . Six weeks were not unusual and the longer the visitors stayed, feasting and idling by day and dancing by night, the greater, supposedly, was their regard for their hosts and hostesses . . .

Wanting in energy and the economic and moral direction which a more fortunate home life can bring with it, many white Creole women fell all too easily into indolent, sensual and barbaric habits of overeating, oversleeping while their slaves fanned them and tickled their feet; daily-dosing with the bottle of laudanum . . . drinking; and a calloused yet avid interest in the lascivious negro amours of the men of their families.

Such a composite picture, and with so many unsupported – even contradictory – assertions! We recognize the unending responsibilities of onerous duties, the drudgery and toil of domestic management, and the gentle, compassionate ministrations to the "unsubduable" female slaves. But here also is the idle, intemperate, often cruel mistress, as well as the sensual and overindulgent creole with a taste for luxury, lacking moral or intellectual rigor and fond of gossip and dress. How do we evaluate so many contradictory versions? How do we determine the extent of interpretive intervention by the authors and editors of these accounts? Clearly the accounts discussed, even allowing for differences in geographical and temporal specifics, suggest that the figure of the white West Indian woman is hardly a stable icon, but rather a *construct*, an amalgam of stereotypical representations that served a number of narrative purposes. This overview of sources merely serves to underline the instability of such constructions, their ideological overdetermination and questionable reliability as "evidence."

For example, the recurrent – if not always overt – distinction between white creole and English women, and the underlying class distinctions, points to authorial bias. Lanaghan's mockery of those women who attempt to rise above their station is evidence of the latter. And Nugent is explicit about the tensions between creole and expatriate white women. The creoles she finds unattractive: they are perspiring and bilious (1966: 10) with "yellow wrinkled faces," the men overindulgent (77), immoral and profane (98), and the women, as noted above, generally stupid (55) and given to frivolous and petty rivalry. But undisguised English contempt elicits creole offence and vindictive revenge. In her journal, Nugent records an incident concerning an English lady, Mrs Horsford, who "had injudiciously talked nonsense about the *natives*, and offended them all [the creole women] very much" (202; emphasis in original). Mrs Horsford is put in her place, however: four days later, an entry reports that "the ladies have got a Directory, in which they have discovered, that Mrs. Horsford's father, Mr. Brocksopp, is a slop-seller at Wapping. I do lament her being so silly, and bringing all this upon herself . . ." (203).

In general, where the degenerate, "evil" or idle plantation mistress stereotype gained narrative ascendancy, it was associated with *creole* women who are portrayed as harsh, cruel, slovenly and, in short, all that the English ideal was not. Tonna's anti-slavery novel *The System* (1827) rehearses the portrayal of creole women as languorous, vacant and lazy, with violent tempers (47). Avaricious and racist (56), they are contrasted with the English estate manager's wife who supports his lenient disposition and promotes the amelioration of the Africans' lot. In *Constance Mordaunt* (1862), "E.J.W. (A Woman)" recounts disparaging comparisons made by the heroine's father between English women and creoles (like his wife). The "cult of pure womanhood" which dictates delicacy and frailty in a lady, runs counter to narrative job-descriptions of the white creole as centering around thrifty domestic management and hard work beyond "moral housework" (supporting and nurturing family, Christianizing slaves and maintaining civilized standards). What emerges then is a process by which the negative, perhaps unfeminine, certainly unladylike aspects of white female behavior tend to be split off and attributed to the white creole. Thus Carby's paradigm of two opposite ideologies of womanhood in the American plantation system (associated with white and black women) is subsumed in these early representations of the white mistress in the West Indies as a far more complex tangle of features and qualities.

Again, the question of narrative positioning is germane here. Writers of these early texts draw "the white woman" in the West Indies from specific vantage points (racial, class-based, national). Given their residence in and familiarity with the society they observe, how do they position *themselves* within their generalizations? As noted, Carmichael and Lanaghan for the most part maintain a position of "invisibility" despite their first-person narratives: they do not place themselves within any of the various categories of local women. But Carmichael's "object-ive" stance is a pose: initially she maintains the conventions of a personal journal, emphatically claiming (1969, vol. 2: 236) that "I had then no intention of writing for the public," hence the need to "recur to a personal narrative in my statement of facts" (vol. 1: 15). However the narrative soon shifts into polemic. It is a clearly public "statement of facts" about slavery in the West Indies. Despite the transparent claim that the published journal is not intended to influence opinions on "the question now before Parliament," [the abolition debate], it conveniently emerges that there is "little that I have written that has not an indirect bearing upon the matters now in progress" (vol. 2: 236). Unintentionally but inevitably, Carmichael places herself firmly within the conservative pro-planter camp, hence rendering her "disinterested" representations of West Indian women compromised by an ideological agenda.

Nugent and Fenwick, given the more intimate nature of their literary forms (the journal and the epistle, never intended for publication), do situate themselves within West Indian society and, largely due to the more introspective nature of these genres, reveal to some extent not only how they construct those they gaze upon, but how they themselves are constructed by their subjects. None the less, their texts do not indicate that they considered themselves to belong to any of the groups of women they describe. Issues of "authority" then, mitigate against easy assertions about the mistress in these texts; we rely for information about white West Indian women on the accounts of writers who deliberately distance themselves from the "tainted" creoles. Ideologically overdetermined by discourses of national/sexual/class and race identity already imprinted within the metanarrative of empire, such accounts suggest an investment in preserving a space for originary nationhood/virtue/purity; it follows naturally that creole women will be less privileged objects of construction. In Chapter 2, I want to explore another aspect of this oppositional relationship of self and Other, as played out in the relationships of white and black women in the West Indies.

2 "With the utmost familiarity"

Black and white women

The crucial interdependence of the West Indies and the "mother country" informs Catherine Hall's conclusion that "English national identity . . . cannot be understood outside of England's colonial dependencies. Jamaica, a small island in the Caribbean, may never have been seen by the majority of the English population yet it occupied a place in their imaginary" (1992: 242–3). Similarly, notions of "whiteness" were inextricably bound up with current definitions of "blackness," so that as we have seen, constructions of the white mistress are necessarily dependent on constructions of the black female slave or servant.

This connection operated at a more literal level too, for eighteenth-and nineteenth-century plantation society in the West Indies was an intimate society. The large number of blacks in relation to whites meant contact at all levels, but in particular between whites and domestic servants. Whites may have given the orders, reports Carmichael (1969, vol. 2: 14), but "upon all other topics negroes converse with the utmost familiarity with the white population, and the white population also with them." In the public sphere, Nugent (1966: 179) was "much diverted with the easy manners and familiarity of the [white] ladies and the shopkeepers, who all seem intimate acquaintances." These shopkeepers would have been predominantly free blacks and coloreds, along with a few poor white hucksters and some Jewish traders. In the more private/domestic realm (the province of women) slaves and mistresses, groups distanced from each other by a whole range of factors, were none the less constantly in each other's company and frequently linked in interdependent relationships.

Nugent vividly portrays the close cohabitation of black and white in Jamaican establishments: "[t]he house is perfectly in the Creole style. A number of negroes, men, women, and children, running and lying about, in all parts of it" (1966: 76); "the negroes in the Creole houses sleep always on the floors, in the passages, galleries, &c." (81). Her sister-in-law, "like all Creole ladies, has a number of servants with her" at all times (146). Nugent herself regularly entertains in her bedroom after dinner "the black, brown and yellow ladies" of the house in which she is visiting, or indeed those who visit her at home (65, 66, 69). And much information does she acquire from these sessions, as when informed on one occasion that her "mulatto friends . . . are all daughters of Members of the Assembly, officers, &c. &c." (78). Of course, this last testifies to another result of black/white intimacy over which the mistress had little control, although white women were reported to exhibit an avid interest in the black amours of the men in their families.

Daily contact obviously resulted in interculturation, the most enduring evidence of which is the development of creole languages. Creolization, explains Brodber (1982: 5), "eroded the polarities between European and non-European, between white skinned people and others and . . . by the end of legal slavery, 1838, it had begun to produce Caribbean forms." If we are to believe Nugent, creolization in the matter of language is evident much earlier. For example, her journal introduces Mrs Sherriff (1966: 76), "a fat, good-humoured [white] Creole woman, saying dis, dat, and toder." Nugent's approximation of creole syntax and pronunciation in itself demonstrates familiarity with the vernacular as, for example, when she records a creole lady remarking on the coolness of the air, "Yes, ma-am, *him rail-y too fra-ish*" (98). If Nugent was acquiring an ear for Jamaican Creole, her children are actually speaking it, as evident in the extended family's amusement back in Europe at "their little funny talk, and Creole ideas and ways" (259). Of course, linguistic interculturation between racial groups does not signify any degree of social equality. Contact between mistress and servant was governed, in theory anyway, by all kinds of rules in an effort to maintain distance, as Nugent discovers when she shocks the white ladies by dancing with an old black retainer at a domestic fete (156). None the less, it serves as a verifiable testament to the extent of consistent interaction.

In a nutshell, "[a]ll classes, free and enslaved, on the plantation and in urban settlements, were 'symbiotically related' by interdependence and emulation" (Bush 1990: 23); at the same time, Bush notes that ambivalence about this interdependence characterized colonial society. Any study of the construction of white women in the West Indies then, must take account of their complex interrelationships with black women at virtually every major stage of life. In the rest of this chapter, I illustrate some narrative accounts of this interdependence in representations of white women at work (domestic management of black women); of white female sexuality (as related to that of black women); and of white women's role as mothers (with black women highly involved).

Work as domestic servitude: managing black women

"Oh!" cried the lady, "never speak to me about that [black] woman, I am a martyr to her. I am the victim of my Negroes.

(Wilkins 1854: 144)

From the lofty vantage-point of a male observer, Schomberg claimed in *Travels in British Guiana, 1840–41* that the West Indian kitchen "only knows the lady of the house and her daughters by name, and the remaining cares of a housewife are just as much unknown to the former as to the latter."[1] However, as noted, women observers record the lot of the plantation mistress as a life of hard work and drudgery. A major part of this work involved the supervision and direction of domestics, who would have been mostly black and female during both the slavery and immediate post-emancipation periods. As Brereton (1995: 67) puts it,

> For white women resident in the Caribbean, the management of the house-
> hold domestics, whether slave or free, was pivotal to their daily existence.
> Control of the domestics was one of the few forms of power they possessed,
> and defiance of their authority by the servants was seen as an assault on their
> power and privileges as women of the elite.

And the domestics most certainly did defy her authority, making the mistress's job very difficult. A few representative texts illustrate the endemic resistance of "management" by black women.

Carmichael's vindication of the white population in St Vincent and Trinidad is, she claims, true for the entire West Indies (1969, vol. 1: 15). As we have seen, her defense of the planters is intended to caution the British Parliament, its Commissions of Enquiry and all the ill-informed British ladies who sign anti-slavery petitions, that blacks in the Caribbean are thus far unprepared for free-dom. Her strategy is cunning, if familiar. She acknowledges her own naive expectations and then disproves them by recourse to "experience":

> I arrived in the West Indies fully convinced that I should find, and indeed
> almost determined to find, every slave groaning under oppression, yet I was
> not one month in St. Vincent, before I was compelled from my own experi-
> ence of negro character, to be somewhat sceptical, whether *it were possible to
> overwork a negro* . . . Employment is their abhorrence – idleness their
> delight . . .
>
> (Carmichael 1969, vol. 1: 96; emphasis in original)

But if it is not the slaves who work the plantation, who *does*? Why, the planters of course, aided by their womenfolk who are worn to a shadow in the effort (vol. 1: 20).

For Carmichael (vol. 1: 263), black women (and men) serving in her household are inveterate thieves, cheats and liars,[2]

> and that with a degree of adroitness that baffles the eye, and the understand-
> ing of any European; and what is worse, they invariably get into a passion if
> you refuse to let them take the book [the Bible], and swear to the truth of
> what you know to be false . . .

In addition, domestics are incurably slothful and determined to do as little as they can get away with. A waiting-maid for instance, "considers she does very well if she assists her mistress in dressing, and does about as much work with her needle in one day, as her mistress in one hour . . . yet this is all that is required of them, and indeed it is all they would do" (vol. 1: 117). Between laziness, thievery and deliberate or feigned stupidity, domestic slaves were "a trial" (vol. 1: 22–3) whether hired, as was the practice in town (vol. 1: 122), or purchased by her husband, as was the case after their removal to Trinidad. Carmichael had a particular antipathy toward those responsible for household laundry: "of all your troublesome establishment, the washerwomen are the most discontented, unmanageable, and idle"; their destruction of clothes was "past belief" as everything was "ill washed" and badly ironed; and nothing could persuade them to stop starching items, even handkerchiefs (vol. 1: 118–20). This complaint is echoed in James's *The Mulberry Tree* albeit with more humor:

> Unless you send eternal and unremitting weekly pleadings, everything you wear is returned to you starched; and what is more, *raw* starched. My handkerchiefs are pieces of cardboard, my nightgowns are hair shirts, and my linen dresses are plaster casts. To insist upon getting your things unstarched is to have to take the chance of their being most indifferently laundered . . . I would like to have the starch monopoly for the West Indies if all the islands are like Jamaica.[3]
>
> (1913: 45; emphasis in original)

In the urban setting, the labor of (frequently intractable) female domestics was also essential to the maintenance of a mistress's role. Nugent's privileged position as Governor's wife spared her the daily grind of one-to-one supervision of household slaves, although she is taken aback by the initial state of King's House on arrival and has her English maid organize the "black ladies" to make it "a little less filthy" (1966: 11). After assuring the slaves of good treatment, Nugent finds them "good-humoured" but cannot help wishing that "they would be a little more alert in clearing away the filth of this otherwise nice and fine house" (13). The Nugents had a core staff of four white servants when they left England, and "the mistress" seems to have used these as go-betweens (or overseers) for the cavalcade of black domestics they were obliged to maintain in Jamaica (150, 155).[4] Nugent is aware that she is more fortunate than most white women, for as she "traveled around Jamaica, staying on plantations, she found many disorderly, uncomfortable houses, with crowds of awkward, dirty servants and badly managed children," and a shrewish mistress constantly scolding the domestics (Brereton 1993: 7). The scolding upset Nugent but she is persuaded black domestics simply would not perform their duties without it. Again Mary Prince's account suggests otherwise. For although Mrs Woods abuses her as totally useless, Mary was none the less the chief "confidential" servant left in charge of the household during the family's frequent absences from home, and they refused to sell her despite several offers. In both cases, the texts reiterate that while black women were indispensable to the mistress's position, their management constituted a disproportionate amount of her time and effort.

Obviously not all white women could achieve the financial security of a "good" marriage and the resultant retinue of personal servants. Several maintained themselves by hiring out their female slaves as higglers, domestics, seamstresses, washerwomen and even, in some cases, as prostitutes. The less well-off the female owner, the more dependent she was on her female slaves/servants for her livelihood. What of those who hired such slave women? An account which details this (frequently frustrating) dependency is that of Eliza Fenwick, in her letters to novelist Mary Hays, written from Barbados between 1814 and 1821.[5] Her husband John Fenwick, an editor and translator, was apparently a drunkard with many debts. Eliza separated from him in 1800 and took a position as governess in Ireland. Meanwhile, her daughter (also Eliza) had been touring the West Indies with a troupe of actors and had met and married a Mr Rutherford in Barbados. Fenwick joined her daughter and son-in-law there in 1814, accompanied by her son Orlando whom she hoped to place with some merchant. Alas, Orlando died of yellow fever in 1816, and her son-in-law, also over-fond of the bottle and "speculations," decamped in 1819 leaving Fenwick, Eliza and her four young children to run the girls' secondary school that provided their income. The direction of the family household (swelled in ranks by a constant stream of boarders) became more and more Fenwick's domain as her daughter was sickly and much occupied with her little ones. Thus Fenwick had a great deal of first-hand experience of the management of domestic servants, hired from their owners or, as was later the case, purchased as family property.

Determined to "secure a living," Fenwick fills her letters with reckonings of debits and credits, with plans to increase the latter and notes on depredations of illness or climate that add to the former. Like Carmichael she stresses the high cost of living in the West Indies, and the necessity of hard work on the part of the mistress: "[w]e who seek for gain in these climates," she writes, "have terrible penalties awaiting us" (1927: 196). But no matter how thriving their finances, "one thing will ever mitigate against my contentment – the negro slaves" (168). Against the grain of many colonialist accounts Fenwick, with Carmichael and Symmonett, acknowledges the graceful appearance and elegant dress of the female slaves, but is forced to conclude (167) that "except demeanour & outward form they are a detestable set of people – idle, ungrateful, dirty, dishonest and profligate in the extreme." Of her own domestics she observes (168) that

> no imagination can form an idea of the unceasing turmoil & vexation their management creates. To kindness & forbearance they return insolence & contempt. Nothing awes or governs them but the lash of the whip or the dread of being sent into the fields to labour. With us, therefore, they pursue a regular course of negligence, lies & plunder, the latter of which they carry on with a cunning & ingenuity that is surprising.

"Pilfering seems habitual & instinctive among domestic slaves," she adds (163), citing examples of theft by two servants even as her daughter was giving birth (171), and the robbery of forty pounds by a 16-year-old nanny (203). When discovered, the girl admits her guilt but boasts "that she knew I would not suffer her to be flogged, & therefore she knew better than to work when she was not made to do it" (175).

The unrelenting business of getting the black women to do their tasks "without being watched and driven" (177) is largely responsible for Fenwick's exhaustion and despondency. The "superintendence of all domestic concerns" is "a labour so great, so constant, so oppressive in this country, where every order must be executed under the eye of the mistress" (191), that she compares it to a kind of slavery: "if you knew the slavery of managing a family in the West Indies with Negro Domestics (& we have seven of them), you would wonder how I support the toil" (188–9). Accounts by contemporary white American women reinforce the claim that "[s]lave women could – and did – behave in ways mistresses found exasperating, and mistresses whose self-esteem as wives, mothers, hostesses, and neighbors depended on slaves' work, were often frustrated" (Weiner 1996: 283).[6]

Fenwick (like Lanaghan) points to the source of the black women's poor work ethic: "[I]t is a horrid system, that of slavery, & the vices & mischiefs now found among the Negroes are all to be traced back to that source" (164). None the less, she cannot do without the domestics. Writing about the situation in the American south, Fox-Genovese gets to the heart of the matter: in the colonies, even more so than in Victorian Britain, "women, to be ladies, had to have servants" (1988: 197). Far more than a badge of status, Fenwick acknowledges that she is at every stage dependent upon servants; in fact, when a hurricane has devastated the island (181–2), the domestics are literally the family's lifeline:

> We have no means of getting at bread or any fresh provisions, & if the servants we have sent out to search the Hucksters' shops down the Bay, do not get biscuits and salt fish, which is all we can hope for, I know not what will be done for the poor children & boarders. My poor & lovely baby is pining in vain for his Milk.

Similarly, Carmichael relates instances of white families in reduced circumstances relying on their ex-slaves for sustenance, a situation drawn by Rhys in the early part of *Wide Sargasso Sea* and by Phillips at the end of *Cambridge*. At length, Fenwick seems to have reduced her dependency on hired female servants by the simple expedient of buying male slaves. She writes uneasily to Mary Hays (207),

> It will no doubt be repugnant to your feelings to hear me talk of *buying* Men. – It was for a long time revolting to mine, but the heavy Sums we have paid for wages of hired servants, who were generally the most worthless of their kind, rendered it necessary. Out of 8 in our household, 5 are now our property, 2 Men, 2 boys and one woman. The latter, should we ever quit this Island, I shall give freedom to, because she is old, & has attentively nursed our little Orlando.

The onerous job of managing black women is not mentioned in the rest of the correspondence. Wilma King paints a similar picture in the southern American states. Writing on Louisiana plantation mistresses in the nineteenth century who, like Fenwick, were responsible at different times for the management of owned and hired slaves, she cites frequent complaints about the work of overseeing a household since "a negro never sees any dirt or grease" (King 1996: 84). The highly personalized nature of the mistress/maid relationship often resulted in discord, King observes, so that in the narratives "control/resistance dynamics were never far from the surface" (83).

In these texts then, the role of the mistress involves constant "turmoil and vexation" in the management of female slave and hired labor. This management was a crucial part of the white woman's "job description" in both the urban household and the plantation Great House, sites which served as symbols of the mistress's privilege, but were also venues for daily confrontation.[7] Domestic management may thus be read as one site of shifting power relations "on the ground," since regardless of the white woman's superior status within colonial discourse, the maintenance of her role was bound up with dependance on an unruly body of black women whom, as these accounts testify, she could rarely control *in fact*. In incident after incident, these black women are shown to resist control and undermine the mistress's authority. Carmichael tells of an offended servant taking revenge on a strict mistress by putting an old bed sheet on the table when she entertained a "large ceremonious party at supper," innocently claiming to "tink sheet as good as table cloth" (1969, vol. 2: 104). As King observes of the American South, it was often difficult for the mistress to act the part of the calm, self-possessed and dignified lady in her dealings with black women; the documents she cites seem to indicate that sometimes, for white women such management seemed hardly worth the trouble.

My particular focus so far has been the inscription of the mistress in her role as domestic manager, the crucial interrelationship of black and white women in this sphere, and the ways in which these relationships unsettle norms of power enshrined in the dominant discourse. Reviewing the status of women in slave societies, Wertz posits that by handing their work over to slaves, "a society thereby raised the position of its freewomen, but at the same time these freewomen became economically useless. The result was a paradoxical change that simultaneously raised and lowered freewomen's status" (1984: 377). On the plantation, she suggests, "the equation of higher social status for women with idleness and with isolation from political power" produces the figure of the pampered, idle and fretful mistress enshrined in one stereotype (378). But the embattled urban or rural mistress vainly attempting the job of efficiently managing recalcitrant female domestics, is clearly another kind of inscription altogether. Bound together in the household, Fox-Genovese avers, conflict between the mistress and slaves/ servants "who wouldn't or couldn't function as compliant extensions of her will and her hands," sometimes simmered and often exploded (1988: 140). Particularly interesting is her conclusion that "[s]lave women, in covert or overt defiance of their ascribed station, achieved in practice something like a perverse equality in their contributions to the tensions of everyday life" (135). Such tensions and the "perverse equality" of black women are amply illustrated in the West Indian narratives discussed. As I have suggested previously (O'Callaghan 1993a: 27), acts of resistance, of subversion, perhaps nothing more overt than a deliberate refusal to invest energy ("laziness"), in effect "mitigate against the depiction of black women as powerless and passive." Several early texts acknowledge that "silenced" black or mulatto women were in fact a formidable presence. They constantly intrude into the personal and domestic lives of white women; male writers, not surprisingly, have little to say on this interdependence. The very constitution of the white woman's role is thus bound up with the complicating factor of the black woman's *participation* in these roles. In a sense, black women both make possible the existence of the "ideal white woman" *and* in their "perverse equality" expose ambivalences within the ideology that promoted this ideal. In the rest of this chapter, I outline the involvement of black women in two other important aspects of white female identity: the role of wife and mother.

Wives and mistresses

Sander Gilman (1986) graphically illustrates the point that female sexuality under slavery was very differently conceived for white and black/brown women: the white wife and mother was chaste, moral, modest, demure even to the point of asexuality; the black mistress was wanton, seductive and promiscuous. Gilman takes this alterity further by suggesting that aggressive female sexuality in the later nineteenth century was considered pathological and that black women and prostitutes figured in the dominant discourse as the apogee of this pathology: their alleged anatomical peculiarities become synonymous with abnormality, uncleanliness, and disease (256).

Certainly, much colonialist writing about the West Indies portrayed black women, in the words of Marsh-Caldwell's *Adelaide Lindsay*, as "very ugly things to look upon." Which, however, did not stop white men from seeking them out for sexual congress: in Hyam's terminology, "[t]he expansion of Europe was not only a matter of 'Christianity and commerce,' it was also a matter of copulation and concubinage" (1991: 2). Gikandi records English comparisons of black women with the Victorian "norm" of white femininity, but notes that in male accounts this was not always to the detriment of the black women. Trollope, for example, conceded their freedom in relation to "starched" English women and Kingsley, though shocked at their (masculine) strength and self-confidence, states categoric- ally that the "Negro women are, without doubt, on a more thorough footing of equality with the men than the women of any white race" (cited in Gikandi 1996: 112). A "Gentleman lately resident on a plantation" in Jamaica (Peter Marsden 1788: 8), observed that white men "are very free with the [black] females, who are remarkably quick and lively; with them they hold a dancing assembly, which is generally much more crowded than the first assembly composed of Creole white ladies of the best families of the island, who in general are very haughty." The preference of white men for the company of less haughty black and brown women is repeatedly attested.

Nugent, the aspiring "Angel in the House," was delighted with her ideal marriage and reflects, on the occasion of their fifth anniversary, "nor have I ever experienced the smallest degree of slight or unkindness from my dear husband;

and this year finds me a happier woman than ever I was in my life. I am so truly blest" (1966: 129). However, "dear N." appears to have been the exception to the rule. Other white men in Jamaica, she notes (29), keep black or mulatto concubines:

> The overseer's *chère amie*, and no man here is without one, is a tall black woman, well made . . . She shewed me her three yellow children, and said, with some ostentation, she should soon have another. The marked attention of the other women, plainly proved her to be the favourite Sultana of this vulgar, ugly, Scotch Sultan, who is about fifty, clumsy, ill made, and dirty.

Young English officers worry Nugent with their "improper connections," as in the case of "foolish Captain Johnson [who] is in great distress, about an ugly mulatto favourite, who has been accused of theft" (173). Even the ex-Governor of the colony, Lord Balcarres, has his menage (38) and in general, "white men of all descriptions, married or single, live in a state of licentiousness with their female slaves" (87). This did not end with slavery. The husband in Long's novel *The Golden Violet* (1936), soon succumbs to the current practice on arrival in post-abolition Jamaica, and to his wife's disgust acquires a mulatto mistress. What reservations, if any, do white women's texts reveal about their men's black sexual partners and the influence wielded by these partners? How did they feel about the "yellow" offspring of such liaisons, who often lived in the family home with their own legitimate children? Who, if anyone, is to blame?

Carmichael lays the guilt squarely on mulatto/brown women, labeling them the worst kind of sexual temptresses: similar sentiments recur in several of the early novels. According to her, colored women are proud, indolent, contemptuous of blacks and materialistic. In general, coloreds "as a population . . . are peculiarly inclined to immorality" (1969, vol. 1: 74), and as for the women, "to allure young men who are newly come to the country, or entice the inexperienced, may be said to be their principal object" (vol. 1: 69). For Carmichael (vol. 2: 178), all blacks are inherently promiscuous, and close contact with them contaminates the lesser orders of whites. Low-status white men on country estates, "having seldom or ever any females in their own situation in life to associate with, and to whom they might be respectably married, they get a negro [woman] . . . to live with them, until they . . . become as the expression is, almost *a white negro*" (vol. 1: 59; emphasis in original). White men of the better classes who lapse, she maintains, behave responsibly to their illegitimate offspring who are "amply furnished with every necessity of life" (vol.1: 94). This is not quite the picture painted by, among others, a disgusted Fenwick:

> What is still more horrible, the Gentlemen are greatly addicted to their women slaves, & give the fruit of their licentiousness to their white children as slaves. I strongly suspect that a very fine Mulatto boy about 14 who comes here to help wait on the breakfast & luncheon of two young Ladies, our pupils, is their own brother, from the likeness he bears to their father. It is a

common case & not thought of as an enormity. It gives me disgusted antipathy & I am ready to hail the Slave & reject the Master.

(1927: 169)

As Ferguson (1992) demonstrates at length, concern for female slaves as sexual victims of white men occupied an increasingly important place in anti-slavery writing by British women in the early nineteenth century. This concern is suggested by Fenwick; and in Mary Prince's narrative, as Brereton reminds us (1993: 13–14), sexual abuse is a submerged but powerful subtext. The missionary context of Prince's publication, and the conventions which demanded that female slaves be depicted as "pure" victims, meant that Mary's sexual experience would have been treated with extreme reticence by her editors. Nevertheless, Brereton "suspects that both Captain I——and Mr. Wood may have been sexually involved with their female chattel" (13) and notes Prince's clear reference to sexual abuse at the hands of Mr D——, who was given to stripping naked and ordering her to bathe him on pain of a beating.

There is plentiful evidence, then, that white men in the West Indies, whether married or single, were openly involved with black or brown mistresses.[8] Taking concubines was sometimes claimed to be the result of a scarcity of white women[9] but even in Barbados where there were more women than men across the races, Fenwick's narrative demonstrates that the practice was just as pervasive. As Bush (1990: 111) puts it, "sexual relations between black and white could create 'perpetual spirals of power and pleasure' " from which white women were excluded. Needless to say, interracial sexual congress for white women would have been tantamount to the kind of social death described in Cassin's late nineteenth-century novel, *With Silent Tread*, where a creole girl who marries a respectable young colored man is disowned by family and society. White women, then, shared their men with one or more black women. How do the early narratives describe their responses? Does cultural contact allow the Victorian patriarch to get away with less upright conduct in the tropics?

Such concerns surface in narratives along gender lines: "issues of miscegenation, . . . outraged virtue, and planter licentiousness are found foregrounded in diaries by Southern white women, while absent or in the background of the records of their planter husbands" (Carby 1987: 46). Certainly one can argue that in the Caribbean, most white as well as black women were in fact the chattels of white men. Hence the awareness of female powerlessness and vulnerability in texts by white British women which focus on the frail status of female slaves:

Granted, situations of middle-class white women and enslaved black women are fundamentally different but in some areas of masculinist exploitation, abuses lap over one another. Lack of protection and rights underpin anxious texts; in their somewhat ironic status as authors with assumed authority, white [women] writers betray the limits of their social power.

(Ferguson 1992: 237)

Ferguson maintains that in this situation,"[b]lack and white women confront comparable sexual predations, even the same predators" (235). So British female writers suggest in their texts awareness of a common – although differently configured – subjugation by white men, or project their own radical inclinations in the face of male oppression onto black female rebellion; both strategies underscore the interconnection of black and white women under slavery. Brereton (1993: 14) observes that in some cases "female slaves were capable, despite their own sexual jeopardy, of empathising with white women victimised by male power," as when Prince pities her mistress, Mrs Williams, for having a harsh and unfaithful husband, or attempts to protect Mr D——'s daughter from her father's savage beatings.

Narrative depictions of white women's sharing of "wifely duties" on the sexual front, can be seen as polarized along ideological lines. In some texts, slavery is to be blamed, and the black and brown women are the most wronged; for example, Fenwick sighs, "It is a horrid & disgraceful System. The female slaves are really encouraged to prostitution . . ." (1927: 169) and she absolutely loathes "these moral evils" (205) that are the system's legacy. But in others like Carmichael's, idealized white women are favorably contrasted with skilled black and brown courtesans, innately immoral, who seduce "their" men. Nugent's account of a white man's cruel treatment of his wife due to infatuation with his brown "favourite" (whom he ends up murdering in a jealous rage) reeks with disapproval of the latter while sympathetic to the wronged wife (1966: 182). And her constant worries about "our" young men being led astray by such "improper connections" indicates little concern for the soon-to-be-abandoned "improper connections" and their offspring. Oddly enough, Nugent is quite sanguine about a female slave, "wretched *little* Hortense," producing "a great German [baby] boy" (201; emphasis in original). Perhaps the fact that the white father is *not* one of "our young men" somewhat mitigates Hortense's folly. Generally speaking then, recognition of common sexual vulnerability is more difficult to "read into" the West Indian texts of white women. Any awareness of shared oppression was undermined by white women's recognition that their status depended on investment in racial "superiority," which prevented more than a sympathetic gaze at the Other.

For the mistress who had bought into the ideal of domestic virtue, yet lived in an intimate setting with her husband's "concubines and bastards," blaming them was perhaps the easiest course to take. Hence, Brereton (1993: 19) is skeptical about Schaw's view of white creole Antiguan women in the 1770s: "jealousy is a passion with which they are entirely unacquainted, and a jealous wife would be a most ridiculous character indeed." What is discreetly hinted here, is that Antiguan ladies were expected to accept and ignore their husbands' amorous entanglements with black and brown women. "A jealous wife" would indeed be inconvenient, but more tellingly, such emotion would be inappropriate for all kinds of reasons, not least that it acknowledged some kind of competition with a supposed inferior and implied that the "Angel in the House" experienced unbecoming sexual passions. But jealousy probably did manifest in less ladylike behavior. The representation of the rural mistress as prone to ill-treating her female slaves has been discussed previously, and Bush states that in the Caribbean white women were repeatedly said to react with jealousy when white men sought out black women (1990: 44, 114). Ferguson concurs that the "image of a cruel planter's wife was a common one. As a group, plantation mistresses were frequently alleged to be deeply jealous of black female slaves and politically powerless" to challenge their men's liaisons (1992: 161). The temptation to lash out at the available scapegoat, the black "mistress," is clearly irresistible for de Lisser's Annie Palmer and subtextually informs the construction of the sadistic plantation wife encountered in other narratives. Taking sexual rivalry to the extreme, *The Jamaica Lady* by "W. P." describes how a deceitful servant "whispered into her master's and mistress's ears, and made each jealous of the other's having too familiar a converse with the slaves, which caused such a disturbance in the family that . . . The master whipped the men, and the mistress the women, and then went to't themselves" (1963: 128–9).

In the urban setting, a wronged wife sometimes chose less violent means of articulating her sense of injustice. For example, Brodber (1982) refers to a Mrs Mary Emily Sampson, who took out an advertisement in the *Barbadian* newspaper in February, 1838. Her marriage to Thomas Sampson (clearly a man of substance, who owned properties in Broad Street and Roebuck Street) had been reported in the local press as taking place in the Cathedral two years previously, and Mary was the daughter of a Bridgetown merchant. For Brodber, this strongly indicates that the couple were "Euro-cultured whites" (10). In answer to Mr Sampson's notice in the press that his wife had left his home and he was not responsible for her debts, Mary spiritedly replies in the same forum that *she* is the injured party, explaining that "Mr. Sampson's extraordinary attachment to a servant has been the sole cause of his unkindness toward me" (9). In 1838 Barbados, the odds are overwhelming that the servant in question was a black woman, again testifying to the involvement of black women in the most intimate aspects of the white woman's life.

Sexual rivalry is the subject of an anonymous late eighteenth century poem discussed by Carolyn Cooper (1991). Put into the mouth of a female slave, the verses tell of her seduction by "massa" and the material rewards (clothes and cash) that accrue. But after she delivers massa's alleged child, the relationship sours: "When pickinniny him come black / My massa starve and fum [beat] me;/ He tear the coat from off my back,/ And naked him did strip me." In time, she reaches an understanding with the overseer and "[h]im get one pickinniny, white!" Thinking the white child is her husband's, "missess" thrashes the slave woman until massa interrupts the punishment, abusing his wife as a "lying bitch!" Here, a text which purports to illuminate the slave woman's consciousness inadvertently highlights the complex power relations that inform black and white female sexual roles. The "Angel in the House" is transformed into a vicious, defeminized white witch by her husband's preference for (supposedly pathological) black women.[10] The playing out of sexual and racial politics in the spheres of the erotic and the domestic (Pratt 1992: 105), demonstrates that easy assumptions about the superior status, power and fixed identity of white women in the

West Indies are all complicated by the crucial role played by her Other, the black slave woman or domestic servant, in the very definition of her sexuality. The mistress did not have the white man's power; nor, in the erotic sphere, did she have the same power *over* him as the black woman. This uneasy but *de facto* "division of labor" relating to conjugal duties in the early texts is another testament to the enforced intimacy of black and white women, of maids and mistresses, which obtained in colonial plantation society.

"Superseding me in one of the most precious parts of my expected duty": mothers and nannies

Perhaps the most vital role of white women in the success of the colonizing project, particularly in the so-called settler colonies, was the bearing and rearing of white children. If women internalized the importance of this function, undoubtedly reinforced by the celebration of motherhood as a crucial aspect of femininity, then one would expect childbirth and child rearing to dominate women's early narratives of the West Indies. Yet there are few references. Perhaps taboos on explicit treatment of sexual and bodily functions discouraged the inclusion of such material. Additionally, the choice of narrative perspective – as in Carmichael's detached observations of "manners and customs" – preclude reflections on such intimate aspects of women's lives. Nugent's diary, although suitably decorous, does give us a glimpse of what it was like.

Desperate about her failure to become pregnant, Nugent is miserable in December 1801 at the thought "that the dear name of mother will never greet my ear" (1966: 47). Her prayers are answered, however, and after intermittent complaints of illness she confides to her journal in July 1802 that "I return thanks fervently to God, and now look forward with more certainty and joy than ever to the arrival of my expected darling baby" (109). No delicate flower, Nugent rides around Jamaica on horseback during her pregnancy without ill effects. She is relatively frank – and highly amusing – on the subject of a "Creole confinement" (124):

> First, the heat is so dreadful, that it is impossible to go to bed. Then, to mitigate it a little, the blinds are kept closed. Then, the dark shade of the room brings swarms of musquitoes . . . Then, the old black nurse brought a cargo of herbs, and wished to try various charms, to expedite the birth of the child, and told me so many stories of pinching and tying women to the bed-post, to hasten matters, that sometimes, in spite of my agony, I could not help laughing, and, at others, I was really in a fright, for fear she would try some of her experiments upon me. But the maids took all her herbs from her, and made her remove all the smoking apparatus she had prepared for my benefit.

Nugent was dissuaded from breast-feeding little George, as "it would be impossible for me to do justice to my dear baby in this horrid climate, and with the many anxieties of a public situation" (119). In contrast, Carmichael claims (1969, vol. 1: 24) that planters' wives are "always suckling their children, and generally to a longer period than is usual in England; and never for any party or pleasure, trusting their infant to the hands of others." However, Carmichael is prone to self-contradiction as well as manipulating "facts" for polemical purposes. Elsewhere, her claim that "Negro children are brought up altogether differently from European infants" in that the black mother, "unless in cases where sickness prevents, always suckles her own child" (vol. 1: 188–9), clearly implies white mothers do *not* generally nurse their infants!

This is the case for Nugent, and an Irish wet nurse is secured. Mother grudgingly surrenders "the delightful idea of nursing" for the good of baby, although she concedes that she feels "half angry at her [the wet nurse] superseding me in one of the most precious parts of my expected duty . . . full of jealousy and worry about nurse Hamilton, for why should I not be a mother indeed" (122). In due course she achieves a close relationship with the woman who feeds her child, but her ambivalence about yielding this basic biological function is apparent. What was it like for white women of less elite status, for whom the wet nurse would very likely have been black? Beckles refers to a typical example, describing a white infant being breast-fed by a black nurse in a Barbadian dining room at the end of the 1790s. What is interesting is the disparity between the embarrassment of foreign onlookers and the casual attitude of the creole ladies, who even assist the process by "slapping, pressing, shaking about and playing with the long black breasts of the slave, with very indelicate familiarity" (1989: 69). Here is a paradigmatic vignette of the relationship of black and white women, once more sharing roles: in this case, the duties of motherhood. The black woman is without rights to her own body, and the white woman is circumscribed by social expectations in the employment of hers, and (once more) has to depend on her supposed "inferior" in this most intimate and "natural" of maternal duties.

Breast-feeding apart, the black nanny/nurse had a great deal of responsibility for the everyday care of white children. Indeed the elite child often had a retinue of female slaves or servants at his/her beck and call: young Dorothy of Lynch's *Years Ago* (1865: 8) casually mentions that "[w]e are obliged at this season to have three or four little [negro] boys, during breakfast-time, to stand round the table, continually waving orange boughs over it to keep off the flies." Nugent bewails the effect of such immoderate attention on her niece Bonella, who is "so spoiled that I am afraid she will be a little tyrant" (1966: 146). Fenwick's own children are grown, but she has the opportunity to observe her grandchildren in a household of black domestics and "dreads for them the sensual indulgences & luxury that most Children here are allowed" (1927: 200–1). Even Carmichael acknowledges that white West Indian children are overindulged by servants, although of course she finds a way to excuse their planter parents: knowing they will eventually have to send their darling abroad to be educated, they cannot bear "to cross the poor child" in the meantime (1969, vol. 1: 27).

Bridges's memoir of a Trinidadian childhood in the late nineteenth century portrays the extent to which white creole children were raised by black nurses and nannies, as does Rhys in *Smile Please* (1979), evoking her Dominican youth during a similar period. So throughout the slavery period and well into the twentieth century, privileged white children of creole or expatriate extraction were largely socialized in their early years by black women of the servant class. Again, language is a direct indicator of the extent of this daily and intimate cultural contact. Like Nugent, Carmichael and Symmonett, Lynch (1847: 17–18) acknowledges the thorough acculturation of white children as manifested in their fluent Creole speech: "although my mother had taken pains to keep me from what is called, amongst West Indians, 'talking negro,' yet, there was a langour and drawl in my manner of speaking, which drew from her the most cutting sarcasms." In the West Indies then, new kinds of cultural production evolved as did new types of relationships and tensions, new ways of identifying with and differentiating oneself; all of this, as is clear in the quote above, alarming to colonialists who vainly sought to maintain the originary purity of European "home" culture.

With regard to new kinds of relationships (and tensions), the narratives depict white mothers depending on black nannies and nurses at every phase of motherhood. How did they feel about this? On the one hand, texts suggest that mutual concern for the young child could unite women of different races and classes. In "Margaret: A Sketch in Black and White" (1896b), Augusta Fraser ("Alice Spinner") describes the close contact between "the mistress" and mulatto Margaret who becomes her baby's nursemaid. In her 1894 novel, *A Study in Colour*, Fraser details at some length a similar relationship between "the Missus" and Justina, her infant's nanny. After the sudden death of the child, we are told, "[g]rief had drawn the two women very near together" and indeed the Missus finds greater consolation "in the sight of poor ignorant Justina's inarticulate woe, than in the more finished sympathy of her English friends" (146). None the less, despite the shared bond of maternal affection, there is no overlooking the implicit gaps in status between "poor ignorant Justina" and the mistress's "English friends." Weiner quotes a Georgian plantation wife in 1856 on the issue of care for pregnant women, expressing "sympathy with my sex, wether [*sic*] white or black" (1996: 278). "[Mrs] Thomas clearly believed that being female led her to view slave women with a degree of sympathy not possible for men," Weiner comments, "in spite of the vast race and class differences that separated her from these women" (278). While Nugent demonstrates a benevolent interest in the new mothers among her household domestics and, in the post-slavery period, Fraser closely attends to Justina's career as a mother, the early West Indian texts do not generally portray empathy between black and white mothers.

This limitation on bonding by virtue of shared maternal roles is blatantly, if unconsciously, apparent in Bridges memories of a childhood nurse, Zabette (1988: 50). Born a slave, Zabette

> had grown up as the playmate of the master's children. Later she had suckled the child of her white foster-sister with one of her own. In due course she had taken over control of my grandfather's domestic staff, had acted as midwife to my mother at the birth of her first children, and returned after each of these confinements to dwell again in my grandfather's household. In her

room in his compound she lived in peace and dignity with all her wants provided.

After having delivered and nursed generations of white babies in the Rostant family, Zabette in her retirement speaks fondly of the mistress and her siblings as "me white chillum," and of her own children as "me black fambly" (50); there is little doubt which took priority. As Mary Prince learned, so too the faithful Zabette accepts that love of her "white chillum" will never suffice to make her part of *their* family.[11] Mary cuts ties with "white family," receiving nothing in recognition of her services. Nearly 100 years later, the loyal ex-retainer Zabette is still firmly in her place, in a room on the compound, with no mention of connections with her "black fambly."

On the other hand, there were many domestics who resisted the role of faithful surrogate-mother. Perhaps shared concern for children sometimes shifted barriers between white and black women, but the narratives also suggest that the division of childcare into the roles of mother and nanny led to increased awareness of, and resentment at the unequal nature of the arrangement. Certainly it appears that black women were aware of the power they held in being responsible for white children, and did not hesitate to convert this into improvement in status. Carmichael (1969, vol. 1: 29) comments that once a female servant was "appropriated for the children, she had twice the authority of either parent," and mentions cases where the "affection of the children towards . . . negro domestics was unbounded, and where they [the children] took no pains to conceal that they preferred the society of these servants to that of any white person." Obviously, nurses exploited this favored position and considered themselves "household aristocrats" who "would not so far forget their dignity as to wash their own clothes, brush out a room or indeed do anything but carry young miss or master" (Carmichael 1969, vol. 1: 121).

The nanny's range of influence extended further for she had, quite literally, the power of life and death over her young charges. The opening passage of an anonymous tale, *The Babes in the Basket* (1881: 6), foregrounds the potential danger represented by the nanny. Entering the room of two sleeping white children, the "striking contrast" between "her black face and . . . the fair children" seems ominous: "Who was that dark intruder, and what was her secret errand, in that quiet room?" Highlighting racial difference to denote ambivalent status, the narrator queries, "whether she came as a friend or an enemy, to the sleeping children of her master" (6). In the event, Daph proves as loyal and devoted as was Mary Prince to her charges. Still,

the unfolding of this complicated emotional and psychological entanglement presented slave holders with much discomfort. Many lived with the fear that nannies would murder their children, and as a result, infant mortalities were commonly enveloped in suspicion of foul play. Poisonings were rarely detected by white doctors . . . When in 1774, for example, a slave nanny described by her owners as a 'favourite' was convicted of poisoning their infant, it was discovered that this was not the only occasion on which she had done so.

(Beckles 1989: 69)

The care of white children, then, was a potential site of dramatically effective resistance against the mistress and master, even if the results were likely to lead to discovery and punishment. To illustrate, Carmichael (vol. 1: 272–3) relates how a servant, in retaliation for some perceived offence, gave her 2-year-old daughter a "delicacy" of mustard and country peppers, blistering the infant's mouth severely. More gravely, poison as a weapon of resistance was greatly feared, not just in the case of white children but for all members of the nanny's "white family." Cassin's novel includes an account of a black cook in a white household poisoning soup in revenge for "some vexation" and only repenting as they are about to drink. A young creole woman wryly explains the complexities of "West Indian [domestic] management" in such a case: to retain the cook despite her attempt means the family will probably be safe, while dismissal will likely inflame determination to complete the job (1890: 84)!

In the domestic world of the narratives, enforced interaction and mutual dependency of white and black women created the means for a destabilization of normative hierarchical categories of power. In handing over her precious children to a black nanny, the white mistress relinquished a great deal of her influence over these children; correspondingly, the nanny implicitly gained both status and the bargaining tool of fear, within the transaction, while presumably relinquishing the care of her own children to others. Attention to the particularities of white women's roles and the close involvement of black women in the performance of these, demonstrates a complex shifting of power relations as well as revealing some of the strategies, whether less overt (deceit, laziness, demands for status and privilege) or more dramatic (child abuse, neglect, poisoning), by which the "powerless" domestic slave/servant could manouevre to her advantage within the restrictions of a racially stratified society.

To conclude: the early texts also tell us something about the education of elite girl children in the West Indies. Brereton's survey (1993: 24–5) notes that Carmichael's young children were taught by an English governess; while this suggests privileged status, one recalls Lanaghan's dismissal of English governesses in Antigua, finding them ill-educated girls down on their luck and willing to take any employment. Fenwick's letters attest to the existence of some decent girls' schools in Barbados, and Carmichael mentions the good reputation of similar establishments in Trinidad. But such education only went so far in the Caribbean. Eventually, Brereton concludes, "elite or would-be elite parents tried to send their girls to England for a 'polish.' " An example is Miss Israell of Clarendon, Jamaica, who was 'educated at a "fashionable" London school, [and] was forever consumed with anxiety lest her country-bumpkin parents embarrass her' (Nugent 1966: 58). Bridges[12] describes her rather desultory late nineteenth-century schooling: a kindergarten in Port of Spain run by two "French Creole" spinsters, followed by a stint of tutoring with the English daughter of the principal of Queen's Royal College, and finally a private school run by Miss Bunkle, an English woman. When the family moved to the country, Yseult was taught sporadically by her father until at 14 came the inevitable: she was shipped off to England to be "finished" before entering society, in order to eradicate "the insidious singsong Creole accent and acquire that poise and complexion, that cachet, which would enhance her chance of making a 'good match' . . . the whole object of a woman's existence" (Bridges 1988: 157). Bridges account ends in 1902, when she left Trinidad. In 1934, Eliot Bliss published *Luminous Isle* which also draws on her own childhood.[13] Born in Jamaica in 1903, she too was sent off to England to be educated although her exile began earlier, at age 9. It is clear from the fictional protagonist's account that the result of this sojourn abroad has little to do with education per se and everything to do with fitting her for the social rounds of "a garrison town in a Crown colony" (Bliss 1984: 87). Again, marriage was the final goal, and in the marriage competition the white creole girls found it hard to "compete with the fresh young English girls wintering in the Island during the cooler months with a trunkful of new clothes" (128). Local schooling or foreign "polishing," for a young white woman in the West Indies the end of both was to make "a good match."

Marriage, "the whole object of a woman's existence," ushered in the tripartite destiny of wife, mother and mistress of a household, a model which explicitly or implicitly informs the ideal in most of the early narratives discussed in this book. In this chapter, I have argued that in the execution of these central roles – of sexual partner, childcare-giver and domestic manager – white women are represented as sharing responsibilities with, and often being undermined or superseded by, black women domestics, slave and free. Given that these roles were intrinsic to the white female's private *and* public sphere, one can argue that the slave system and its aftermath impinged crucially on the world of the mistress, perhaps at an even more fundamental level than that of the master whose public and private spheres were more differentiated. Further, we can extrapolate from the accounts that since the roles which were central to white women's self-construction depended as much – if not more – on the participation of black women as on white men, diffuse shifts and exchanges of power across race and gender occurred. The white woman, powerless under patriarchy, *had* power over black women and men; the black woman, powerless in a racially stratified society, *had* power over white men; the white woman, empowered as domestic manager, yet was powerless to fulfill her role without dependence on the black woman. Certainly, the female-authored narratives discussed rarely portray black women as passive and ineffectual; neither do they represent black women as considering *themselves* to be inferior or powerless. Troublesome they might be, dangerous, incorrigible, deceitful and more, perhaps, but hardly passive victims. To the extent that this textual selection proves representative of the writing under study, one can argue for a revision of some of the previously fixed coordinates used to inscribe the mistress/servant relationship, and of stereotypical constructions of white as well as black women bound by such relationships during the nineteenth and early twentieth centuries.

3 "This is another world"

Travel narratives, women and the construction of tropical landscape

Sailing sunny seas: women's travel writing

Moving on from early representations of white women in the West Indies, I turn now to a central concern of this book: how such women represented the *place*. How did women writers see the West Indies, how did they feel about what they saw, and how did they tell it? In particular, how did they represent the place within a specific kind of narrative, that of the travelogue? Of course, in naming the genre I risk falling at the first hurdle, as travel writing is a notoriously tricky genre. A few quotations indicate the difficulty of defining the category. For Percy Adams, noting its ties with history, geography and the evolving novel, "[t]he literature of travel is gigantic; it has a thousand forms and faces" (1983: 281). As narrative genre, it eludes categorization to the point where Adams is forced to "define it by negatives" (279): so that the "recit de voyage" (his preferred term) is not just a first-person journal or diary, is not only in prose, is not just a set of notes jotted down by the traveler, is not simply an objective report of people and places seen (it has a subjective component), is not only present-tense "observation" but switches back and forth in time with interpolations of all kinds, and so on and on. In short, for Adams, this is not "a literary genre with a fixed definition any more than the novel is" (282). Pratt would seem to agree, since her study aims "not to circumscribe travel writing as a genre but to suggest its heterogeneity and its interactions with other kinds of expression" (1992: 11). Reviewing a recent crop of representative critical studies, Glenn Hooper reiterates the constantly evolving, hybrid, volatile nature of the narratives grouped within under this head (2001: 57).

None the less, let me briefly outline some of the main types of travel writing, starting with Pratt's overview of texts produced in the period of European colonization of the New World. The earlier sub-genre of "survival" literature, dealing with voyage, shipwreck and the contingencies of the traveler's struggle with a new environment, is epitomized by Defoe's *Robinson Crusoe* (1720). It generally utilizes a first-person narrator, detailing hardships and dangers endured as well as marvels and curiosities encountered. Then there is the more "scientific" exploration account, generally "objective" and descriptive, which catalogues data: measurements, climatic conditions, species of flora and fauna, topographical features and the like. This type of narrative of the new place, Pratt considers part of "a

European knowledge-building" in the eighteenth century: a "systematizing of nature" within "a finite totalizing order of European making" (38). In this writing, human presence – observer, observed – is marginal.

By contrast, the authority of the "sentimental" travel narrative "lies in the authenticity of somebody's felt experience" (Pratt 1992: 76). This writing details accounts of a particular traveler's sojourn and adventures in foreign parts. Crudely put, the scientific exploration account collects specimens; the sentimental travel narrative collects sympathetic stories. Finally, there is the "natural history" text in which the travel writer focuses on landscape or produces an ethnographic "manners-and-customs" account of the (populated) new place. As Pratt puts it, such writing is more obviously imperial in intention: "one produces land as landscape and territory, scanning for prospects; the other produces the indigenous inhabitants as bodyscapes, scanned also for prospects" (64). In the nineteenth century, the investment of nature with transcendent values further colors landscape in travel narratives, fusing scientific observation with "the esthetics of the sublime" (121). This "primal nature" is what Victorian travel writers "discovered."

One can simplify, perhaps, by attending to the style of narration of a travelogue. Some present the narrative as dispassionate reportage, factual and transparent, and tend to be third-person, present-tense accounts, very specific as to locations and physical features described, with minimal inclusion of the narrator's personal reactions. Indeed, the narrator of such texts is, in Pratt's terms, a "landscanning, self-effacing producer of information" (78). Others utilize a first-person and thus more "personal" voice, spontaneously articulating apparently random sights, events and observations which are juxtaposed in a manner that suggests the (apparent) absence of any overall narrative plan. Sara Mills's *Discourses of Difference* (1991), which deals specifically with women's accounts of their travels during the "high imperial" period of British colonization (mid-nineteenth to early twentieth centuries), again observes the distinction between the two types of author function: the impersonal or the foregrounded. In the first, statements emanate from a distanced gaze and people are simply traces on the landscape described; in the second, the narrator interacts with place and people visited, and statements originate in a personal source. By the nineteenth century, travel writings tended to slot into one of these two models: either "factual guides" or more impressionistic "literary" accounts.

It seems then, that the scholarship generally agrees on certain points. Firstly, that travel writing by men or women tends to be intertextual, in that narratives draw on earlier texts. Travelers came with preconceived images of what they expected to see, culled from books, stories, pictures and the media. Mimi Sheller notes one observer describing his impressions of Barbados in 1804, freely confessing his expectations and acknowledging their sources: earlier "historical" texts and "youthful visions" from illustrated books, the latter helping to explain why, as with many so travel writers, landscape is described as if in a painted composition. The West Indies, then, is "already mapped in their 'unconscious' before ever setting foot there" (Sheller 2001: 16). As Gikandi comments, personal experience and observation of the new territory serves to confirm what is already known, so that in the case of colonies like the West Indies, travel narratives are "haunted by prior accounts from the imperial archive" and what is recorded actually serves as "a rediscovery of the already discovered" (1996: 97). Hence, for Mills, earlier descriptions form the basis for reading the new space, which is seen "through a previously written conceptual grid" (73).[1] Indeed, for each territory there is an agenda of sites/sights considered worth seeing and to which the present narrative can only add some wittily variant observation or update some previous insight.

Secondly, as Gikandi argues, since British colonies played a crucial role in the formation of English identities, the trope of travel generates narratives concerned with "self realization in the spaces of the other" (1996: 8). And this "realized" self was normatively male: the traveler situated himself in a long line of heroic adventurers through Raleigh, Drake and Rodney. "The essence of Englishness – and, alas, masculinity – is predicated," he claims, "on a certain affiliation with the romantic history of empire" (103). In the travelogue, one could compensate for anxieties about the present state of England by reliving dreams of past valor, and hence reassure the intended English audience (and oneself) that despite problems at home the alternative abroad is barbarism and decay. Accordingly, texts tend to follow a common plot, detailing adventures in a remote setting, with challenges to the traveler necessitating heroic exploits that demonstrate (male) virtues of courage, fortitude, leadership and quick thinking. Like Pratt, Mills notes the "genre expectation" that such adventures should occur in a primal landscape which is duly mastered (as are the native inhabitants on its margins) by compiling information about it, by "knowing" it. Logically, travel narratives are related to quest journeys: here, the quest is for something strange to describe (which, of course, affirms the societal norm "at home"), thereby demonstrating both the author's superior categories of knowledge, and the "reality" of the country visited.

Lastly, travel narratives tend to be complicit in the consolidation of imperial rule in their methodology of reduction and homogenization. The new is described as different, but in a pejorative sense. In such texts, as Pratt points out (1992: 120), others are homogenized into a collective "they," distilled even further into an iconic "he," "the Negro," or "the native." The Other rarely acts as an individual, but demonstrates instances of pre-given traits. This is also the case, adds Mills, with the assignment of the "Other place" to a different time – different from the narrator's own – by the use of temporal aspects like "primitive," "backward" and "developing." Native others are represented as children, not yet in the temporal space of adult Europeans and thus, like children, often inferior in terms of rationality, cleanliness and moral scruples. The strange landscape is also depicted as less evolved, less "human" than the European, according to which it is consistently judged and found lacking. Certainly this is the gist of Paravisini-Gebert and Romero-Cesareo's take on "narratives of travel" (2001: 7) in which the complex Caribbean ("imagined, historical, coveted, fragmented, multilingual, hybrid – at once object of desire and confined space from which to escape"), is seen through imperial eyes "as a homogeneous territory, peopled by 'others' of distinctly separate race and culture, easily fitted into colonial hierarchies and within rigid categories." In the rest of this chapter, I want to test these general observations about travel writing against a range of early constructions of the West Indies by women.

Certainly women traveled – and wrote – in large numbers in the eighteenth and nineteenth centuries. Chaudhuri and Strobel (1992) point out that there were multiple reasons for women embarking on voyages to empire. Some traveled for "adventure, authority, and enhanced status" in professions such as nursing (9); women missionaries "went to the colonies to transplant Western values and culture" (10) as well as to reform and improve women's lives in these far-flung corners of the world; some, particularly the wives, daughters and sisters of men attached to colonial institutions, undoubtedly wished to help in the task of explicating empire to those at home; some traveled for their health, and others for "travel's own sake," usually after the death of parents or husbands allowed access to the necessary money and independence. Undoubtedly, a certain fascination with the exotic – witness the fad for "chinoiserie" and "Ottoman furnishings" in the late nineteenth century – as well as a simple wish to escape the restrictions of British society, fueled the desire of many women to venture abroad. But do their travelers' tales manifest the general trends outlined: intertextuality, projection of (male) self-affirmation, and complicity in imperial homogenization of the Other? Appropriating Susan Blake's title (1992), I am asking "what difference does gender make?"

What difference does gender make?

W. J. McCormack (1985: 73–4) characterizes the traveler as one who "enacts that expansive, aggressive spirit which characterizes the rise of the bourgeois individual," acknowledging the new as simply a field for his activity rather than the product of a fully mutual subject/object relationship. There is, of course, a crucial connection between this "expansive, aggressive spirit" and the colonizing mission, and Blake is but one critic who maintains "the implicit imperialism of all travel by Europeans in the empire" (1992: 20). In the African context, for example, the travel narrator resembles imperial agent in that both

> undertake to conquer, grasp, or assimilate challenging lands and alien peoples. They exercise the power they have (wealth, stamina, ingenuity, flexibility) to gain more power (knowledge of land, people, flora, fauna; knowledge of self; sense of achievement). They requisition food, shelter, carriers, and guides and return cash, medical attention, and glimpses and tokens of European culture. Like the empire, they both assert authority over and depend upon the people they encounter.
>
> (Blake 1992: 21–2)

Pratt too sees travel writers thematizing European expansionist designs: for her, travel writing participates in "the rhetoric of discovery" and "a goal-oriented rhetoric of conquest and achievement." Destinations, in place of kingdoms, are conquered textually; logistical, rather than military challenges are overcome (1992: 148). However, within colonialist discourse lie the seeds of its own deconstruction. Hence Pratt notices certain ideological cracks in earlier travel narratives which sometimes "affirm plausible worlds of African agency and experience" (84). Chaudhuri and Strobel observe that some texts can even be read for resistance, since they mix "endorsement of empire with accounts of personal experience that undercut imperial notions of superiority" (1992: 6). So despite the propensity of the travel narrator to draw authority from investment in a "superior" British identity, perhaps the writing itself is not always necessarily invested in the imperial enterprise? Steve Clark, for one, questions reductive generalizations which insist that travel narratives invariably "promote, confirm and lament the exercise of imperial power; and that this ideology pervades their representational practices at every level" (1999: 3). Rather, he wishes to examine such writing for "certain generic resistances to any simplistic equation with the exercise of power" (4). In this chapter, I attend to the complex nature of the "exercise of power" in the work of women travel writers.

Consider for instance how Winifred James opens her account of a trip to the Caribbean: "Knowledge of geography I have none," she confesses, "for no place has any meaning to me till I have actually seen it" (1913: 7). The declaration is disingenuous, given that the exotic is already partially mapped out in terms of imperialist discourse. Hence the "ignorant" James none the less knows in advance of her visit some vital information about Jamaica: it is "a hot place and belonging to Us" (7). At the same time, James's narrative persona, whose plans for the voyage involve overcoming her terror lest she encounter cockroaches, is hardly representative of the "expansive, aggressive spirit" of the (male) colonizing zealot. Does gender then make a difference to the travelogue's supposedly implicit promotion of the imperial norm? For Blake (1992: 19), such a question suggests "the hope that women, colonized themselves by gender, might recognize and oppose colonization based on race." The word "hope" here is revealing. What is suggested is that women's travel narratives are frequently read through a critical template with its own (feminist) political agenda. Laura Donaldson, in her introduction to *Decolonizing Feminisms* (1992), comments on the trend in feminist studies to adopt the metaphor of man = colonizer, woman = colonized, citing sources which conflate the colonization of underdeveloped countries and female oppression within capitalism. According to this logic, women as a group would share an awareness of oppression with other marginalized groups.

Despite this questionable assumption, the point has been made that women participated in colonial ideology or praxis differently from the way that men did. Mills argues that

> In the colonial context, British women were only allowed to figure as symbols of home and purity; women as active participants can barely be conceived of. This is because of social conventions for conceptualising imperialism, which seem to be as much about constructing *masculine* British identity as constructing a national identity *per se* . . . women's writing and their involvement in

colonialism was markedly different from men's . . . women travel writers were unable to adopt the imperialist voice with the ease with which male writers did. The writing which they produced tended to be more tentative than male writing, less able to assert "truths" of British rule without qualification.

(1931: 3; emphasis in original)

For Mills, gender inequality and women's marginal position in relation to imperialism, problematize easy application to these narratives of Said's blanket term, "Orientalism." Given the difficulty of women writers assuming an official voice,[2] attempts to represent themselves as imperial mouthpieces are subject to textual fissures. Indeed Mills argues that "Orientalism itself . . . was an exclusively male province" (57). Hence, it was a natural progression from the "rightness" of male authority in the domestic sphere to the rightness of male domination of the subject peoples of the world (Chaudhuri and Strobel 1992: 11). So, while some women might envisage empire as an opportunity for adventure, freedom and advancement, their own subordinate position makes it impossible for them to "unconditionally valorize the imperial voice" in their texts (Gikandi 1996: 123).

As noted, much women's travel writing has been enthusiastically coopted by feminist scholarship. For example Mills notes how the more autobiographical accounts have been read as proto-feminist "adventure narratives depicting strong, resourceful, women characters in situations rarely found in the literature of the period"(1991: 4). Moira Ferguson (1992: 206) also asserts that women travel writers "as subjects who write, speak, negotiate, travel and refuse to be used [,] privilege themselves within a stringently patriarchal community." Writers who foreground a resourceful, independent female agent, may indeed force readers to reconsider sexist perceptions about travel: at the least, they call attention to such perceptions. An amusing incident from James's *The Mulberry Tree* may serve as an example on a small scale. In her preface (1913: 4), she recalls a childhood desire for travel and adventure while realizing that travel was a man's prerogative so that even her imaginary voyages had to be conducted through a male persona. Now, finally voyaging in person, James emphasizes the particular stresses a woman encounters in the field. Sensitive to the "type of British male one meets traveling" (23) who considers the ship's deck to be masculine territory in the early morning, James challenges this hegemony and steadfastly holds her position at the rail, ignoring the claims of "all men in ill-fitting, unbecoming garments [pajamas] and of slippered feet and unshaven face" (24). If she claims a little space for women travelers here, she is also sending up any pretensions to heroic status in their accounts. For as Mills points out (1991: 119), in the nineteenth and early twentieth centuries, women's self-representation in terms of an "expansive, aggressive spirit" – however modern readers might approve such a subversive role – would have been considered eccentric, abnormal, even slightly ridiculous and their narratives cast in doubt as exaggerated "women's tales" (112).

James is in fact a recognizably feminist travel writer, and inserts herself into her account with energy and wit. The eponymous mulberry tree which doubled as imaginary ship during childhood, serves as a metaphor for her early and unladylike yearning for travel and adventure. No longer only a dream, "this time I go my distances and make my adventure in my body as well as in my mind, with the same happy ignorance as to what will befall" (1913: 7). Here, James calls on a recurring trope in nineteenth-century travel writing by women: the contrast between the constricting world of European home and the exciting unknown abroad, onto which is projected the desire for freedom, for a space from which to explore new "subject positions." After all, the very act of journeying is in some way "motivated by (and thus an admission of) deficiency and lack" (Clark 1999: 14–15). And what is the deficiency in the situation of this elite Englishwoman that prompts a desire to escape? Self-mockingly, James explains her motivation: "I am tired of chintz and telephones and maids who breathe heavily when they are shown the dust on the piano top. I will go down into the city and talk with the fates" (4). Here again, the questing adventurer gives way to the more common narrative persona of helpless lady. Her brave determination to travel translates into passively entrusting a firm of shipping agents to decide "my most immediate destiny," leaving her with "but the consideration of clothes" (7), and a niggling worry about cockroaches: "they have such horrible black bodies and scrawly legs – men don't understand us." Such concerns are clearly trivial to the decision makers ("the fates") who frostily inform her that "[t]here are no cockroaches on Our ships" (15). The exchange is amusing but also clearly self-deprecating: assuming a timid but well-meaning persona reinforces the femininity of the narrator. As Kröller points out (1990: 96), the bemused and "muddled" observations of the helpless lady traveler, and the self-deprecating references to herself and her text, can serve to place the undertaking of the journey within ironic brackets, belittling any pretensions to "serious" exploration and adventure.[3]

Much of the travel writing discussed in this chapter utilizes this persona. Wilcox opens her account with the edict of "Himself" (her husband) that "we would take a little voyage to Cuba" (1909: 11), and stresses throughout that "Himself was, as usual, right and, as usual, my reward came from obeying him" (226). In terms of her own authority she makes it clear that "this chronicle of sailing in sunny seas claims to be nothing but personal experiences, impressions and adventures" (195). Similarly, Margaret Newton's introduction to *Glimpses of Bermuda and the Tropics* (1897) also constructs her narrative persona within a feminine model: diffident about offering her text, she presents herself as needing to be cared for, assiduously listing everyone who "kindly agreed to help" or "generously transported" her, even when it is clear that she paid for such services. Like many women travelers, she inserts repeated disclaimers and apologies for failings in the accuracy or comprehensiveness of her findings. Newton's strategy is to portray herself in the role of artist, a sensitive and impressionable – and feminine – viewer of beautiful scenes, which she then sketches for the enjoyment of others.

From a feminist perspective then, assuming the "helpless lady" persona does mark the gendered nature of narrative, but in a feminine rather than a feminist manner. None the less, however helpless as women, neither Newton nor the other "feminine" travelers question their presence in the colonies. From a postcolonial perspective, the racial, national and economic privilege that makes their journeys possible belies the powerlessness that this persona suggests. That there are complex interconnections between discourses of feminism and femininity, colonialism and anti-colonialism in women's travel narratives should by now be apparent. I argued in my introduction that problems of appropriation chiefly arise when rigid critical readings attempt to claim the writing for unitary ideological purposes: for example, the desire on the part of interested critics to read into a body of narrative either imperialist consolidation or complicity in feminine submission, or to read "against the grain" for postcolonial or feminist resistance. A more productive strategy, it seems obvious, is to approach the material in a historically contextualized manner which attends to interactions of gender, race and class within different types of colonialisms.[4]

Mills takes this sensible path in noting that "the clash of feminine and colonial discourses constructs texts which are at one and the same time presenting a self which transgresses and which conforms both to patriarchal and imperial discourses" (1991: 106). I should mention here Seacole's 1857 travel journal, although it is only tangentially concerned with constructing the West Indies. None the less, it illustrates intersecting discourses in that Seacole too undercuts the masculinist genre of the adventure quest by representing herself as an independent and resourceful female traveler, thus complicating Victorian notions of "femininity": "[m]y present life was not agreeable for a woman with the least delicacy and refinement" (1984: 100). In addition, she undermines colonialist discourse by proudly asserting her creole status and appropriating the gaze of the discoverer to comment on European space. Recording reactions to herself in Constantinople, she privileges her own cosmopolitan sophistication by essentializing the European "natives" (132):

> Somewhat surprised, also, seemed the cunning-eyed Greeks, who throng the streets of Pera, at the unprotected Creole woman who took Constantinople so coolly (it would require something more to surprise her); while the grave English raised their eyebrows wonderingly, and the more vivacious French shrugged their pliant shoulders into the strangest contortions. I accepted it all as a compliment to a stout female tourist . . .

However, her narrative is also informed by a certain ambivalence when it comes to national and colonial loyalties. Attention to just such intersecting discourses deflects rigid superintendence of political/theoretical boundaries in reading how women wrote "the West Indies."

"Female features": the confessional, ambivalence and relationship to the land

Mills's case is that women writers who inserted themselves into the "masculinist" constraints of the travel narrative had difficulty with a number of generic conventions, including the adoption of the voice of the (male) hero. Additionally, there was a tension between the woman writer's need to fulfil cultural expectations of the "feminine" (properly concerned with domestic and interpersonal relations) at the same time as describing her deliberate entry into a world of novelty, difficulty and even danger abroad. Negotiating between the powerful discourses of colonialism and femininity, women had to modify and manipulate the genre. For example, Blake (1992: 20) notes that male travel writers follow a pattern whereby the hero overcomes obstacles (the intractable landscape, or native) and proves his manhood by "getting things done" through either force or superior knowledge. For the female, such options are closed; thus women's travel writing tends to be more concerned with interpersonal relations, acknowledging the value of judicious reciprocity on the trail, and in the text. The woman traveler, in other words, is always a lady.

For the female traveler, maintains Clark (1999: 21–2), an "element of doubling is always present: the persona of adventurer may be inhabited, but always with a degree of circumspection . . . If the desire to depart may plausibly be seen as a repudiation of femininity on a number of levels – maternal embrace, conjugal fidelity – the female traveller is at the very least a site of generic contradiction." I want to return later to the implications of this slippery narrative voice, which leads, one could argue, to a fundamentally plural reading of the text and that which the text constructs: "the West Indies." For the moment, however, let us attend to what the women writers did with the genre. Gillian Whitlock (1994: 90), for example, points to Mary Gaunt's explicit desire to record "trivial daily happenings" as against the "serious matter" of male travel writers. James too, has an informing "domestic eye" in her travel account, self-consciously recording little details of furniture arrangement, appearance and fashion, prices and cost-cutting measures and so on. A similar interest in detailing "trivial things" characterizes Nugent's journal, and indeed as James openly expresses admiration for this journal, it is interesting to speculate on intertextual links between the two.[5]

By attending to such modifications of generic conventions, critics have isolated a number of features common to female-authored travel narratives. In the rest of this section, I want to discuss three of these features – the "spontaneous," confessional form of women's travel narratives; ambivalence about "truth value" of the works; and relationship with landscape in the texts – as manifested in my selection of travelogues. Studies of nineteenth-century women travelers and their texts – by Pratt, Mills, Chaudri and Strobel and others – neglect narratives set in the West Indies. As a corrective, I focus in this chapter on a number of works by Jamaican creole writers, as well as by English, Irish, American and Australian women who wrote about the region. Chronologically, the texts under discussion range from Mrs Lynch's *The Mountain Pastor* (1852) and *The Wonders of the West Indies* (1861) to the second of Gaunt's two Caribbean travel narratives, *Reflection – in Jamaica* (1932).[6]

The Mountain Pastor is a collection of moral tales put into the mouth of the eponymous rector, and can only be termed a travel narrative in the prefatory letter, which invites "my young friends" to leave the crowded streets of London and "search with me in a far distant island of the West" (Jamaica) for the beautiful tropical highlands where the Mountain Pastor has his home (3). These mountains are described in a style that shifts between lyrical rhapsody, natural history and a Romantic predilection to see God everywhere in nature. *The Wonders of the West Indies* (1861: 3), is also prefaced by a letter distinguished by an overblown lyricism ("The tropical dews, resting like heavy rain on the morning world") and a propensity to praise the Almighty for his creation. There follows a potted history of the various peoples and territories of the region, their provenance, folklore, crops and so on. Both of Lynch's introductory narratives speak for the narrator *and* for a group (an "us" to whom this beauteous tropical world is strange and new). It is on these initial sections of the texts that I will focus.

Symmonett's *Jamaica: Queen of the Carib Sea* (1895) announces itself as "a synopsis of the actual manners, customs and appearance of the natives, with a few of the most prominent sceneric features of attraction" (4). But the narrative proper takes the form of a dramatized shipboard dialogue between travelers, some of whom are Jamaica-bound and others who warn that this "Isle of Springs" is a "God-forsaken hole" (6), full of cannibals, drunken savages, disease, alligators, wild hogs and the like. This is followed by a description of arrival in Jamaica, the first sight of which demonstrate the horror-stories to have been a hoax, and ends with a lengthy letter combining "manners-and-customs" information with hyperbolic praise for the island's social amenities and physical attributes.

Glimpses of Life in Bermuda and the Tropics (1897) is Newton's "record of my wanderings in the regions of unending summer," based on some twelve month's residence. The diffident first-person narrator gives us "glimpses" of several West Indian islands, purportedly to encourage other visitors, liberally interspersing the mix of "manners-and-customs," natural history and "painterly" descriptions with her own black and white sketches. Her methodology is to describe "rambles" taken in pursuit of "subjects" which are then painted or sketched, accompanied by various subjective impressions and nuggets of information. Like all the other narratives, hers waxes lyrical about the natural beauty of the Caribbean.

May Crommelin's short account of a week's holiday in the Blue Mountains soon after her arrival in "the dream-island," is aptly titled "The Mountain-Heart of Jamaica" (1898).[7] A first-person account, it is a breathless whirl through the (sensationalized) history of the island, subjective impressions of encountered natives – often seen through the semi-fictional filter of historical romances – and effusive praise for the "other worldly" mountain scenery. Several photographs are included.

Also supplemented by her own photographs and verses, Wilcox's *Sailing Sunny Seas: A Story of Travel* (1909), is an account of a series of cruises to Cuba, Jamaica, Haiti, Porto Rico [*sic*], Dominica, Trinidad, Santo Domingo, St Thomas and Martinique, as well as Honolulu. The motive is a respite from cold New York winters: "Oh, the joy of it, as we sailed away on December 20th, knowing that we had the whole beautiful winter ahead of us in summer lands, to dream, rest, saunter, read and write, and do as impulse and fancy willed" (37). The first-person narrative is straightforwardly from the point of view of the tourist, although response to the islands is biased in favor of the superior "management" of American territories.

James's *The Mulberry Tree* (1913) is an (often irreverent) travel account which recounts impressions of and adventures in Jamaica, with side trips to Haiti, Costa Rica and the Panama Canal. Several photographs are appended. James's narrative persona quite specifically owns the tourist gaze. She travels, we are told, "to satisfy my curiosity" and "for fun . . . not to gather statistics. I want to see what other places are like and how other people live" (175). Hers is an ostensibly light and consciously witty travelogue, although her fascination with the variety of human-kind – including her fellow tourists – is sometimes tinged with asperity. The passage describing an American influx into the Myrtle Bank Hotel astutely observes tourist behavior at its worst, long before Jamaica Kincaid's modern satire of West Indian tourism in *A Small Place*. The narrator distances herself from such gauche types (29):

> Young men with padded shoulders, enormous trousers and bulgy-toed shoes tied with sash ribbons, spinsters out in their middle age to know the world, all except the cynical children, sworn as one man to see the most that could be seen and do the most that could be done in the time, all looking out for information with the same intentness as lizards look for flies, all with the same awful intelligence and the same nerve-destroying voices.

Her intended English audience is invited to enjoy a bit of fun at the expense of the Americans.

Gaunt's *Reflection – in Jamaica* (1932) is the longest of the texts, preceded by an introductory account of the narrator's lifelong wish to travel to "wild" and roman-tic places, which – as Whitlock discusses – is exactly how she constructs the island of Jamaica on this, the occasion of her second visit. Emphasizing her gender and her intention to depart from the format of her hero (a male travel writer, Captain Speke), she proposes to "write about trivial things" and to impart a "tale of Jamaica" which "is not a tale of what the ordinary tourist sees" (viii). Indeed, the travel narrative is very much about Gaunt herself and her tour of the island, conveyed in a series of rambling anecdotes in which places and people are fre-quently excuses for forays into a melodramatic, romantic fantasy of the island's past. Once again, the text praises the gorgeous natural glory of this exotic place, and includes a number of photographs.

From these brief synopses, it is clear that the writers favor the "sentimental" rather than the "scientific," the "literary" or poetic rather than the factual mode, and frequently assume a spontaneous, personal, confessional style. Even so, there are no hard and fast rules. As noted previously, Carmichael's apparently private journal is clearly written for the public eye, though she acknowledges the need to "recur to a personal narrative in my statement of facts" (1969, vol. 1: 115). On the other hand, Newton's "poetic" sentiments do not disguise her fascination with recording biological, botanical and ethnological details. Generally speaking, how-ever, the "personal" mode dominates, and the use of letters, journals, diaries or other confessional forms is common among the sample I have read. These vehicles were considered appropriate for women, given that the accretive epistolary/anecdotal form was, as Mills (1991: 104) points out, perceived to be "loose enough to contain their unstructured narratives." The confessional style tends to avoid specialized language (like statistical data), claiming to be just a collection of random notes; although Newton's assertion that her "glimpses" were "written at the time with a view to keep the memory fresh for me than with any distinct idea of publication" (1897: 2) hardly disguises the fact that her text is a consciously worked, selective document. Additionally, women's travel writing was thought to border on the fictional in its use of dramatized dialogue, poetic language and detailed descriptive passages, a claim that James's and Symmonett's narratives certainly support. And since such "feminine" forms invited reception as autobiography or fiction, the "truth value" of women's travel writing was often in question.

So for example, when Gaunt observes "objectively" that "[b]lood is hot in the Tropics" (1932: 109) there is a certain amount of doubt about the basis of her "ethnographic" assertion, since it is supported by reference to an imagined vignette in which "two men set their hearts on the same woman . . . The hussy very likely doesn't play fair . . . A wild burst of temper and a deed is done that many a man has expiated on the gallows" (110). Kröller correctly points to the "confessional" form allowing for a certain discursiveness, redundancy and spontaneous response which have much in common with literary narratives. Certainly, Crommelin's description of horse-riding in the mountains (1898: 526) plainly invites a "literary" response:

> As each swift minute took us deeper into the heart of the hills, the opposite mountain side became a green sloping sea of tropical foliage – here leafy swells, there high palm-breakers. Beetling cliffs rose high over our heads, overgrown with forest giants . . .

A swift plunge into the threatening sea of vegetation, turbulent with swells and breakers, and ominous beetling cliffs all around: surely this portends some storm, some crisis? But no, the expedition ends with a somewhat mundane account of a Jamaican breakfast of "Akee, mixed with saltfish"!

Attempting to authorize an account by foregrounding herself, explains Mills (1991: 112), "in turn poses problems of credibility because strong women narrator figures conflict with the cultural norms for women." After all, as Lady Anne Barnard writes from Cape Town at the end of the eighteenth century, "expert knowledge which is always claimed by the male traveller, must be avoided by a woman" as any pretension to expertise will be resented (Lenta 1991: 3). So writers who draw on male models (using the persona of an adventurer or employing a scientific account of discovery) would be viewed as odd and thus untrustworthy. But others who adopt the discourse of femininity and write "like a woman" (using the confessional mode, opting for a sentimental or poetic style) are suspected of the exaggeration to which their sex is prone. Clark (1999: 21) disputes this: for him, the perceived "falsehood" of women's travel narratives "is intrinsic to the *genre*" (my emphasis). Still, in the case of women's appropriation of a suspect genre, the doubt about veracity was undoubtedly greater. Anxiety about the reception of their texts may account for the inclusion of maps, photographs and drawings in order to authenticate the "objective" truth of observations made "subjectively." I will return to this issue of the ambivalent "truth claims" of women's travel writing and the corollary tendency to read their texts for contradictions. First, however, I want to turn to a third feature of this writing: narrative relationship to landscape.

Women in nineteenth-century, middle-class Europe were popularly constructed as more sensitive to nature, and to spiritual matters, than their male counterparts. Add to this the influence of the Romantic poets, and it became increasingly common to see depictions of landscape in women's travel writing in terms of "the sublime" and/or linked with religious sentiment, tropes that had no place in "scientific" narratives. Of course, despite this apparently innocent aesthetic appropriation of the foreign landscape, the relationship encodes certain ideological factors. For one thing, as Mills reminds us, depicting a colonial landscape within a universalizing Romantic framework erases "the specificity of the country"(1991: 183). So when Lynch (1852: ix) invites us to "look down the tremendous steep into that ravine – the river-course below. In His hands are the deep places of the earth," attention is deliberately shifted away from the particulars of the *Jamaican* mountain scene towards a transcendent spiritual meditation. Newton also finds the "Arcadian" aspect of tropical scenes lead naturally to the contemplation of "the Author of such perfection" (1897: 146,147) and her Romantic bent is evidenced in her invocation of Wordsworth (216).

Even where the sublime is eschewed for another type of aesthetic depiction – as when Newton writes about the Bathsheba coast in Barbados in terms from Matthew Arnold and the Greek myth of Andromeda and Perseus (1897: 160–1) – this "possession" of landscape by rendering it within an already-known framework, is still obvious. A notable characteristic of Newton's prose is her painterly eye for the "picturesque." The word is used ad nauseam, up to three times in one paragraph (38). A beauty spot, a person, a church, a plant or a view, it is picturesque if it makes a good subject for her verbal (and sometimes pen and ink) sketch. The flattening out of the landscape's inhabitants is striking: they serve only as another feature of a composition. So "some dark-hued natives, graceful and picturesque, at work" are tasteful additions to a description of the Bermudan countryside (12), "giving just the touch of humanity and colour to the peaceful scene which it needs" (13). A fisherman in Grenada likewise, "gave a charming bit of colour and strength of tone to the scene" (23). The landscape is valued precisely because it can fit a particular aesthetic model; the natives are afterthoughts, there to add color contrast.

Another kind of relationship to landscape characterizes Gaunt's *Reflection* and Crommelin's "Mountain-Heart": here the specific is filtered through the lens of romance, drawn from a stereotypical Caribbean "history." Crommelin projects onto the mountain scene an atmosphere of timelessness and danger, a place "always on the verge of an air-world, vapours with mists, into which, if our steeds stumbled, or there chanced an earth-slip of the crumbling track, we should be inevitably hurld" (1898: 529). It is a short step to sense in such a "fictional" space the presence of fearsome figures culled from tales of "terrible negro risings of old, when the fetish oath was taken at dead of night, under a sacred cotton-tree, the vow pledged in a cup of rum and blood" (528)! In *Reflection*, Gaunt inhabits the present but, as Whitlock argues, constantly overlays it (often eschewing transitional markers) with a fiction of the past:

> When the tropical darkness fell, the candles were lighted and they were still at their feasting . . . The ladies in their hoops and high head-dresses retired. The gentlemen loosened their lace vests; perhaps took off their wigs, for the weather was sure to be hot, and gave themselves up to the pleasures of the table.
>
> (Gaunt 1932: 204)

Gaunt is, at least, relatively honest about what she is doing. "I don't know really if it was a bit like that," she confesses (73), after narrating a dramatized scene, complete with dialogue, of Cristoval Yssassi's last days in Jamaica. The island, its landscape, places and people are, in a sense, simply "material" for her literary visions. Just the sound of the name of the district of Harmony fires her imagination: "I am going to try to write a book about Harmony," she promises (153). She did so, soon after; but *Harmony* (1933) is not about the actual district; rather, it is a sensationalized version of "old slave days in Jamaica," a tale of domestic drama and social intrigue.

Whitlock's argument (1994: 89) is that the female narrator can only share textually in "the wilds" she desires to enter through representing the landscape in terms of fantasies of adventure and romance. Between models of historical romance, Romantic poetry, and nature as God's mirror, female travel narrators had several templates for producing exotic landscape. And the choice of template as well as the relationship between narrator and landscape is not innocent. Pratt (1992: 205) demonstrates that the aesthetic qualities of landscape constitute (metaphorically, anyway) the value of its discovery for the explorer's home culture. The more lovely the description, the worthier the prize seems: and the more one can anticipate improving and developing it. What you see is, in a sense, what you get. Since Columbus's diary, of course, the distinction between the region's "value" as a source of aesthetic and material wealth have been blurred. So Lynch's description of the tropical landscape in terms of precious jewels ("emerald and amethyst, with touches of ruby light;" "transparent veil of gold;" "arrayed in diamonds . . . crystal treasure . . . pearl-drops") clearly posits natural beauty as the region's treasure or capital (1861: 3). In Gaunt's novel *Harmony* (1933: 11), similar metaphorical constructions operate in the first sighting of Jamaica: "[t]he sea was sapphire and turquoise; in the opal shallows lay the Bogue Islands, a cluster of jewels, rich emeralds; the shore was green with the greenness of Eden, golden with the sunshine of Heaven."

The West Indies was also a valuable resource for the writer who needed a pool of material. Hence Gaunt and Gertrude Atherton,[8] for example, recycle data gathered during visits in novels, histories and travelogues. Similarly, Crommelin's novel, *A Daughter of England* (1902), recycles material from her earlier travelogue:

descriptions of Jamaican mountainscapes in the novel are lifted word for word from "The Mountain-Heart of Jamaica," and the same local sayings are cited in both texts. Further, the perception of landscape as capital to be marketed informs the more obviously tourist-directed writing. In her rapturous depiction of the tropical climate (1909: 30), Wilcox portrays a region which restores both health and spirits, that makes young again the jaded European who – significantly linked with the colonial project via her reference to Kipling – brings back souvenirs as a material record of the adventure:

> When the flying fishes began to leap from the water and soar above the waves in flocks, great excitement prevailed among the passengers; and we two were among the most excited.
>
> We were living in an atmosphere of that wonderful poem of Kipling's, "On the Road to Mandalay."
>
> A fish flew upon the deck and was carried off by one of the crew, and afterward we secured it, all mounted, as a souvenir for our Bungalow-on-the-Sound.
>
> The skies grew more lustrous, the sea more rainbow colored, the sun hotter . . . Life seemed to have become a June morning in youth for all of us.

The West Indies, then, is constructed for a variety of narrative purposes in these women's travel writings: as a collage of "picturesque" painterly scenes and "subjects" to be captured on paper by Newton's brushes and pencil and pen; as a scenic backdrop for melodramatic historical tableaux in the fevered imaginations of Crommelin and Gaunt; as an otherworldly Eden in which one apprehends God/the sublime, in the homiletic writings of Lynch and (some of) Newton. These supposedly "spontaneous" responses none the less appropriate the landscape as "already known," writing it within a number of already charted and ideologically encoded aesthetic categories.

Symmonett's narrative, *Jamaica: Queen of the Carib Sea*, is an interesting amalgam of several of the constructions noted above, but rather than simply illustrating these features, I want to conclude this section by discussing the text in light of the claim that women's travel writing is inherently multiple, if not contradictory, in terms of production and reception. Kröller (1990) makes an interesting observation about the confessional form favored by women travel writers, claiming such narrative to be self-referentially split or multiple discourse. Her contention is that the first-person travel diarist is both protagonist and narrator, and as a woman, doubly self-conscious in both roles: as protagonist in an alien environment and as narrator in the unsettling, potentially embarrassing public textual sphere. Kröller sees a shifting, shuttling movement in this writing between the public and private, where protagonist effaces narrator and vice versa.

It seems to me that the *creole* travel writer – Lynch, Symmonett[9] – epitomizes this paradigm of the spilt, ambivalent narrator in her relationship with the West Indian landscape. Pratt (1992) reminds us that while the tendency has normally been to see European culture emanating out to the periphery from a self-generating center, this has obscured the movement of people and idea *from* the colony to the center. Thus, while I have described Lynch and Newton depicting West Indian natural phenomena through a veil of European Romanticism, Pratt (138) would maintain that to an extent Romanticism was a *product* of the contact zone, of the encounter with a "primal landscape." But as she acknowledges (193), creole writers from the mid-nineteenth century would find it problematic to use this trope of the "primal landscape" for a thoroughly familiar homeland. And surely, the equation with the female body ("virgin territory"), would make the situation even more fraught for the female writer.

The concept of the "transculturation" of European material in creole representations is crucial to Pratt's interpretation and, to an extent, one can see Symmonett's narrative "transculturating" European prescriptions of the West Indies as a place of savagery, death and disease. The ridiculous, even comic, articulation of colonial prejudice undermines its "truth." En route to Jamaica, Mrs Chandler is warned about

> every few yards encountering with a cesspool of black stagnant water, swarmed with mosquitoes, out of which pop up the heads of those hideous batrachian reptiles – toads; and foul malaria also arising: or coming in contact with a rut, or gully – regular breaknecks . . .
>
> (Symmonett 1895: 11)

The exaggerated horror, the sheer rhetorical excess, clearly signals that the description is to be read with reservations. And in fact, Mrs Chandler discovers (and later writes home to testify) that Jamaica is in fact both lovely and civilized. Another creole, Una Marson, uses a similar strategy in "Sojourn" (1931) in which an Englishman is amazed by the "modernity of the city" of Kingston, and that the population "were as smartly dressed as though they were in London in the summer, nor were these all black in colour as he had feared, but of shades varying from black to white" (8–9).

There is a positively nationalistic fervor in Symmonett's narrative, which accounts for a somewhat idealized overview of island life in Mrs Chandler's letter to England. The health and welfare systems are properly run; "colleges for boys and girls . . . are so satisfactory, that we are rendered quite independent of sending home our children for that object" (21); well-qualified professionals of all kinds are in practice; polite divisions of society obtain, as do all forms of amusement; although "the negro peasantry of the interior country districts present in themselves a very forbidding, repulsive appearance" (22) they work hard; the towns are well laid out with architectural merit, and the countryside – especially the mountains – is lovely.

Lynch (1861) demonstrates a similar pride in her West Indian landscape, and indeed her text is introduced by "Right Rev. the Lord Bishop of Jamaica" (Aubrey G. Jamaica, 1856) as vindicating these "enchanting islands" (i), "these magnificent islands" (ii) of which thus far "very little has been investigated and less made known" (i). Lynch boasts, what is the oak-tree of our England when compared with the cedar or mahogany; the gigantic cotton-tree, whose very stem has produced a boat capable of containing more than a hundred persons; or the wild fig-tree, in itself almost a forest, of which Milton thus writes . . .

(1861: 2)

And here one pauses. The West Indian cedar and mahogany are valorized in comparison to the English oak, but the English oak is "ours." The cotton-tree and the wild-fig, native vegetation, are praised but evidence of their magnificence is illustrated by a quote from an English poet. Perhaps Lynch uses "our" less as a national marker and more as a narrative device to invite reader participation, but this only underscores the fact that her texts are directed at, and shaped by the expectations of, a British audience. Similarly, Symmonett praises the Jamaican town of Mandeville for "its bracing English climate" (1895: 30), and ends her account with a hymn to Jamaica that turns out to be the composition of a "tourist, a naturalist, who but a few months ago visited this island home" (34). The local ("this island home") is familiarized through comparison with European climate, flora and fauna, or by filtering it through the scientific or literary authorities of the metropole.

Leaving aside other kinds of split/contradictory/polyphonic features in women's travel writing, it seems to me that we see here an undermining of the patriotic, even proto-nationalistic impulse (the impulse of which is to negate Eurocentric constructions of the West Indies) by an implicitly colonial need to present "us" *for* Europe. It is tempting to see here what Pratt (1992: 61–2) describes as the rendering of landscape as spectacle, as a panorama in which is implicitly coded its potential commodification for foreign visitors. Symmonett then, despite her pride in her homeland, shares with other European travel writers the rhetoric of discovery for a European audience, a textual "discovery" of what the locals actually know in a far less romantic way. For the nineteenth-century creole writer, there are multiple meanings in James's delineation of the Caribbean as "belonging to Us." While Gaunt, Newton and Crommelin project onto the West Indian landscape their own desires – desire for romance, for the sublime, for painterly inspiration, for adventure – Symmonett and, to an extent Lynch construct their home as an exotic paradise which they "discover" for others, and sell to a potential tourist market. I will return to the ambivalence of creole writing in the following chapter; at present, I want to suggest that, in reading women's travel writing of the period, we need to attend to the complex interaction of discourses which inform the narratives and to the different, even contradictory, meanings that are simultaneously encoded.

The West Indies as paradise/tropical nightmare

Finally, I return to "the West Indies" in travel narratives and (extending the frame of reference a little) in journals and novels not previously discussed in this chapter, which share with the travel narratives a tendency to construct the exotic primarily for (metropolitan) home consumption. I focus on a number of recurrent patterns of representation centered around polar images of the infernal and the paradisal. Joyce Walker Johnson, discussing early fictional representations of the West Indies (1994: 2), argues that popular narratives circulated ideology by creating/re-inscribing myths about the "queer" place and its inhabitants. The perpetuation of value-specific mythical representations of "there" served to unify readers in consolidating the innate superiority of "here." Whether in historical or travel writing, fictional or autobiographical, the accounts of the tropics discussed below insist, with James, that "[t]his is another world" (1913: 30). What is striking about this other world is how the same place can support such multiple and contradictory representations.[10]

"A country of unceasing terror"

> My spirits are much depressed on hearing that the dreadful fever has broken out at English Harbour – and as this is our hot season, I dread its becoming contagious and prevalent, [for] this is a country of unceasing terror, without any pleasing circumstances to rejoice the heart or gratify the eyes, worn out with the scorching sun and want of verdure, shade, or water.[11]

Pre-scripted notions of the West Indies as exotic but dangerous, even fatal, inform descriptions of its hostile climate. While it is true that travel/adventure narratives conventionally increase the value of the narrator's exploits by insisting on hardships endured and dangers faced, travelers to the Caribbean consistently portrayed the climate as (quite literally) deadly. Overviewing sources on tourist travel to Jamaica in the 1890s, W. J. Hanna (1989: 19) notes the island's reputation as a place where a traveler "might contract some sudden, deadly fever. It was no wonder that there were those who felt a visit to Jamaica almost a sentence of death." Crommelin (1898: 527) reports that

> In days not so long past, folk at home used to suppose Jamaica a hot-bed of yellow fever. As a matter of fact, its authorities declare that in the whole history of the island there never was a real epidemic of "Yellow Jack," although he visited the troops severely in 1842.

This contradicts Nugent, writing at the beginning of the nineteenth century. Worrying about the impact of the climate on her own ability to breast-feed her firstborn (1966: 119), she is "much shocked to hear of Captain Bartlett's being seized with the yellow fever. He only left us at 8 o'clock last night, in perfect health, and now they say that his life is almost despaired of."

In 1850 Nancy Prince, a black American woman visiting Jamaica as part of a missionary exercise, wrote in praise of a "hot bath" near Spanish Town which "gives relief in the complaint called the dry bowels malady, which, excepting the bilious and yellow fevers, is one of the most terrible distempers of Jamaica" (62).

And in 1857, Seacole personifies yellow fever as having made "a more determined effort to exterminate the English in Jamaica" (1984: 108). For the British military, the main enemy was "a climate that refused to adopt them"; indeed, she observes, "the mother country pays a dear price for the possession of her colonies." As late as 1909, Wilcox reports that "yellow fever prevailed to a slight degree on the island" of "Barbadoes" (224). In addition, she comments on the presence of leprosy in the Caribbean, a claim substantiated in Cassin's 1890 novel.

Fearful diseases seemed to thrive in the tropical climate, and death was commonplace. Only a month after arriving, Nugent's journal (1966: 18) reads thus:

> Rise at 6, and was told, at breakfast, that the ususal occurrence of a death had taken place. Poor Mr. Sandford had died at 4 o'clock this morning. My dear N. and I feel it very much, but all around us appeared to be quite callous.

The "usual occurrence" is a refrain throughout her journal,[12] but she never achieves the indifference toward illness and death that characterized more seasoned residents. What frightened Nugent was "this deceitful dreadful climate" (21); the new place cannot be trusted and ordinary "home" behavior can have lethal consequences. Even a cooling breeze or a simple walk in the sunshine can lead to illness (15). Indeed, Carmichael (1969) almost implies that the very atmosphere can cause abnormalities in young people: from "eight o'clock till nearly five, all exercise out of doors is prejudicial to the health of a child . . . After twelve years of age, children appear to require a change of climate, they grow too fast" (vol. 2: 321–2).

The "deceitful climate" makes Nugent lethargic (1966: 17), and loss of appetite invokes terror "that the climate had seized upon me" (59). In this case, she is only pregnant, which introduces a fresh source of anxiety. Indeed, there is pathos in the account of a doctor pronouncing her unborn child "very flourishing" while "Alas! poor man, he appears sadly declining" (112). Gaunt's *Harmony* (1933) is carefully researched from earlier sources (including Nugent's journal) and thus serves as a distillation in popular fiction of some of the most pervasive stereotypes of the West Indies. Set in the early nineteenth century, her story encodes a similarly hostile climate: the threatening "pox" soon strikes the estate (18). Given the climate of fear, extreme behavior is commonplace so that excessive drinking is a way "to keep at bay fever and all the other thousand ills the land was heir to" (14).

A more personal account of sudden illness and death is found in Fenwick's letters of the early nineteenth century. Fenwick is well aware of the rigors of the Barbadian climate; indeed, this is the subject of continuous complaint throughout her correspondence. On arrival, she commits the grave error of opening her jalousie windows to the balmy night air which "produced an inflamation in my blood" (1927: 164), resulting in grave illness. Her daughter Eliza is constantly succumbing to some infirmity, which worries Fenwick terribly. Eventually death touches the family. Despite her son's heeding warnings to live temperately, he is struck down: "The heaviest calamity of my life has fallen upon me . . . Orlando is dead! Lost! gone for ever!– A cruel malignant fever, which spares the aged &

devours the young, has made me wretched" (183). Dancing on a Wednesday night, Orlando was smitten on Thursday with a "raging heat," bled on Friday, "the fatal black vomittings [*sic*] commenced" on Monday and he expired on Tuesday. The letter describing his end is particularly moving for Fenwick holds nothing back: his pitiful last words, his delirium and apparent agony, her own grief, the horror of internal mortification are all graphically portrayed. After this loss, Fenwick finds tropical conditions harder to bear: "[n]ow the hot season is commencing I suffer from it much more than I did last year, from my being less relaxed probably" (192), she writes, longing for a more healthy climate. Noting how the children suffered from a virulent "eruption," she reflects that "[w]e who seek for gain in these climates have terrible penalties awaiting us" (196). Lynch's *The Family Sepulchre* (1848) echoes this sentiment: "those who have resided between the tropics . . . follow each other in quick succession to the grave" (231). Lynch's account suggests it is not only expatriates who fear the climate: "alas! we are familiar with death in this country" (222).

Nugent's anthropomorphic depiction of the tropical climate as a predator,[13] demonstrates the frightening otherness of this alien land. Nor is the terror of disease the only misery to be borne. Repeatedly she notes "[t]he heat dreadful" (1966: 119, 120), and describes the city of Kingston in similarly extreme language as "the most broiling place in the universe" (228).[14] The combination of heat, overspiced food and a crowded dining room is almost infernal: "never shall I forget the combination of a crowd of Creoles, and a mob of blackies, with turtle-soup, pepper-pot, and callipash and callipee, at Mr. Mowat's, as long as I live in this world!" (90). Like the climate, the homogenized "Creoles" and "blackies" who enjoy all she finds loathsome, are ranged against civilized and temperate norms. Frequently, Nugent's delicate sensibilities are assaulted by natural forces taken for granted by locals. For example, sudden thunderstorms with rain "like a torrent . . . most tremendous thunder, with flashes of lightning almost blinding" (120), reduce her to a weeping wreck cowering under a table. Similarly, Agnes Satchell's *Reminiscences of Missionary Life in the Caribbean Islands* (1858: 55) describes a hurricane in Antigua in melodramatic terms:

> the lurid lightning flashed in quick succession; the loud thunder rolled in terrific grandeur over our heads; the wind, veering to every part of the compass, blew with maddened fury; and the rain descended in torrents, finding its way through the minutest crevice, insomuch that the chamber in which our dear children slept was flooded . . .

And the insects! These seem to have a particular horror for the women writers. Nugent details the misery of mosquitoes (1966: 31), terrifying scorpions (58, 202), the torture of black ants (64), alarm at a large centipede (141), and the lethal bite of a spider (209). Marsh-Caldwell's novel[15] opens with the newly arrived heroine's letter (dated "183_") from Jamaica, one theme of which is the bane of tropical insects, casually juxtaposed with yet another irritation: "mosquitoes sing and sting all day and night, and the black ant devours every thing that is left in its way. Black servants also, are very ugly things to look upon; but I am getting reconciled to these" (1850: 7).

Writing from Barbados in 1815, Fenwick also links the two (175), complaining that "[n]ext to the Negroes, the intolerable and numerous tribes of insects are great annoyances"; she rails against thieving red ants and fearsome "Cockroaches" but quite likes the "Spiders, some as large as a moderate sized saucer" since they prey on the other pests. Some fifteen years later, Carmichael considers the insects and reptiles of the tropics the worst feature of the West Indies, and Newton recounts stories of the deadly *fer de lance* snake in St Lucia (1897: 55), a fearsome rattlesnake in Demerara (72), as well as mosquitoes, centipedes, scorpions and tarantula spiders (187), although she concedes that these last are a problem only in dirty houses. In 1909, Wilcox rehearses the common complaint about mosquitoes, but has more worries about Jamaican "ticks" (44):

> This vicious speck of animal life is smaller than the smallest atom of black pepper; and attached to a human foot or ankle, it proceeds to bore under the cuticle and hide itself; and unless immediately removed (a difficult process) it produces angry swelling and intolerable itching.

She illustrates the danger by telling of an English lady who unknowingly tramped the countryside and as a result of the parasite "was obliged to lie in bed with bandaged limbs for more than a week" (44).[16]

Newton is by and large a very polite commentator on the West Indies: her artist's eye favors the "picturesque." But lest she should be held to have "dwelt too absolutely on the bright side of the picture" (1897: 3), she also mentions hardships:

> One must be prepared to endure the onslaught of mosquitoes, to be blinded by clouds of dust and the effects of heat so great that one often feels like having a Turkish bath, though the nights are refreshingly cool . . . There are fevers, too, and chills to be combatted, and there is an enervating tendency in the perpetual heat, which makes study of any kind twice as difficult as in a more bracing atmosphere.

As noted above, Symmonett's novella (1895: 7) initially constructs the tropics as a living nightmare. Jamaica is a place where

> alligators are said to lie along the shores in a dormant state, just presenting the appearance of logs of wood, which so deceive the natives, that as a frequent occurrence, whilst out walking, they suddenly disappear from sight, as if spirited away – swallowed and digested.

The natives themselves, all cannibals, hardly merit sympathy: "[t]he bodies of poor unfortunate children after being dissected, are sold and eaten as pork" (7). These heathens are supposedly even less "susceptible to civilisation" than Africans

(9), and are described as black "with wool on their heads, in lieu of hair, of which they come short – as of sense" (10). The entire population drink rum to excess, "which is so inebriating, that the men, women, and children are to be daily seen lying all along the public roads, as the lowest, nastiest, and most degraded wrecks of humanity" (10). At this point, the naive Mrs Chandler wonders why missionaries did not introduce them to tea as an alternative! Tales of disease, ferocious insects, wild hogs that rush "out of mires, . . . goring the legs of passers by" reduce the children of the family to "terrifically [*sic*] exclaim – 'Oh! Father! Father! Will you take us to such an awful place? Is it not better that we get drowned, than to live such a life, and perhaps be cruelly murdered by the savages? Such an awful death to die!' " (11). Of course, all this proves a complete fabrication, but Symmonett accurately pinpoints the grossly pejorative stereotypes faced by newcomers to the tropics, whose initial response to the very concept of the West Indies is terror. Indeed, as Carmichael wryly comments (1969, vol. 2: 314), "[t]he greater number of people who die in the West Indies, die from apprehension."

The narratives stress those tropical discomforts which are particularly fearsome or repugnant to women: the climate which threatens loved ones, the terrible heat that reduces the capable traveler to lassitude and the storms that make her quail, the insects and reptiles which a male-authored text might mention in passing but which the "helpless lady" persona registers as deeply disturbing. Dirt and disorder, as noted in the previous chapter, are anathema to the housewifely virtues enshrined in the "cult of pure womanhood."[17] Again, the particular concern for the domestic space evidenced in female authored texts points to the differences between travel writing by men and women. Pratt (1992: 159) argues that "domestic settings have a much more prominent presence in the women's travel accounts," so that interiors and rooms become, she suggests, allegories of the narrator's subjective state, or a refuge to which she can retire "after the heat and the glare and the dirt" (James 1913: 157).

Recounting her travels in the region (1887: 29), Layard complains about filthy conditions and poor service in Trinidad, and in Guyana rehearses the now familiar domestic refrain (46): " 'To soothe the savage beast' may be a highly creditable feat, but to make the negro work is a far harder task." Dirt and disorder are specifically associated with black West Indians. "So far as cleanliness is concerned," opines Carmichael (1969, vol. 1: 105), "the negro is perfectly indifferent." And if cleanliness is next to godliness, as writers like Wilcox reiterate at every opportunity, it is a short step to equating blacks with godlessness. Carmichael (1969, vol. 2: 196) points out evidence of such savagery in a slave who bites a piece out of another's shoulder during a disagreement, and the barbarism of black women's cruelty to their children (vol. 2: 200). Other writers, like Newton at the end of the nineteenth century, are more circumspect. Generally she finds the natives a friendly lot but when they get too close whilst she is painting on a Georgetown street, she is glad of police protection – "fine reliable brown men" – to keep back the mob: "[I]t was a great relief, as a Demerara crowd of scantily attired and much-heated humanity, however picturesque, is best studied from a distance" (1897: 70).

It is interesting that in the conflicted self-representation of women narrators, helplessness is positively *claimed* as a feminine trait but vulnerability as a white *woman* is rarely mentioned. Newton passes over it, although the subtext of an illustrative sentence is revealing: "*I was alone*, driven by *a black man* over a *lonely* tropic road – through valleys so shaded sometimes that the moon *was lost to view – yet* it was all so full of peace and loveliness" (1897: 244; my emphasis). The portrayal of essentialized natives as happy childlike people precludes acknowledging that blacks can be dangerous, although fears of an invasion lead Nugent to confess that "I am sure the blacks are to be as much dreaded as the French" (1966: 237). James *does* allude to the vulnerability of the female traveler, conceding that it "makes things difficult at times. Not in all professions is it taken as a matter of course that all students shall have the right to study their profession from exactly the same angle, irrespective of sex" (1913: 168). So, during a solitary walk from Newcastle (98), her light tone cannot disguise anxiety when she becomes aware of her position as a white woman potentially at the mercy of the Other, here in the form of a black male:

> Sometimes the solitude and the silence frightened me a little. It would have been so useless to cry for help if help were needed. For a long way I met no one, but once, in one of the most lonely stretches, I heard footsteps coming round one of the bends in the path. It was a fine, tall negro walking in the leisurely fashion that is the only way in which to accomplish long distances. I wished him good-day and he answered pleasantly as he passed. There is very little to be feared from the villager, but when one remembers what things do happen everywhere, and also that all men who walk in the country are not necessarily of the country, one cannot help a sudden fear.

What things do happen everywhere, and what underlies her reassurances about the nature of "the villager"? Clearly, repressed racialized sexuality is at issue here; while she comforts herself that black Jamaican villagers are harmless, those from *outside* the country (not "belonging to Us") constitute a threat.

The "heathen" practices of black West Indians also point to savagery. Newton's apologetic tone hardens when she cites their superstitious nature as evidence of the natives' primitive state. "Coolies" in Trinidad are thus categorized (1897: 123), as are blacks, and we are told that until recently the power of the obeah man "over the natives was so great, that a good deal of difficulty was caused by it" (75). Carmichael quarrels that despite the threat of the death penalty, obeah men/ women frequently elude detection (1969, vol. 2: 253). In the twentieth century, Elspeth Fielding is still citing obeah to illustrate the backwardness of black Jamaicans. In *Short Stories of Jamaica and 'The War'* (1915: 55), she despairs that "our people are to a great extent affected by this terrible curse" (47). Obeah, wakes and nine nights, and belief in ghosts and duppies are directly linked to savage African practices (48), and the "barbarous custom" of the wake is banned in the city (49). In Fielding's stories, wakes are almost diabolic: "Look at those old hags dressed up in thin white gowns, with their heads tied up . . . all ready to set up their devilish howling" (55). Chapter 6 will question this fixation with obeah, but at present I want to conclude the survey of negative constructions of tropical landscape by emphasizing the duality of imagery which characterises the early narratives. From her perch in the Jamaican mountains, James gazes down and comments:

> It is hot down there upon the plain. The white dust has been swirling along the roads, and the sun has been beating all day upon the tired earth. There, it is weariness and anxious thoughts of men.
>
> But up here, folded away in the dark, cool hills, it seems as if no anxiety could come near . . . it is like seeing the Infinite from a nurse's arms.
>
> (James 1913: 79)

Her portrayal of the hot and sweaty life of toil on the plain echoes the construction of the Antiguan landscape in the epigraph which prefaces this section: "worn out with the scorching sun and want of verdure, shade, or water." But the vantage-point from which her gaze is directed is celestial, close to God and transcends human woe. And it is to such heavenly images that I now turn.

"This country is like fairyland"

> There were drives . . . each more wonderful than the other, and life seemed dyed in opalescent hues; and there was no world of care, and nothing commonplace, from horizon to horizon, or from dawn to dawn.
>
> (Wilcox 1909: 32)

> This country is like fairyland . . . Bright, unclouded skies – scenery of the most romantic wildness – glen, cliff and waterfall festooned with garlands of brilliant flowers.
>
> (Marsh-Caldwell 1850, vol. 1: 2)

The scorching, debilitating scenario illustrated above, could not be more different from the pleasant picture painted by Symmonett's Mrs Chandler. After a year in Jamaica she writes home that Kingston has "a genial climate" (1895: 23), that one may also enjoy "the pure untainted mountain air" (26) or "a jolly invigorating mineral spring bath" (23), and that Constant Spring, in particular, has been her salvation (29–30):

> Where! In what part of the West Indies, or of the Southern States can foreigners find a more appropriate health, or winter resort? A place so salubrious in every respect, the entire picture eloquizing health! It has rescued me – nor am I singular – from an untimely grave: and now here I am looking the living picture of health. Our lives have indeed fallen in a pleasant place.

Heat and dust there may be, but Jamaica is also a land of cool waters. As Marsh-Caldwell's heroine writes to her friend in England (1850, vol. 1: 4), Jamaica means "land of springs." And Newton responds poetically to a confluence of rivers: "a wild rush of blended unison, a wider, broader stretch of water, a harmony of many rills merged into one, and rushing madly jubilant with wild exhilaration towards the sea" (1897: 201). Even heat is welcome to those fleeing the cold and damp of Europe or North America where the "weather was unusually severe and cruel . . . making life for man and beast a continual warfare with the elements" (Wilcox 1909: 25). By comparison, the islands are blissfully habitable. So when James registers her early impressions and observes that "[t]his is another world," she means it literally: only "sixteen days away from ice and snow and fog" (30), the tropics are so different as to render them fantastic.

For Nugent, the tropical scene is "all so new to a European eye, that it seemed like a paradise" (1966: 25). Wilcox too images Jamaica as "another Paradise afar" (1909: 25), and arriving in Port Antonio bay, the scene "seemed as it might to a wandering soul reaching Paradise at twilight (37). The connubial bliss of the Nugents seems to have impressed itself on the local audience, as evidenced by the "fine speeches" of Admiral Duckworth who, Nugent records (1966: 63), claims that Jamaica "was a Paradise, and General N. and I were the Adam and Eve of it, we were so happy and so much in love with each other!!"[18] Even if Nugent mentions this conferral of mythical status because of vanity (which she frequently abhors, but none the less indulges in occasionally), the image is appropriate to the Admiral's speech. As a representative of the colonial dream, he has *invested* in the conflation of the tropical island with paradise on earth. His image of a divine state achieved in the here and now rather than the hereafter, justifies the colonial enterprise and the presence of its agents in the region. The recurrence of the paradisal simile in the early narratives marks it as a trope which points to a particular desired construction of the West Indies. It also points, significantly, to the *emptiness* of paradise, and thus its malleability to the designs of Adam and Eve.

Sheller (2001: 2) explains that certain iconic Caribbean images (the palm-fringed beach, the verdant forest) "pick up on longstanding visual and literary themes in Western culture based on the idea of tropical islands as microcosms of earthly Paradise."[19] And "the myth of tropical fecundity and excessive fruitfulness," she elaborates, conjure up other advantages of Paradise, namely "sustenance without labour." This also serves also to tempt investors to "consume" the resources, to *commodify* the landscape. Up until the mid-nineteenth century, the region had been known as a source of wealth, textually inscribed as natural beauty. Introducing Lynch's *The Wonders of the West Indies*, the Lord Bishop of Jamaica moves smoothly from "the history of the Antilles" and its associations with fortunes gained and lost, to a more *enduring* bounty, "the natural endowments of these magnificent islands [which] are of a character to command the admiration of every beholder, and to afford a theme which the most eloquent description could scarcely surpass" (1861: ii–iii). I want to connect two tropes in this quote – the paradisal beauty of the West Indies as a precious resource, and the difficulty of conveying its bounty in words – with a much earlier travel narrative, the journal of Christopher Columbus.

As Robert Benson astutely points out (1992), Columbus's account is an important precursor for subsequent literary treatments of the New World. Benson's concern is less with preconceptions which Columbus brought with him "than with his encounter with what he truly 'discovered' ": that is,

> the shock of a completely new place forcing his language to its known limits, where it breaks down in the face of the unutterable. He could not come *to* terms with the New World because he did not come *with* the terms that could express the novelty of his experience.
>
> (Benson 1992: 49; emphasis in original)

Initially, Benson suggests, the drive is to reconcile the new with the pre-scripted vision of the Orient, but gradually this exercise gives way to a perception of an even stranger, more exotic world. Like the travel narratives by women, Columbus first attempts to familiarize the new by establishing resemblance with the already known, but then slips into the awed speechlessness of the tourist who finds the novel spectacle lovely, too lovely to express. Absorbed with its glory, he discovers new rhetorical strategies for writing about it. Instead of profits, his interest is drawn to marvels, wonders and enchantments. His attempts to come to terms with the gorgeous but essentially *different* nature of the landscape initiate a literary territory that, Benson avers (52), was hitherto absent from the European imagination. Even more so, women's texts can be seen to construct the exotic West Indian landscape as a magical "fairyland." Cassin's *With Silent Tread* records English expectations of the Caribbean as "a topsy-turvy land with fishes that fly, and crazy cashews growing their seeds outside instead of in" (1890: 125). Similarly, the heroine of Minna Smith's *Mary Paget* (1900: 242) describes "the Bermudas" in terms of flying fish, lunar rainbows and sea monsters, an altogether magical realm of spells and enchantments and light "given of angels" (184).

There is a sense in which several of the early texts by women *lose control* of language. For example, in Symmonett's celebration of Jamaica's charms (1895: 31), the narrator admits to being lost for words (although this does not stop her trying):

> I was transported with delight – I was involuntarily thrown into ecstasy by the prospect and beauty in the novelties of nature, in verdure wrought amid the hills and dales, the broad plains of evergreen grass whereon the cattle graze and browse. Fields beyond fields rich in vegetation, the pure fresh air breathed, heavy with moisture, perfumed by the spicy odour of the large pimento groves, and that of ripe fruit predominating. Then on to the diversity of the dense forest, carpeted by the dried leaves of ages old, uninhabited by man or beast: adorned with oases of wood of such description, as to strike or gratify the fancy of any explorer . . . in short, I, unaware, was an initiated rhapsodist, at the complicated sight of babbling innocent streams, and

sluggish ones, all kissing affectionately in meeting at the rendezvous of the bar, tumbling into their mother ocean.

The piece is clotted and overwritten, but does evoke a sense of natural richness and a bountiful picture of unspoilt beauty, which recur in many of the other narratives. Stephenson's novel *Undine* also tends to "purple prose" describing "the glories of Nature," although the heroine's perception of "this Eden," "the sweet dreamland of these happy hills" (1911: 59), is heightened by being in love.

Where the writer is, like Columbus, lost for the appropriate language to envision this paradise, she often makes do with a catalogue that is the syntactic equivalent of luxuriant natural profusion. For instance, Nugent attempts a description of a tropical garden:

> The garden contains a great variety of flowering shrubs and fruit trees, and the hedge round it is of lime trees . . . The limes were ripe, and the yellow tint mixed with bright green had a beautiful effect. Here and there the logwood was seen, which is something like our hawthorn. In other places are seen rows of orange trees, the fruit just turning yellow; mangoes, red and purple; forbidden and grape fruit, in clusters; the acqui, a tree that bears a large scarlet fruit, the inside of which, they say, when dressed is like a sweet-bread; and the avocado pear . . . which poor Lord Hugh told me he ate for his breakfast on toast, instead of butter. There were also pomegranates, shaddocks &c. in abundance . . . *But it is quite impossible to describe* the great variety of beautiful plants, trees and shrubs, that at this moment delight my eyes, and regale my nose.
>
> (1966: 26; emphasis in original)

Beginning with an attempt to catalogue, she becomes bogged down by the excess of colors and textures; again she attempts to control the scene by naturalizing the new in terms of the familiar ("like our hawthorn"), or explain it by reference to authority ("they say"; "Lord Hugh told me"); finally, she resorts to simply listing before giving up in the face of such over-stimulation. As Lynch (1861: 3) confesses, "words cannot do justice" to such scenes. Newton (1897: 201) comments on "the riotous wealth of vegetation" before attempting to impose order by listing different types of ferns, mosses and trees until she too runs out of breath: "Nature has lavished her choicest forms of vegetation, in an almost rampant profusion" (203). It is almost *too much*.[20] James (1913: 73) also portrays a panorama of "cane, bamboo, cocoanut and mango, and gay with scarlet hibiscus," while Fielding (1915: 5) favors superlatives: "I trust the reader will pardon this spontaneous outburst, on the scenic beauties of this far-famed land of beautiful cascades, sparkling rivulets, deep-seated gullies, possessing an inexhaustive supply of umbrageous wealth, of tropical foliage." Lush, fertile, with jewelled colors and heady scents, the West Indian landscape was constructed as a fabulous resource, an inexhaustible ("umbrageous") wealth of natural beauty.

Such praise is not always spontaneous and original. Travel narratives invariably utilize conventional set-pieces, the scribal equivalent of postcards. Newton, for example, devotes two pages (1897: 108–9) to a tropical sunset, as does Symmonett (1895: 25–6), and both segue into evocative pictures of moonlight on the sea. The arrival scene is also common. Conventionally, the islands are best seen first from the ocean. So Nugent (1966: 10) recalls the excitement of the shipboard community when Jamaica appears on the horizon: "We were all up, and on the lookout by 6 o'clock. It appears beautiful. – Such hills, such mountains, such verdure; every thing so bright and gay, it is delightful!"[21] Fielding (1915: 10) pushes the envelope by combining a sunrise with a first view of the island "looking purple in the light of the rising sun ... and the sky a mixture of reddish gold looked wonderful as the sun rose majestically," making her long to be an "Artist; so that I could immortalize the glorious panaramo [sic]."

A close second to sunset and dawn, the hills and mountains of the West Indies seem to have been especially inspiring. For Fielding mountain scenery is "the *most* picturesque." (1915: 5; emphasis in original) Crommelin devotes the majority of her short narrative to it, and Symmonett's scenic tour through Jamaica concludes with an evocation of the dazzling Blue Mountains (1895: 32–4): the peak calls forth the rhetorical question, "[w]hich eyes of an admirer of nature, would not fain be centred thereon, on this elysium of earth! on this El Dorado of the 'Queen of the Carib Sea?' " (34). For Wilcox, the mountains at night constitute "a silver world of entrancing beauty" (1909: 61), while the pleasures of mountain scenery for James (1913: 74) have to do with its familiarity: "I drank my tea in an English spring, looking out over an English rose-garden." But there is a note of peevishness in some accounts when the tropical is *too* much like home. So when Symmonett describes a Jamaican town noted for its "bracing English climate" (1895: 30), she comments that its "sceneries [are] by far less romantic than most of the country districts" (31). Newton corroborates this impression, noting that "Mandeville is so like an English village that it is perhaps a little disappointing to the artist whose soul longs for what is tropical and strange" (1897: 174).

Enchantment with nature has its roots in the Romantic poets' notion that contemplating unspoilt beauty is beneficial to the human soul. Hence, the sea by moonlight leads Symmonett to posit that "[t]is there the author reads the volumes written by nature. Tis there the atheist denies no longer the existence of a Supreme Being" (1895: 26). Apart from spiritual inspiration, beauty has a calming effect on the careworn observer. Wilcox recalls morning at Port Antonio thus: "Rising at the first break of day to look out of the window, the overwhelming beauty of this tropic scene seemed a compensation for every dark and dreary hour that life had ever known in the past" (1909: 31). For Stephenson's Undine the Jamaican countryside – far from the bustle of city and town – is a refuge: "Here, Nature is at her best, her grandest, free from the jar of the commonplace. 'Tis a spot where for a space one is tempted to believe in the peace, perfect peace, of the Elysium plains" (1911: 21). Notably, the creole heroine's rhapsody ends in a fulmination against the changes wrought by tourism: "How could any one turn

a home in this Eden of beauty into a public resort, I cannot understand!"
Much earlier, Lanaghan (1844, vol. 2: 205–6) comments on the "country-seats" of
Antiguan planters as embracing

> prospects of inexpressible loveliness. Nothing of what is generally termed the
> sublime, it is true – no frowning precipices or gigantic mountains . . . the
> scene is of a more quiet nature, one where there is such a rich harmony of
> colouring, such a blending of earth, and sea, and sky . . . that as the eye gazes
> thereon, a pleasing calm comes over the beholder and every discordant pas-
> sion sinks to rest.

Somewhat curmudgeonly, Newton tempers such praise by arguing (1897: 188–9)
that what "we" really want is "calm but not stagnation – and in these regions of
perpetual heat there is undoubtedly a tendency to become indolent mentally and
physically, and perhaps in both ways." Overindulgence, that old creole vice, even
if it is overindulgence in beauty, leads to the debilitation of Western faculties.

One final aspect of the construction of the West Indies as unspoilt paradise: it is
a strangely unpopulated landscape. "Natives" are a picturesque afterthought in
Newton's verbal canvas. Even when they intrude on her vision en masse – as in "a
chain" of black men loading banana boats in Port Antonio (1897: 250–2) – there
is more empathy for the oxen employed in the enterprise than for the human
beasts of burden. Similarly, Wilcox is more repulsed at the cruelty of labourers to
"ill-fed and overworked animals" in Cuba and Jamaica, than by the hard lot of
the workers:

> The optimistic patience and courage of the peasants seemed pathetic as we
> saw them in our drives, trudging joyously over twenty miles of mountain and
> valley to bring a shilling's worth of produce to market; and trudging cheer-
> fully back again at the close of the day, with their small purchases.
>
> (Wilcox 1909: 32)

Pity is mollified by rehearsing the usual conflation of natives with happy
children, who "greeted us always with pleasant words and smiles" (ibid.) Like
children, they accept their places; but like children, they need correcting. In
relation to their cruelty, she prides herself on planting "a little seed of thought on
the subject of our responsibility toward animals in a few crude minds" (51).
Ironically, such lessons indicate a certain amount of violence in the teacher herself, which consolidates the ambivalent and constantly slipping combination
of power and powerlessness, sensitivity and harshness which characterize white
women's roles in colonial culture. Witness an incident in "Porto Rico" for
example (Wilcox 1909: 189),

> I repeatedly begged one driver I had engaged to put up his whip, and let his
> willing horse trot along unmolested. I had engaged him by the hour, and I
> was in no haste. After the third sullen defiance of my request, I reached over

and administered a sharp slap on the fellow's cheek. For the remainder of the drive his horse was free from the lashing of the whip. Sometimes it requires an object lesson to teach certain types of mind that you are in earnest in your determination to protect animals against more brutal animals.

Given such "types of mind," it often seems that the narrators would prefer all evidence of the local population to remain mere background color, just as James (1913: 73) depicts native huts "hidden away" in the vegetation. When the protagonist of Jenkin's *Cousin Stella* (1859, vol. 2: 121) wanders the Jamaican mountains communing with nature, a deformed black man crosses her path; the sight, she observes, is "not very pastoral" and in fact "turns all to ugliness." Symmonett's Mrs Chandler also prefers to relegate the forbidding "native peasantry" to the interior country (1895: 22), while in town, natives are occasionally observed as servants and "characters." For Wilcox, the "dreadful squalor of the houses in which the peasant population of Jamaica lives" are regrettable because the "unsightly" hovels compromise the "picturesque sights of Jamaica" (1909: 134).

By contrast, the presence of white inhabitants is approvingly noted, perhaps to assure prospective visitors of appropriate company in the wilderness. So one of the first surprises to Symmonett's arriving family is the sight of *civilized* creoles. Observing "some fashionable people tripping across the busy streets" of Kingston, young Harold asks, "[d]o they not look like any of us?"; and indeed, these white "sons and daughters of the soil . . . speak as good English as we do" (1895: 19). More often, the presence of whites is signalled not by people but by their buildings. For Lanaghan (1844, vol. 2: 205), Antiguan proprietors' "dwellings, situated upon their several estates, in the most cultivated parts of the island, are mansions which would not disgrace the parks of our English country gentlemen." A predominant theme in early depictions of the West Indies, Sheller observes (2001: 8–9), is the *cultivated*, ordered nature of the landscape; however romantic, wild or waste land signifies a failure of colonial civilization to master the exuberant exotic. And for a woman writer, where better to note details of civilization than in the home. So Cassin's novel dwells lovingly on the beauty of a well-kept great house with its polished floors, shining mahogany furniture and glittering silverware (1890: 26–7). Describing the pens (estates) of the elite in rural Jamaica, Symmonett singles out their elegant houses and gardens for praise (1895: 28), noting that these add a human touch to the pastoral scene.

Public spaces too, bear the marks of cultivation. Trinidad's "beau monde" can be seen driving around the Queen's Park Savannah in the afternoons, Newton informs the reader (1897: 189), and playing cricket as the band serenades them from nearby Government House. Here we have a West Indian "variation of the old Hyde Park scene" (190). Gaunt's historical romance, *Harmony* (1933: 106), conjures up scenes of elite Jamaican society during the golden age of empire, in an imaginary reconstruction of the annual Falmouth Ball. A spectacular interior landscape is lovingly detailed complete with polished mahogany furniture, sparkling crystal and brilliant chandeliers. This is another kind of postcard scene, projecting the tropical as a setting for privileged luxury. Indeed, her tale artlessly advertises itself as such. The players in the scene do not matter; it is the *setting* that is timeless: "[t]he people for the moment were nothing, simply clusters . . . of gay colours against the dark paneled walls" (107).

In a sense, several of the narratives discussed in this chapter serve as early tourist promotions, in that they clearly present the West Indian landscape, past and present, human and natural, urban and rural, in terms of a European desire for difference, for the exotic, and for physical and aesthetic pleasure. Clearly the work of Lynch (1861), Symmonett and Gaunt fall into this category, different as they are in terms of generic and narrative positioning. As late as 1957, Fielding follows the pattern in *Romance in Jamaica*, a novel written "many years ago for the purpose of advertising Jamaica, when the island was not as tourist-minded as it is now" (6). The nostalgic evocation of an era when the Myrtle Bank hotel was home to the cream of society is contemporary with Eliot Bliss's *Luminous Isle* (1984); Bliss's treatment of this class of Jamaican society in the 1920s is far more critical, however, while Fielding recalls "the good old days" when such privilege was assured by an "unspoilt" pool of black servants who knew their place. Jamaica Kincaid's *A Small Place* (1988), itself a wicked parody of some travelogue conventions, demonstrates that in the modern period it is still the case that even genuine admiration for the new and exotic, yet privileges a metropolitan "home" as the norm and projects onto the tropical landscape the tourist's wish-fulfillment fantasies or, indeed, her fears.

Expectations and projections

Over and over the narratives demonstrate that female as well as male visitors come to the West Indies with clear mental pictures of what they expected to see. Such images, as James acknowledges (1913: 99), are drawn from a combination of visual/literary archives and the imagination:

> I . . . had seen myself reclining under the shade of giant trees while dazzling birds flew from branch to branch, monkeys pelted me with coco-nuts and obsequious negroes salaamed before me. Sunday afternoon in one's extreme youth, with *Religion in Many Lands*, and all the woodcuts that went to make it palatable, create an impression not willingly wiped out.

Encountering only one monkey throughout her tour, she is forced to acknowledge the disparity between expectation and reality and ruefully comments, "[s]o does one have one's imagination denuded" (99). For all her levity, James points to the pervasiveness of the already-written, already-seen Caribbean. Similarly, Atherton (1932: 335) records the first sight of Charlotte Amalie on the island of St Thomas in terms of "a great seraglio, a collection of pleasure houses of some Eastern potentate." However, the town (337)

> so enchanting from a distance, was anything but picturesque at close quarters. The streets were full of rubbish, the houses that had looked so fairy-like

from the harbor, were of stone painted in crude primal colors, worn off in spots; the palms were dusty and ragged, and the long flights of steps swarmed with naked brown children . . . and frowzy Negresses.

Again the "exotic" declines to fit the expected/projected fantasy.[22]

How could it be otherwise, given the innately contradictory configuration of such fantasies in terms of extreme stereotyping of the region: debased and sinister, or pristine Eden. One can argue that by the late nineteenth century, the West Indies had to a large extent been "domesticated" and familiarized by just such writings as these. But as JanMohamed has argued (1986: 83), colonialist literature by its nature represents the colony as a world at the edge of civilization, "a world therefore perceived as uncontrollable, chaotic, unattainable, and ultimately evil."[23] Difference, it would seem, generally encodes lack. It is interesting that whatever the shortcomings of the *British* West Indies, the non-British territories are more severely censured. In 1909, Wilcox's account of Cuba notes that under the Spanish, conditions were dirty, cruel and dreadful (14–15) but "under American management" it is much improved (17), and despite Cuban resentment of her countrymen a few educated citizens of Havana now "realize and appreciate the debt all Cuba owes America" (19). Perhaps less impressed by "American management," Maclean (1910: 66) claims that while "Barbados negroes are said to be the best workers in the West Indies," Cubans are lazy people who have made no progress, while "Hayti" is "a nightmare of sin" ruled entirely by blacks who continue in the savage practices of their African ancestors.[24]

The narrative demonization of Haiti, onto which all negative constructions of the tropics become displaced, is revealing. For if, as James puts it, places like Jamaica belong "to Us," then the non-English-speaking Caribbean, and in particular, Haiti, which belongs to "Them," must be viewed with suspicion. For Haiti is ultimately "Other," a black republic with a history of violent resistance to European colonial rule. In English travelogues, explains Gikandi (1996: 113), Haiti serves as "a radical site of alterity . . . the spectral metaphor of blackness – an imminent threat to the idea of Englishness." Displacing this fear makes possible the textual preservation of "Our" safe part of the Caribbean as paradise, which – JanMohamed would argue – justifies continued control since the civilizing mission is always under threat (from forces such as those at work in Haiti) and thus infinitely prolonged. Hence Wilcox smugly deduces from a visit to Haiti that "[t]here is small hope for the [African] race save as it is guided, directed and assisted by the Anglo Saxons" (1909: 150). Despite the laudable freedom of "the Haitian Negroes," the plantations are ruinate, the roads impassable, the town and population are filthy and "foul stenches pollute the soft air" (151–2). Here indeed, is Paradise lost, fallen, reverted to barbarism; significantly, the terms used speak, once again, to a domestic concern with dirt, wastefulness, an absence of hygiene, and indeed a lack of taste and decorum. Less strident than Wilcox, other women writers also project their political antipathy onto the Haitian landscape. Four years after Wilcox's diatribe, James's first impressions of the island (1913: 22) are couched in apocalyptic imagery:

A dark mass of mountains silhouetted against the sky and over it a great black cloud from which shot forked white tongues of flame. It was as if all the unrest and fever of men's minds had risen and gathered there like smoke from evil fires . . . the feeling of things sinister and unknown come creeping back to the mind.

The picture is, of course, far more suggestive of European fears of Haitian political history – although James admires l'Ouverture – than representative of its hills and coastline. But when she goes ashore, James too finds a scene of squalor, filth and neglect. The town of Jeremie (156–7) consists of

a long unpaved street with open stagnant gutters in which dabbled pigs and chickens and children all together; women squatting on chairs that bridged the gutters or sitting beside them with open baskets of foodstuffs poised on the brink and ready to slip in with the first shove; mangy little curs lying palpitating with heat under ramshackle verandahs; and dirt everywhere.

For elite women, the terror of revolutionary ideas and anti-European sentiments spreading from "Them" to "Us"[25] underlies negative portrayals of Haiti from Nugent's journal right through to the early twentieth century. Writing in 1801–2, Nugent (1966: 60) reflects on Toussaint's revolution against French government: "[h]ow dreadful a business it is altogether; and, indeed, it makes one shudder, to think of all the horrible bloodshed and misery that must take place, before any thing can be at all settled in that wretched island." Lynch's *Years Ago* (1865: 40) comments on "the unsettled and dangerous state of things in St. Domingo" in 1790, and ventriloquizes the white Jamaican population's fear "of the negroes comprehending in any way these insurrectionary feelings, lest it should incite them to rebellion" (27). The date of Lynch's novel – the year of the Morant Bay rebellion in Jamaica – is ironically appropriate to such a sentiment. And in Fielding's stories (1915), we witness the same displacement of all that is evil and savage in the tropics onto the much maligned republic. In contrast to Jamaica which, despite its shortcomings, is "our own dear little Isle," we are warned about "a blood red Island, not very far from our own shores, a land where Vodonism, Cannibalism, and the offering up of sacrifices to a heathen god, exists [*sic*] even to this day" (47). For Wilcox too, the rites and ceremonies of "Vaudouxism in Haiti" – to which she devotes a whole section, mostly based on second-hand sources and histories – is "associated with revolting crime, and indescribable obscenity. They begin with drunkenness, proceed with licenciousness [*sic*] and end, often with murder and canibalism [*sic*]" (1909: 161). "If in the midst of such civilized centres as Louisiana and Jamaica," she commiserates, "the Vaudoux evil cannot be eradicated, how vain the idea which is trying to be forced upon the public, that it has ceased to exist in Haiti" (163). In Haiti, then, the narratives give full rein to all the negative and fearful aspects of the West Indies which, because of their investment in empire, can only be hinted at in constructions of "Our" islands. Only if left in the proper ("Our") hands, can the West Indies continue to provide the right mix of unspoilt yet unthreatening paradisal pleasures for the consumption of the literary (or actual) tourist.

To conclude, I return yet again to James's formula for the West Indian colony as "a hot place and belonging to Us." "A hot place" is shorthand for the exotic: the tropics, a fantasy realm onto which is projected desire for the (sometimes dangerously exciting) strange and other. "Belonging to Us" counterbalances this otherness by translating it in terms of familiar prescriptions, making it safe because ultimately it is framed within the categories of European rule and of European knowledge-building (hence the inclusion of "facts," details of flora and fauna, ethnographic manners and customs). The exotic is familiarized (for Us); the tropics are textually appropriated and made safe (for Us). And always in the background, Haiti is the cautionary reminder of what can go wrong.

The coexistence of opposing mythical constructions, and the encoded contra-dictions of the women's travel narratives examined here, demonstrate the enig-matic constructions of the specific, the places and peoples loosely grouped under the term "the West Indies." Within this net of projections onto the landscape – projections which are themselves the product of discursive and stylistic clashes and interfacing of pre-texts – what of the *real* "West Indies"? One is reminded of the anguished cry of the husband in Rhys's *Wide Sargasso Sea*, "I want what it hides." But the West Indies is not lurking somewhere within these multiple and various constructions. Partly the product of these (and other) representations, yet eluding definitive appropriation, "the West Indies" endlessly repeats and reflects such constructions in patterns old and new, into the imagination of the world.

4 A female "El Dorado"

"Terrestrial paradise": myths of new beginnings

The narratives discussed in the previous chapter manifest the complex, and often contradictory projection of prescriptions, desires and fears onto the West Indian landscape. In this chapter I consider the female configuration of one such projection: the New World as promised land, as El Dorado. What is interesting about this enduring symbol is its gender associations. A historical illustration: the frontispiece to Peter Hulme's *Colonial Encounters* (1986) reproduces an image now almost archetypal of the colonial encounter. The engraving, by Jan van der Straet (Stradanus) is dated around 1600 and entitled "America." In it, a naked and fleshy Amerindian woman starts up from a hammock, as a clothed and armed European male stands over her. She is surrounded by "American" props (parrots, bows and arrows) and a cannibal feast is in progress in the background. As Hulme observes (1), the sexual nature of the encounter – the male gazes down at the semi-reclining female body – and the manner in which the allegorical woman figures both "native" and "land," are apparent. Similarly, Columbus's journal configures the Gulf of Paria as the entrance to "the terrestrial paradise" (another inscription of El Dorado), and fittingly "from his reading of geographers and theologians, he had come to the conclusion that the earth here was shaped like a woman's breast, with the terrestrial paradise at the top of the nipple" (Naipaul 1962: 38). The tropics as woman's body, a bountiful source of sustenance and pleasure, and the construction of the encounter between Old World and New in terms of male conquest of seductive "virgin territory," may have had its origin in Walter Ralegh's account of his 1595 "Discoveries of the Large, Rich, and Beautiful Empire of Guiana."[1] Here he described "a country that has yet her maydenhead," the site of the fabled El Dorado, the city of gold. In any case, it was a familiar trope by 1669 when John Donne's "Elegie: To His Mistris Going to Bed" compared the exploration of his lover's female body with that of the Conquistadors' forays into the new continent:

> Oh my America, my new found lande,
> My kingdom, safeliest when with one man mann'd,
> My myne of precious stones, my Empiree,
> How blest am I in this discovering thee.

Here, America is depicted in terms of the uncharted, and thus tempting female body, as a sensual paradise *and* a source of wealth. The gendered landscape is to be discovered, explored, conquered and its riches yielded up. El Dorado is in this instance feminized.

How did women respond to this inscription of the colonial encounter? With male domination and exploitation so blatantly encoded in such imaginative visions, how could they identify with the imperial project? In Hulme's frontispiece, we see white man and "native" woman; there is no place for the white woman. Perhaps European women longed to participate in some way in the adventure of empire, yearned to experience the novelties and the riches of El Dorado, but they could hardly identify in an unproblematic manner with this deeply gendered pre-scription of the encounter. And surely the relationship was even more complex for writers who were creoles, white "natives"? Or did women appropriate the trope in a different way?

I argue that while women shared the concept of the region as a site of opportunities from which they were excluded (on the grounds of class and/or gender) within the "mother country," their narratives *reconfigure* the trope of El Dorado/virgin territory/promised land in more prosaic and domestic terms. Certainly the far-flung lands of empire offered an imaginative escape from the confines of a claustrophobic Victorian Britain and, for women travelers, an ideal of a new beginning, away from the demands of families, brothers, fathers, suitors and husbands. As Gikandi observes in his discussion of colonial women's writing, such narratives "are propelled by the belief that empire opens up new opportunities for female subjects in the nineteenth century; women travelers seek to consolidate their notions of freedom in the realm of the other" (1996: 49). But, he continues, "they also have to contend with the fact that empire is a male affair," as are its dominant representations, including a gendered landscape.

Let us reconsider some of the idealized portrayals of the West Indies by women writers. One dominant strain of imagery, as noted, relates not to a potential source of wealth but to a site invested – at least initially – with magic and potential adventure. In Jenkin's novel (1859), the chapter detailing Stella's departure for Jamaica is entitled "Bound for Fairy Land." Prior to her journey to the colonies in Smith's *Mary Paget* (1900), the heroine is outfitted with a wardrobe "fit for a fairy princess about to enter upon an idyllic life in an enchanted island" (234). Part of the enchanting prospect, on a practical level, is the possibility of becoming "somebody." So Alice, the orphan heroine of Crommelin's *A Daughter of England* (1902) escapes her job as caretaker to a miserly uncle through an inheritance of income from Jamaican estates, and travels there in the expectation of a new life of pleasure and social attention after years of sobriety and deprivation: "how often had she tasted the bitterness of being a nobody" (248). For white women – and men – in the colonies, increased status conferred by virtue of race was one benefit. And for these women – and men – enhanced standing is at the expense of an undifferentiated mass of black inferiors.[2]

Thus the vain, affected heroine of Long's *The Golden Violet* (1936: 21), set in pre-emancipation Jamaica, fancies that she will be a queen ministering to savages and looks forward to increased prestige and power: "how stupid her past seemed in contrast to this brilliant future" (21). Nugent's journal is but one account that suggests almost obsessive concerns with rank and status amongst white women in the colonies as witnessed by the exaggerated deference shown to herself, and the anxieties of other women to cultivate her patronage. Loathing the constant rounds of "making the agreeable" with visiting and local dignitaries, she ridicules the awe in which she is held (1966: 81):

> If I were the Queen of Sheba, I could not be made more fuss with than I am here. It is really overpowering. A word from me decides every thing with the ladies, and a look sets all the gentlemen flying to anticipate my commands.

Nugent recoils from this eminence, resolving to "avoid cabals" and "live alone at my private hours, and so put an end to all these silly jealousies" (30). The fawning of Mrs Pye, a major's wife, repulses her (15) and she attempts to separate the adulation she receives as "the Governor's lady" from that due her as an individual woman (218). Nugent's awareness of her almost deified status is humorously treated in her account of an old black servant spying upon her in her bath in order to see *all* of the "Governor's lady" (67).

The splitting off of this *rara avis*, "the Governor's lady" from that of the narrator, Maria Nugent, is a neat metaphor for the kind of fantasy in several narratives whereby "ordinary" women are automatically elevated in the West Indies by virtue of race and nationality, but attribute the promotion to innate qualities, heretofore overlooked. Lanaghan (1844, vol. 2: 198–9) is caustic about ill-bred whites who immediately assume superior airs on arrival in the colony: she compares them to pale mushrooms (*"fungi"*) which spring up overnight from muck. As previously noted, the male upstarts are exceeded by their wives in pretensions to social class. Simply residing in the West Indies, some narratives suggest, confers social advancement. Nugent, on her return to Britain, notes with amusement that her English maid has been passing herself off to fellow servants "for having been a maid of honour, in foreign parts, where, she assured them, I had been a queen!" (1966: 264).

If the texts by women rework the trope of "terrestrial paradise" into a more pragmatically conceived site of novelty and increased social standing, how do they rehearse the sexual overtones implicit in Hulme's frontispiece: the new space as an erotic field? While European women could hardly buy into the fantasy of sexual adventure, surely the "exotic" suggested an attractive alternative to the grey realities of Victorian prudery? Certainly, Phillips's reconstruction of an Englishwoman's voyage of discovery to the New World (1991), does explore this possibility. In the West Indies, Emily learns as much about her sexuality as she does about her anomalous place in imperial power relations. Less explicitly, I suggest that most early narratives by women map the Caribbean in terms of self-discovery; what is encountered in the new land is a new possibility of self-fulfillment.

One sustained elaboration of the West Indies as promised land occurs in Bridges' "Victorian Memoirs" (1988). Bridges recounts the story of her English grandfather who is smitten with the island's natural charms on an official visit to Trinidad just after Emancipation. On his return, his evocation of the paradisal scenery – "luxuriant fertility . . . pellucid stream . . . rare orchids . . . exotic birds" (72) – seduces his wife, and the couple immediately purchase and settle on an estate in Diego Martin. But the dream by stages becomes disillusionment, particularly for the wife. Her intention is to rebuild the plantation house "and to surround it with a park-like pleasance, to enclose which she ordered from England an elaborate wrought-iron fence" (73). Tropical rains, the collapse of country roads, the dishonesty of overseers and the failure of crops puts paid to such ambitions. "[L]aboriously conveyed to the estate," the numerous sections of the wrought-iron fence "were left to rust where they lay for everything was already up for sale to liquidate as many debts as possible" (74). Without her grand project and frustrated in the society "of people whose interests and outlook were severely limited" (75), the wife wanders the countryside in search of artistic inspiration instead of doing the expected: "relaxing into the genteel indolence proper to a lady" (76). Still pursuing adventure and enchantment, at the age of 63 she "conceived the notion of exploring the upper reaches of the Orinoco river in Venezuela, into which no white man, let alone woman, had ever ventured for any distance" (76) and *does* so, going missing for over a year! Clearly, the imaginative lure of El Dorado continues to exert a powerful influence on some women.

Escape from dependency, acquisition of social mobility, self-fulfillment through adventure: these desires inform white women's narrative appropriation of the West Indies as El Dorado. And one practical avenue to achieving these goals was through meaningful employment.

"Liberation through migration": the lure of work

There is not scope here to detail the position of middle-class women in nineteenth-century Britain but, generalizing hugely, one can state that a woman's socially sanctioned identity was dependant on "belonging" to a man: she was a man's daughter, sister, wife or mother. In *Early Victorian Britain 1832–51*, Harrison describes the strictly hierarchical nature of the middle-class family and its effectiveness as an instrument of social discipline and conformity. "But," he continues, "this outward success was only achieved at a price, and the internal stresses and strains of family life were seldom far below the surface" (1971: 116–7). For women, Harrison asserts, "the middle class family provided a strangely restricted and debilitating role . . . the middle class wife had difficulty in avoiding a life of utter triviality and boredom." Daughters were subordinates, dependant on and ruled by their fathers regarding choice of mate; once married, "a middle class woman was securely within a gilded cage from which there was no escape," divorce being virtually impossible until 1857 and the divorce courts little utilized for some time after (117). And fulfilling and challenging (that is, *paid*) work was frowned on for the married or single middle-class woman.

Once the perfunctory education of girls was complete, Harrison observes that "there was little to fill their heads but thoughts of marriage" (1971: 117). The unenviable lot of the middle-aged spinster and the poorer governess, unmarried woman dependent on the charity of relatives or the vagaries of underpaid and low-status employment, was to be pitied if not viewed with suspicion and, sometimes, scorn. Nineteenth-century novels such as Jane Austen's *Emma*, Brönte's *Jane Eyre* and William Thackeray's *Vanity Fair* testify to the humiliation and exploitation associated with the position of governess: for a woman with intelligence and ambition, such a career spelt misery. Yet few other kinds of income-generating employment were considered respectable. For many, marriage was considered the only option. Again, Phillips's *Cambridge* (1991: 3) vividly imagines the state of mind of a nineteenth-century spinster approaching 30. Faced with the prospect of "a fifty-year-old widower with three children as a mode of transportation through life," Emily seizes the chance for a temporary respite in a voyage to the West Indies, ostensibly to visit her father's plantation. The "truth was she was fleeing the lonely regime which fastened her into backboards, corsets and stays to improve her posture" (3–4). Other women too undoubtedly craved escape, such as the unfortunate governesses seeking release from what Brönte herself described as "this wretched bondage." And in *Constance Mordaunt* by "E.J.W. (A Woman),'" an equally desperate widow survives by traveling as paid chaperone from the West Indies to England, resigned "to go into service or starve" (1862: 89ff).

Catherine Hall (1992: 241) and Renk (1999: 8) evoke the model of the hierarchical Victorian family as a neat paradigm for English colonial relations: as Renk puts it, "the family is a metashrine which serves as a transmitter of English culture and as an apparatus that exerted control over what the patriarchy considered the 'unmanageable,' the Other: white women, slaves of both sexes, and the colonies." For dependant women then, the New World may indeed have suggested an alternative to patriarchal tyranny, domestic drudgery, and a claustrophobic life of petty restrictions at home. And as Pratt reminds us (1992: 170–1), by 1828 there *were* a few precedents in women who had found ways to earn a living abroad: "the Spinster Adventuress, her back to Europe, fleeing the confines of her time and returning – sometimes – to write about it." As noted previously, travel writing and the literature of discovery had long propagated the myth of personal and financial renewal through imperial adventure; and the West Indies was synonymous in popular thought with potential wealth. Why should women not imagine it in similar terms? Travel writing often coded the journey as a project of self-actualization beyond the restrictions of class in England; why not beyond the limitations of the class-bound female role? As Beckles admits (1998a: 2), historical studies have tended to suggest "that the lure of a West India fortune, which gripped the heart and soul of the propertied classes in English society, had engendered positive responses only from enterprising menfolk" and very little is known of "those white women who, as part of the rural gentry and urban middling classes, chose the West Indies as a place to repair broken domestic economies or pursue new fortunes." Some early narratives by women can help in addressing this gap.

Making one's fortune in the West Indies was the subject of many tales in the eighteenth and nineteenth centuries, and some featured women's success. The picaresque narrative of a female protagonist who makes good in the colonies gained some popularity in Europe following the publication of Defoe's *Moll Flanders* in 1722. Even earlier, in 1720, *The Jamaica Lady, or The Life of Bavia* detailed "An Account of her Intrigues, Cheats, Amours in England, Jamaica, and the Royal Navy" ("W.P." 1963). Bavia does not quite succeed in making her fortune in Jamaica, although she enjoys periods of prosperity. In contrast is Polly Haycock, the heroine of *Fortunate Transport* ("Creole" 1755). Born into poverty and transported as a felon, "in spite of all that, [Polly] now rolls in Ease, Splendor, and Luxury; and laughs at dull Moralists, who would persuade Mankind that the way to be happy is to be good" (5). After surviving a cruel indenture in Virginia, she robs her lover and travels to Jamaica where, by a combination of business acumen and sexual manipulation of rich men, she acquires land, wealth and social standing until she can count herself among "the first Rank in the Island" (40). 1757 saw the publication of *The History of Miss Katty N*——by "herself" (Katherine M-x-well [Maxwell]). The subtitle specifies the content: it is a rollicking account of "her Amours, Adventures, and various Turns of Fortune, in Scotland, Ireland, Jamaica, and in England." The Jamaican section relates that the narrator, a woman no more respectable than Bavia or Polly, none the less lived very well in the West Indies: "My house was furnished like a Palace, and not one in Kingston lived more genteely than I did" (1757: 208).

But the West Indies does not yield its riches easily to poor white women. Lanaghan's account of her West Indian residence (1844, vol. 2: 197) suggests that a poor English governess is no better off in Antigua than at home. And as we have seen, Fenwick's letters from Barbados in the early nineteenth century temper rosy dreams of prosperity with frequent records of financial crises. As a representative of the middle-class expatriate in the West Indies, Fenwick's insights are quite different from those of the aristocratic Nugent, or Carmichael the planter's wife. Nugent's work is of the diplomatic sort, and she certainly lives in luxury. Carmichael is comfortably off even though she complains – not entirely convincingly – that whites in the West Indies lead a far meaner life than those in England. But even Fenwick enjoys "the comforts of a good table, a large and handsome house" (1927: 191), and "the luxuries of our present dwelling" (205). Elsewhere, however, she expresses her disillusionment with El Dorado: "I recollect perfectly that in struggles & pecuniary difficulties I used to think any place would be paradise where I could secure a living. The means are abundant, but Barbados is not my paradise" (174). After drought, hurricane, the departure of her alcoholic son-in-law and collapsed speculations increase their expenses, the means are less "abundant" and Fenwick has the "daily penance to read over my list of unpaid debts" (203). Towards the end of her stay she is willing to exchange all this "for a cottage and narrower means at home" (205): this is largely rhetoric, for she has become accustomed to the good life and her plans for another school in Bristol or Connecticut necessarily involve a large house with gardens and accessible "good society" in order to maintain "that decent &

comfortable order which we think highly salutary to the habits & good taste of our children" (211).

Among the fictions, Jenkin's *Cousin Stella* (1859, vol. 3: 149)[3] contrasts the virginal heroine with worldly-wise Olympia, who walks out on an exploitative and unfaithful husband in England and achieves independence in the West Indies. Employed for some time as a bookkeeper, an equal in business acumen with the men of the estate, her ambitions (and her past) eventually catch up with her. In *His Promise* (1925), Winnifred Duff ("Freda Granville") also portrays the West Indies as a land of opportunities for English girls down on their luck. The heroine, one of a struggling clergyman's large family, accepts with alacrity a post as governess in Jamaica. She soon loses the job, and in desperation marries the first man who offers himself.[4] For the protagonist of Fraser's *Lucilla*, the West Indies is likewise conceived in terms of economic and social betterment. The English music mistress arrives in "San José" to teach in a college for non-white girls, expecting to find adventure and financial reward but soon disillusioned, lonely and with "no money, no prospects," grasps "rashly at the first change that offered": marriage to a man from a well-to-do colored family (1896a, vol. 2: 5). Similarly, the heroine of Stephenson's *Undine* returns to the West Indies only to find herself impoverished and forced to work as a daily governess, and is quick to exchange a life of hardship and privation and her attic room in "upper Duke Street, Kingston, Jamaica" to marry the unprepossessing father of a pupil (1911: 12).

While the earlier fictions romanticize the West Indies as a veritable goldmine for enterprising women of dubious virtue, and the accounts of Fenwick and Lanaghan detail the hard work necessary to improve one's status in the colonies, the later nineteenth- and early twentieth-century fictions portray paid employment coming a poor second-best to the ideal of marriage in El Dorado as in England. But there was another option for respectable women who sought fulfilment outside of her "proper" place in the home: missionary work.

The missionary "family"

Walter Houghton (1957: 351) argues that a central characteristic of the middle-class female role in the literature of mid-nineteenth century England, was "to counteract the debasing influence on religion as well as morals of a masculine life preoccupied with worldly goods and worldly ambitions." A woman was to raise the "tone of mind" of men in the household to considerations of a more moral and spiritual nature, since after all, the female birthright was "the power to love, to serve, and to save." In the colonial context too women's role as "moral housekeeper" helped to dignify the crass business of exploitation. This vital influence was crucial to the missionary cause, with its stress on feminine virtues of self-sacrifice, piety and charitable concern for the less fortunate. Accordingly, association with such institutions provided a permissible avenue to travel, adventure and new experiences for women. Thus St John Rivers shrewdly tempts Jane Eyre, who hungers for liberty from the prison of her gendered social space, with "the destiny of the pioneer." What this actually means for a woman translates into assisting his "glorious" ambition of bettering the heathen race by bringing knowledge and piety into the realms godlessness and superstition (Brönte 1987: 329). In the early nineteenth century, Catherine Hall tells us (1992: 274), British missionaries "tended to come from the lower to middle class and were exclusively men. Gradually, missionary work became a realm of possibility for women; they were able to go out as school teachers, assistants, and later full-blown missionaries." Again, the more acceptable way was through marriage. Hall (252) cites the example of Mary Ann Hutchins (née Middleditch), who yearned for the missionary life and wrote "that I would rather go to Jamaica than dwell in England." As Hall explains, "her route was through marriage, but in her letter to her parents explaining her decision to go it was love of Christ which was emphasized, not of her husband-to-be."

Women who traveled to the West Indies to fulfill God's work tended to do so as an adjunct to a man and/ or as part of what Hall calls "the mission family" (254). In *The Youthful Female Missionary* (1839) Hutchins writes of being taken into the Baptist community in Jamaica, and treated like a daughter by Thomas Burchell and his wife. Hall's likening the network of Baptist missionaries to an extended family corresponds with the accounts of Anne Hart Gilbert and Elizabeth Hart Thwaites, Antiguan women of mixed race who were pillars of the local Methodist mission. Agnes Satchell's *Reminiscences of Missionary Life in the Caribbean Islands* (1858) records her love of missionary work as well as the physical freedom it allowed: she rides, climbs mountains and travels by boat in the wild terrain of Dominica, all in the service of the Lord. However, like the Hart sisters and Hutchins, her role is primarily one of duty to her own nuclear family and the "brothers and sisters" of the Wesleyan-Methodist mission. As Hall points out, the "structure of the mission family, as with the early nineteenth-century English family from which it was derived, was strictly patriarchal" (1992: 256), with everyone contributing to the collective enterprise in properly gendered ways. Missionary women then, may have found new possibilities for work, spiritual satisfaction and a breadth of experience in the West Indies, but they were still defined and bound by their (secondary) place in the home and family. El Dorado translates into a new home-space, with all its attendant responsibilities and restrictions.

Further, the missionary "family" was not an egalitarian system but a hierarchical one in terms of gender and race. Just as women missionaries were there as "junior partners," so blacks were children to be guided towards freedom/ adulthood. "Spiritual equality might be one thing," Catherine Hall observes drily, but "[e]conomic and cultural equality were quite another" (1992: 262). This is evident in the language used by Hutchins to describe native converts: "[w]e find some of the Negroes very interesting, quick creatures, and are quite delighted with their simplicity" (1839: 98). Satchell's nostalgic memories similarly encode a maternal relation to inferiors: "I often fancy I see the bronze and sable faces of the dear people among whom we have laboured, and hear their happy salutations, 'Morrow, mi Missis,' sounding in my ears" (1858: 40). The patriarchal and colonial limitations within which even the most zealous operated, once again foregrounds the ambivalent nature of the white woman's empowerment through ministering to those who, however "saved," could never be equals.

Therefore, while some white women in the West Indies found new avenues for worthwhile, fulfilling work in missionary activities, their accounts testify to the fact that such goals could be achieved only by negotiating within expectations about a woman's proper – and subordinate – position within a family. And even then, the region continues to proves an elusive promised land for many missionary women. As noted, the corrupting effect of West Indian society on the morals of new arrivals was a frequent complaint:

> It is the extraordinary to witness the immediate effect that the climate and habit of living in this country have upon the minds and manners of Europeans, particularly of the lower orders. In the upper ranks, they become indolent and inactive, regardless of every thing but eating, drinking, and indulging themselves, and are almost entirely under the dominion of their mulatto favourites. In the lower orders, they are the same, with the addition of conceit and tyranny . . .
>
> (Nugent 1966: 98)

Missionary women were particularly disgusted by the seemingly intractable immorality of all social groups. Nancy Prince, an American woman of mixed race, determined to travel to post-emancipation Jamaica as a Baptist missionary.[5] Her *Narrative* (1850: 37) captures the lure of missionary work – "A field of usefulness seemed spread out before me" – as well as her disillusionment with the reality of local practices in Jamaica. Prince details with cutting sarcasm the exploitation of the black poor by greedy church and missionary leaders of all races for whom the salvation of souls is secondary to lining their own pockets, via taxes, tithes, collections and even charging for baptism and monthly communion. She unambiguously blames this on colonial collusion in slavery and her outspoken condemnation, perhaps fueled by anger after a contentious break with the missionary "family" in Jamaica, strikes at the core of the colonial enterprise and the corruption of the church within it. For missionary women, this rottenness at the heart of empire must have tainted constructions of the West Indies as terrestrial paradise.

"A home of one's own": the tropics domesticated

> Those of the North with the call of the tropics in their blood have never a moment of strangeness; they are content, at home there.
>
> (Atherton 1908: 28–9)

If marriage and a home of one's own remained the ultimate ideal, most white women had better chances of finding a mate (demographically speaking) in the colonies. Husband-hunting in the West Indies remains a consistent theme, from *Fortunate Transport* and *The History of Miss Katty N——*onwards. Nugent reproaches such behavior:

Mrs. Wright, the young widow staying here . . . has, I am afraid, taken a fancy to Mr. Rocket [the newly arrived medical Inspector-General], and all the gentlemen of the staff are already making a joke of her *attentions* to him. I am sorry she makes herself so foolish, but it can't be helped.

(1966: 217; emphasis in original)

The poor widow is out of luck, for soon after Nugent remarks on Mrs Wright's dejection since "Mr. Rocket was particularly cold yesterday, and she shed many tears in remarking upon his conduct; but I dare say she will soon forget all about it, as she seems rather *volage* in her feelings." Others do manage to make a marriage, like the nursery maid who weds a German ensign and is thrilled by her transition to "an officer's lady" (238). Alas, her new status is illusory as two weeks later, Nugent writes "the account of poor Mrs. Brockmüller, who is not even allowed to sit down to table with her lord and master, the Ensign, but is obliged to wait behind his chair; and he has in fact married her to have a good servant, poor thing!" (240). In Lynch's novel *Years Ago* (1865: 2), young Doss relates in her journal that since she and her sisters have all been educated by their father, there was no need for a governess; and in any case, "mother always said that nineteen out of twenty of them would have been seeking husbands, and have left us to go on with our lessons as best we might." These husband-hunting governesses may have found a measure of economic security in wedlock, but inevitably it was on patriarchal terms. In the colonies, as much as in England, fathers and husbands had complete control over their women: Mary Prince's slave narrative testifies to the mistreatment and abuse meted out to wives of white men, and relates how she had to intervene in a cruel whipping one planter was administering to his daughter.

Further, male approval was required before a young woman *could* marry. Doss's father in Lynch's (1865) text strikes and then incarcerates a daughter who has secretly chosen her own husband, and the novel condones this punishment by demonstrating the unsuitability of her union. Doss herself is pressured over several years to wed her father's choice, and finally submits. She conveniently discovers that she loves Hugh, her reward (as well as her own secure home) for obeying male authority which, after all, knows best. A young wife, Doss reflects that "It is so good of him [her husband] to let me sit in his library" (232), and recounts "how I strive to anticipate his wishes" in everything (235). Their relationship is successful only in so far as she curbs her will, and continues in the role of Hugh's "docile pupil" (229). Ultimately, the myth of El Dorado is prosaically reconfigured with a husband and hearth as the treasure, and female submission the price.

Sometimes this price is high. In Duff's romance, *His Promise* (1925), a governess rescued by marriage from penury and unsuitable male attentions, "gloried in her new surroundings, and it was a joy to put the little feminine touches" to her new home. None the less, she has married an older man whom she does not love in a baldly utilitarian exchange. In *Cousin Stella*, marriage is viewed with some cynicism by older women. Stella's youthful aunt Celia explains that if she does not put my foot on your uncle's neck, he would ill-treat me. People talk of happiness: I wish they would tell me where it is to be found. I never saw it anywhere but in a novel; in real life things never go as one wants them, or expects them! The warmest heart woman can have is very soon frozen. Instead of being cared for, she must make herself a slave to every whim her husband chooses to have: she dare not have an opinion of her own, nothing but contradiction, til in self-defense she is forced to act the virago.

(Jenkin 1859, vol. 1: 307)

Again, one notes the equation of women's lot with slavery. Stella discovers soon after arrival in the West Indies that "Fairy Land" is not the Eden she imagined. Recognizing that as a woman "her only chance of not giving offense, or of being the cause of evil, was to remain passive." She comes to revolt against this submissive role: "She was depressed and discouraged: any toil or danger was preferable to this colourless life" (vol. 2: 137). But as soon as she falls in love with her authoritative cousin Louis, Stella *embraces* her passivity: "she entertained that species of veneration for her cousin which made her, what her original nature did not, gentle and yielding" (vol. 2: 219). Craving "a home of my own" (vol. 1: 214), Stella comes to see Louis's estate as a refuge, "a holy sanctuary" (221). Louis rules Stella absolutely: "I have decided that it is right you should go," he informs her when danger threatens (vol. 3: 81). And to this as all else, she willingly submits: "Stella was in a sort of ecstacy of suffering: she enjoyed it; it was for him!" (vol. 3: 83). Unlike her aunt, Stella does find home and happiness with Louis, but again such bliss comes only with unconditional surrender of female will and any pretense to equality: "she had dreamed of being allowed to love him—of him accepting her devotion—but never, never that he would call her 'his darling' . . . He must not—she was such a silly girl—so inferior to him" (vol. 3: 282).

This almost risible normalization of female servility is hard for modern readers to swallow, but other narratives are less sanguine about marriage as a paradise. Lucilla, for example, in Fraser's novel, soon comes to realize that her hasty wedding offers no salvation. She has bought into the myth that the West Indies is a place where English girls tired of drudgery may find wealth and status through a good match, but learns that she "had made a miserable mistake from the first" (Fraser 1896a, vol. 2: 40). Marriage turns out to be as dull, unprofitable and unsatisfying as her former teaching career. Worse, by her union she has "finally and completely cut herself off from all her own race" (vol. 2: 146) and, to her horror, her quadroon husband reverts to "native" African ways, eating with his fingers out of a calabash on the verandah (vol. 2: 194). After enduring humiliation and abuse Lucilla runs away. All too soon, she realizes that she has not found her El Dorado, a home and family of her own; quite the opposite, in fact, as she constantly comments on the "unhomelike surroundings" of her husband's residences. The novel closes with her wandering around Europe, desperately avoiding any West Indians who may know the true story of her tropical adventure.

What lesson does the novel convey? Obviously, it is a cautionary tale for headstrong English women who marry into West Indian families of means but dubious bloodlines. The threat of miscegenation still haunts colonialist discourse at the close of the nineteenth century. More interestingly, however, is the implicit disillusionment of Lucilla (and Stella's aunt) with the romance formula. Bitterly reflecting on the novels she has read, Lucilla confesses that "the phrase, 'they were married and lived happily ever afterwards,' conveys now to her aught else than the cruellest irony" (1896a, vol. 2: 212). Perhaps the vapid Stella, who has also uncritically imbibed her notions of romantic love from sentimental novels, is in for a rude awakening along the lines of her cynical aunt? Certainly Jenkin's text indicts the romantic fiction consumed by women as a source of impossible expectations concerning life, love and marriage, and indeed the West Indies themselves. In women's constructions of the region as a place of adventure and enchantment, the magic often has to do with romance and passion. Like Bridges's grandmother, Mary Paget is entranced with her beloved's account of the Bermudas (Smith 1900: 16) and (literally) escapes opposition at home to join him there. The island's loveliness is but a backdrop for their romance, which transforms it into "the Eden of our hearts" (240).

Similarly, in Crommelin's *A Daughter of England*, Alice feels herself thaw in the islands, capable now of experiencing love and passion which do not thrive in the "sober northern soil" she has left behind (1902: 316). Consider also Atherton's ponderously titled historical novel, *The Gorgeous Isle: A Romance, scene, Nevis, B.W.I., 1842*. Arriving in the Caribbean from "the harsh salt winds" of her English home where she lived "a life of Spartan simplicity," the heroine feels her senses awaken. "There are certain people born for the tropics, even though bred within the empire of the midnight sun," she reflects, as "[m]ind and body respond the moment they enter that mysterious belt which divides the moderate zones" (1908: 26). In love with a dream (an island poet she has long admired from afar), she invests landscape with her own repressed desires: "this warm, fragrant, poetic, land. It was made for such as she, whose whole nature was tuned to poetry and romance, even if denied the gift of expression or consummation!" (26). Appropriating the West Indies for her own fantasy, she is able to convince the poet of her affections, marries him and is delighted that "his home was her own" (170). But the pattern of dream-to-disillusionment is repeated here. Her husband turns out to be a dissipated wreck, drunken and tormented, a great soul in a "polluted tenement." Romantic fantasies fail, inevitably, to live up to expectation.

So while several narratives conflate the exotic with the erotic/romantic, all too often the reality clashes with the romance formulae. In *Undine*,[6] Stephenson's Jamaican heroine conceives a melodramatic passion for a handsome English stranger, not in the dusty town in which she labors as a governess, but on a visit to the Jamaican countryside. In this magical space, her feelings are projected onto the pastoral scenery and, it seems, actually suffuse the very air she breathes: "a purple haze is enwrapping her senses, and all things are melting into a calm, smooth current" (1911: 27). Like George Eliot's Maggie, the river of passion carries women away, but to their detriment.[7] So it proves for Undine. Committed elsewhere, the handsome stranger reluctantly departs. The novel suggests this is just as well anyway since Undine believes that in daily life, all affections become "sordid, commonplace . . . the imagination is the only real enjoyment we have in life; let me have the dream to remember, it is the best" (55). True love cannot blossom in the dusty streets of Kingston: unrequited passion is more fittingly enacted in the verdant hills. In the text, "real" love remains idealized, unattainable, well within the conventions of the romance formula in a pastoral setting.

The most biting exposé of the dangers of mistaking romantic fantasy for actuality occurs in *The Golden Violet* by Gabrielle Long[8] (published under a male pseudonym, "Joseph Shearing"). The protagonist is a "lady novelist" steeped in the worst excesses and clichés of the popular romance, whose eyes are opened by a brutal encounter with West Indian reality. The romance genre is mercilessly satirized in excerpts from Angelica Cowley's writing, full of stock heroines with impossible virtues and fluttering hearts, on whom she initially patterns herself. Soon disillusioned with the inferior position she is expected to adopt by her philandering husband, and the violence and corruption of colonial slave society, she becomes sexually involved with a "quadroon" of anti-slavery sentiments. The West Indian experience forces her to realize the ridiculous nature of her fictions:

> the world of phantasy in which Angel[ica] had for so long wandered at ease now quite escaped her. She scribbled pages about the Troubadours and tore them up; as she became more interested in herself and her surroundings, she became less interested in those creatures of her imagination in which she had once taken so much delight. Only when she had to describe her hero did she please herself, for she gave him all the physical attributes of [her lover] John Gordon and endowed him with all the qualities she believed that young man possessed.
>
> (Long 1936: 105)

Once again, the West Indies resists idealized notions of a romantic life in the colonies. The black subjects Angelica thought to patronize repudiate and mock her, the husband she saw as a shining knight proves a womanizing brute, and his estate yields her neither the fortune nor the status she imagined. Marriage as an escape from her job as a hack novelist proves a worse bondage. Indeed, Long's text makes explicit connections between female subjugation and black slavery, commenting on men's ignorance of their wives' "bitter resentment when that dependence was abused, of their instinctive hostility towards their masters, whom they feared, despised and needed" (1936: 51).

Angelica dreams of the West Indies as a place of liberation: "she wanted indeed to be a different creature from what she was, with a different destiny altogether from what she had" (1936: 24). And for all her disillusionment, Jamaica does indeed prove to be Angelica's El Dorado, in the conquistadorial associations of the term. She encounters all the adventure she could dream off, sensual pleasures never imagined, acquires a great deal of practical wisdom as well as wealth and social status. But her strategies for achieving these goals is linked with that of slaves and women: shrewd deployment of "duplicity . . . subtleness and intrigue . . . the weapons of the weak" (75). Ultimately, Angelica gains freedom by shedding cumbersome gender roles (the submissively feminine heroine) and reinventing herself as an independent woman. The result is not very flattering, but it is certainly an improvement and Angelica herself vindicates the transformative powers of the West Indies: "she had no desire to be meek or generous or pious or forgiving, nor anything she had been. She believed that in escaping from England, she had escaped from sham" (121). In casting off the conventional attributes of the nineteenth century "Angel in the House" – although she keeps up appearances when necessary – she resembles Polly Haycock and Bavia and Katty N—— of the earlier narratives. For her, the quest for El Dorado is undertaken with some of the (unfeminine) swashbuckling passion of the buccaneers: and she reaps the rewards. *The Golden Violet* then constructs the West Indies as a site of empowerment for women only if they break with redundant models of womanhood brought from the Old World.

Casting the West Indies in terms of the myth of El Dorado meant depicting it as a venue in which adventure, wealth and pleasure might be enjoyed by virtue of exploring and mastering "virgin territory." The texts I have examined rework this deeply gendered trope. Most follow a general pattern, a kind of female rite of passage in which a journey takes place from the Old World/center (to escape from poverty or restrictions of class or gender) to a New World/empire which is conceived in terms of potential: as a site of liberty, personal or spiritual self-fulfillment, financial security, exotic/erotic adventure, a safe home of own's own, and so on. The quest tends to end in one of three ways: disillusionment, partial integration or self-discovery.

Where protagonists insist on familiarizing the new by imposing upon it the template of the old, or mapping it in terms of desires and fantasies that bear no relation to the place, the journey results in disappointment and disillusionment. The West Indies will not conform to rigid pre-scriptions, no matter how enchanting. In such writings, constructions of the Caribbean landscape as a new "home" prove illusory. The place and its people will not fit the projected mold and resist being appropriated as a home-away-from-home, and for the most part a process of disenchantment ensues.[9] This clash between expectation and reality informs disparate narratives by Fenwick (1927), Carmichael (1969), Atherton (1908), Fraser (1896a) and, for rather different reasons, Nancy Prince (1850). For their protagonists, a *new* migration becomes necessary, either to another potential El Dorado or in retreat to the metropolitan home. A letter from Fenwick in 1819 conveys desire to return to familiar places and people in England (1927: 196):

> When, when my dear Friend, have I since my first arrival in this island, which has been the grave of so many proud & dearly cherished expectations, sat down to write to you with such a glow as at this moment spreads from my heart to my visage? – Yes! I feel my pale face is glowing with the expectation that makes me seem to be above feeling the clogs, embarrassments, labours & anxieties that, in reality, surround me for Oh, my dear Mary, I shall I believe once more see you . . . We are coming to England!

But dreams die hard. Fenwick ends up in another colony, America, still in pursuit of fortune and status.

A second option is to attempt (partial) integration into the society of the New World. It is significant that in text after text, women travel to the West Indies to join family. The impulse to assimilation is the subject of most of the narratives surveyed: protagonists seek in El Dorado a renewal of old family ties and/or the establishment of new ones. Introducing Bliss's semi-autobiographical novel *Luminous Isle* (1984), Alexandra Pringle tells us that Bliss's mother, Eva Lees traveled to Jamaica to live with her married brother, and there met, married and started a family with an English officer of the West India regiment. In Jenkin's novel, Stella returns from an English education to Jamaica, the land of her birth, to join her father and stepmother, and in due course marries her cousin. Mary Paget, in Smith's novel of the same name, voyages to Bermuda to join her fiancé. So too Fenwick journeys to Barbados to live and work with her married daughter and family. Angelica Cowley of *the Golden Violet* accompanies her new husband to his West Indian estate, and in *Undine* the heroine anticipates returning from Europe to a life of ease in her father's Kingston home. The "missionary family" welcomes female arrivals and encourages them to marry into it. For these women the unexplored new land of empire is less an El Dorado needing to be conquered, than an extension of home requiring tending and cultivation.

However, in many fictions (by Jenkin, Fraser, Lynch, Atherton and Long) the achievement of home and husband carries a price tag of female submission and servitude. A recurring image of this domestic bondage is the huge bunch of keys which the mistress of the household was obliged to carry with her at all times, the badge of her accountability for *his* goods and property. For accepting the keys to a man's home meant running his household, and managing his slaves/servants: accepting her secondary place in the home as in the colonial hierarchy.

Finally, and more rarely, some women's narratives represent the quest for a terrestrial paradise in the Caribbean as an empowering rite of passage into self-knowledge. In *The Golden Violet* and *The Gorgeous Isle* the heroines, like Phillips's Emily, are faced with their own repressed sexuality. The encounter, then, is not only with the new territory but with the buried territory of the female body. Long's heroine, like those of "Creole," "WP" and Katherine Maxwell find it possible to adopt behavior that subverts gender norms. Like all oppressed groups (and unlike the saintly ideal of European femininity) they undermine and exploit colonial society – which is, fundamentally, about exploitation and profit – for their own ends, and benefit from this strategy. Using their sexuality as much as "feminine" cunning and flattery, and learning a shrewd business sense from necessity, such women are constructed as manipulating middle-class patriarchal rules in their own quest for new beginnings, for physical and financial renewal in the colonies. Even if some of the eighteenth-century picaresque tales were written by men, they share with the narratives of several women a radical reconfiguration of the West Indies as a theater where women can perform other identities than the saintly destiny of loving, serving and saving souls.

"Not at home": the in-betweenity of the white creole woman writer

> She never blinks at all it seems to me. Long, sad, dark alien eyes. Creole of pure English descent she may be, but they are not English or European either.
>
> (Rhys 1968: 56)

Another dimension of the multiple signification of "home" and "homemaking" within the context of the colonial space, concerns the ambivalent self-identification of the white creole woman. Rhys's Antoinette has become representative of this group, a "white cockroach" to the blacks and a "white nigger" to the English, wondering "who I am and where is my country and where do I belong and why was I ever born at all" (Rhys 1968: 85). The ambivalence of the white creole woman is figured as a kind of double consciousness, a division of loyalties and affiliations: to places, to people, to cultural practices. The protagonists in the novels of Bliss, Allfrey and Rhys are only at home in their tropical world during childhood; all too soon, that sense of belonging is eroded and alienation ensues.[10]

Although distinct from the colored progeny of illicit black–white unions, one could never be sure that there was not "a touch of the tar-brush" somewhere in the ancestry of even the oldest settler dynasty. Additionally, white creoles were distinct from Europeans "gone native," though they shared many vices in common. But they were also distinct from "real" Europeans serving empire in the tropics. However "pure in blood" (to use Lanaghan's term), "[t]hese people who have lived here for generations are a very different people to us" (Bliss 1984: 71). The "difference" might be revealed in physical features, as with Antoinette's eyes in the quotation above;[11] similarly, the anonymous author of *The Koromantyn Slaves* (1823: 32) claimed that the eye sockets of creoles were apparently deeper than those of Europeans, "thus shading the eye from the ill effects of an ardent and glaring solar light." Physically, whites in the West Indies seemed to evolve downwards toward the bestial; and this applied to character also. So creoles in the region are represented as *less* well-bred, intelligent, active, sensitive, moral – generally less in *every* way – than the British and American writers who pronounce on them. Nevertheless, by virtue of their whiteness, these creoles take for granted a claim to the mother country as home. Given such complex identification, what exactly were white West Indian creoles? Where were they placed, and where did they place themselves in narratives of the Caribbean?

Gikandi (1996: 98) cites Trollope's caustic references to white creole behavior as a "burlesquing of the English in the West Indies," another variant of Fanon's colonial "mimic men" and Bhabha's native mimicry. The adoption of the trappings of colonial culture, a partial and deliberate approximation, categorizes the white creole too as *"almost the same but not quite."*[12] West Indian society in early narratives by women demonstrates to a great extent the "failure" of black and colored natives to acquire civilization beyond insolent and inappropriate mimicry; rather, the natives frequently contaminate the colonizers, whose descendants mutate into something else again: they became *creolized*. I use the term "white creole," as do Nugent and Rhys, in the original meaning of a locally born white.[13] Over time, the label became more inclusive. For example, Seacole refers to herself as a creole, meaning one of mixed blood; and indeed miscegenation often blurred the distinctions between colored and white creoles, hence the husband's suspicion of his wife in *Wide Sargasso Sea*. She is not black, but neither is she English; she is white, but a different *kind* of white and has colored relations: "almost the same but not quite." Occupying an in-between position, neither black native (but undeniably native) nor white European (but still white), how does the creole woman writer construct herself and her home?

Again, Rhys and her writing have come to serve as a typical illustration of white creole consciousness. For instance, Gregg suggests that in Rhys's autobiographical writings, white creole identity participates in colonialist discourse in the sense of grounding itself in the "Othering" of black West Indians (1995: 71). At the same time, the creole played the role of "Other" to the European so that Rhys's work, according to Gregg, "is consumed by the determination to free the self and the West Indies, as she knows and imagines both, from their containment within dominant discourses of European history and of subjectivity" (72–3). For Gregg, Rhys's reminder in a letter that "all Creoles are not negroes," indicates an "insistent desire to seek legitimacy for the articulation of the West Indian world from the Creole's perspective" (40). But what *is* this "Creole's perspective"? For most critics, it is one which articulates the occupation of "a cultural space between European and black Caribbean societies" and which "quite consciously complicates the dichotomy between 'colonizer' and 'colonized' " (Raiskin 1991: 51–2). While Rhys's West Indian writing falls outside my period, it is these tensions and ambivalences in creole culture I want to attend to in the remainder of this chapter. Primarily, my argument is that narratives by *locally born* women writers, while participating in colonialist discourse, also express an ambivalence about the culture of the English metropolis, and sometimes turn a unique and critical gaze on this center, reconfiguring to some extent the significance of El Dorado and "home."[14]

A few textual examples should suffice. When Rhys's creole protagonist refers to the England she has never seen as a "dream," she distills an unease that is representative of earlier narrators. Just as English women draw on fiction to imagine the Caribbean, West Indian girls in the nineteenth century learned about the mother country from books so out of date as to appear fictional. What did they learn? Not much, apparently. At the end of the nineteenth century, Cassin (1890: 35) has a visiting Englishwoman noting that until recently schools for women "out here" were rare, and that most creole girls are as ignorant and shallow as the unfortunately named Terpsichore Cadwallader. After a day in her company, Marion pities "the cramped, imprisoned, undeveloped life, of this girl who knew nothing of the beautiful world of art, of literature, or science in which she might have lived" (70). All this can only be acquired abroad, it seems. Bliss's *Luminous Isle* also paints an unflattering picture of colonial life in Jamaica in the early twentieth century. For Em, the artistic creole protagonist, the colony represents the stifling class and gender restrictions which she longs to escape for the sexless, classless "life of the mind," the world of "[b]ooks—the real world, the world of chronicle and analysis which she had left behind" in England (1984: 177).

In 1803 Nugent received "a packet of books from England, for the instruction of poor children . . . but alas, they can be of little use to us here!" (1966: 140). Carmichael too, in 1833, complains about the unsuitability of English school-books for teaching West Indian children (1969, vol. 2: 250). At the end of the century, Mehetabel Burslem's account of her first eleven years in Barbados is sketched in the brief typescript, *A West Indian Childhood.*[15] At age 5 or 6, she attended several dame schools and was taught by her mother. Her account of her syllabus is fascinating, drawn largely from books her own mother used at school in England in the 1840s and 1850s: *The Child's Book of Knowledge* ("How is bread made?"; "What is Caviare?"), spelling tables, scripture, French Grammar and Mrs Markham's History (7). Bridges, in her memoir of a Victorian girlhood in Trinidad, terms her education a "haphazard and spasmodic process" (1988: 97), again consisting of kindergarten at a dame school followed by private lessons and then an unsuccessful stint as her father's pupil, until she departs for school in England aged 14. It was also dated and entirely Eurocentric in content: "King Alfred and the cakes, Canute and the sea, Bruce and the spider . . . that London was on the Thames and that part of England was called the 'Black Country' " (99). Bridges's imaginary world is peopled with characters from archaic English stories: she gallops "wildly through Windsor Forest with Herne the Hunter on his 'swart horse,' voyaged the seas as Mr. Midshipman Easy, or became Jo in *Little Women*" (38). Clearly, the construction of England and Europe in the schoolroom text had little basis in contemporary fact – for the English, and even less so for the West Indian child – a theme which recurs in twentieth-century Caribbean litera-ture. Indeed, the disparity between the (tropical) world of real life and the fantasy (English) world of books in Merle Hodges's *Crick Crack Monkey* (1970: 61) is a phenomenon with which Burslem and Bridges could identify:

> Books transported you always into the familiar solidity of chimneys and apple trees, the enviable normality of real Girls and Boys who went a-sleighing and built snowmen, ate potatoes, not rice, went about in socks and shoes from morning until night and called things by their proper names . . . Books trans-ported you always into Reality and Rightness, which were to be found Abroad."

But like Rhys after them, Burslem and Bridges are also educated from a young age into the culture and folklore of black West Indians. Burslem's family home in Whitepark borders on a tenantry behind the garden wall, and an under-nurse explains all about the wakes and other events that take place in this other society (2). Bridges too is socialized into African-Caribbean culture by servants, who relate local superstitions (148) and tell stories about Compère Lapin and Compère Tigre (1988: 53). Like the white creoles in Crommelin's *A Daughter of England*, who utilize "bush" remedies for fever, Bridges's family are treated for illness with herbal cures (51), and Yseult learns about East Indian culture at first hand from the tenants on her family's country estate (185–8). Doss's grandmother in *Years Ago* (Lynch 1865: 101) passes on much of the Maroon lore of Jamaica to the girls, and even has a photograph of their leader Cudjoe. Bliss describes a white creole child's firm belief in "Duppies" despite adult contempt for such "silly nigger talk" (1984: 216). However, all these narrators are sensitive to their distinctness from this kind of "native" culture and of the class barriers separating them from "half-castes and poor whites" (Bridges 1988: 49).

Living in multiple worlds at home, some white creoles simply dismiss the relevance of books which conjure up an imaginary world outside the West Indies. The creole "lady-kind of the island," reflects an observer, have no interest in reading about a place they have never experienced:

> "Where's the interest of a description of a snow-storm or a ship wreck to these folks who have never seen snow or been to sea in their lives? They only jump over it to see if the hero or heroine escaped, or if they were married and lived happily ever after and shut up the book believing they have extracted all the interest which lies between its two covers. Where is the charm of a novel with any [British] dialect, or French or German quotations, or classical allusions to them? As soon as they come to the 'stupid scotch' or the 'silly old Latin' they throw the books down in disgust and send back to the long suffering library for more, if they are fortunate enough to have a library near."
>
> (Cassin 1890: 78)

Armed only with impressions drawn from archaic text books, British magazines and popular romances, the creole protagonists are ill prepared for the England they do encounter when they travel.

For go they must. In 1878, Burslem is sent to school in England at age 11. This was her mother's fate too, obliged to spend over ten years, including extended school holidays, away from her family with only one trip home to Barbados during this time. Bridges finds the wrench of being "shed" by home and family painful (1988: 202–4), but is told it is "for your good." Popular wisdom (157) dictates that young creole women of her class

> should spend at least a year in England, preferably three or four, being "finished." There only would she have a chance to eradicate the insidious singsong Creole accent and acquire that poise and complexion, that *cachet*, which would enhance her chances of making a "good match": which, if she failed to do, would mean that she had failed in the whole object of a woman's existence, and after a season or two would be relegated to the background of the home, there to live parasitically or to eke out a genteel existence in some ladylike way.

Again, gender considerations inform the purpose of this training. England here is not conceived of as a physical or social space in its own right, but as a further educational stage in the elite colonial woman's curriculum, the final goal of which is to graduate with a "good match" into real womanhood and a privileged place in island society. Lynch's *The Cotton-Tree; or, Emily, the Little West Indian* (1847) describes a happy tropical childhood until the little creole is sent away for seven years of "finishing school" in England. As in Bridges account, Lynch's Emily is lectured on the importance of the "accomplishments" needed "for the *establishment* of a young lady in Jamaica; by which I understood she meant *marriage*" (1847: 69; emphasis in original).

Burslem and Bridges end their stories with departure from the West Indies, but a few other narratives give us a glimpse of creole girls' responses to the "New World" of England. For the younger ones, it is a miserable experience. At age 13, Emily receives notice of her impending exile and can hardly "attempt to describe the intensity of my suffering at this time" (Lynch 1847: 20). After a heartbreaking farewell to her beloved mother, she arrives in England lonely and homesick: even the strange flowers, "beautiful but unknown . . . filled my heart with an oppressive sense of desolation" (34). Emily calls herself "the lonely stranger child . . . under alien skies" (36). In another of Lynch's novels, the narrator's aunt tells of being "sent from my dear mother to be, like many other little West Indians, an alien in England, a stranger in the land whose very name is *home*" (1848: 135; emphasis in original). What exacerbates Emily's sense of alienation is the reception she receives at school where she is preconceived as an outsider on the basis of her tropical birth:

> They laughed when I spoke; and I felt the blush of shame mount to my forehead when I discovered that my Creole accent was the cause of their merriment . . . I could stand this no longer, and, in an indignant tone I told them, that children from the country they affected to despise, would not behave in so rude a manner; that they would not thus laugh at a stranger. Upon this, some of the young ladies asked me, if I thought I had my little slaves around me, that I spoke thus hastily; and made many bitter observations . . .
>
> (Lynch 1847: 42–3)

Her schoolmates enquire "if my father were a negro; and Madame herself expressed astonishment at the fairness of my complexion, as she thought one born in the West Indies must necessarily wear the shadow of Africa's sable daughters" (44). Timidly, Emily resists the ignorant and condescending, even contemptuous attitude of the English to the creole.

Morea in Cassin's text is more spirited. Leaving the Caribbean, she refers to "going home to England" (1890: 106), but once there meets with English prescriptions of herself as a stereotypical creole, a *different* creature. The English Selwyn – who will later propose – expects Morea to be short, yellow and indolent, "utterly incapable of helping herself" without "six or seven black maids lolling about," drawling in her speech and fond of giving orders (116). Morea, like Emily, "refuses to fit into that niche" (119), and fights back. She continually praises the West

Indies to the detriment of England; takes pleasure in comparing the "sun at home" with its English imitation, a "poor watery thing" (121); insists she will continue to love her West Indian friends, including her black nurse, "quite as much as anybody in this muddy England" (137); and even mocks preconstructed notions of English manhood, that ideal of "strength, vigour and athletic ability. I hope I am not doomed to prove him a mere delusion and a fraud" (120). Laughingly, she advises Selwyn, "You are sadly in need of a little travel to enlarge your mind" (125), neatly turning the tables on the superior Englishman. Similarly, in *Constance Mordaunt* (E.J.W. 1862: 95), the child from St Vincent is viewed as a curiosity in England, as someone from "outlandish parts," for the author tells us (stretching credibility) that in those "bygone days" the West Indies was as unknown as China! The encounter with such ignorance and prejudiced stereotyping has remained a motif in modern Caribbean literature; so too, England – or, more recently, North America – is portrayed as the site of growing self-awareness of a *Caribbean* identity on the part of the immigrant: "[t]he creation of the colonial subject . . . takes place not only in the colony but in the 'Mother Country' as well" (Raiskin 1991: 59). Educated to belong to the center, it is in the center that creole migrants are forcefully made aware of their marginality, their otherness.

On the one hand then, white creole women proudly assert their nationality and culture. Symmonett's patriotic impulse has already been noted; Stephenson, another Jamaican, prefaces her romantic novel (1911) with a verse praising "Jamaica! Land of wood and stream" and her heroine proudly introduces herself, "I am Undine Varden, and I belong to Kingston, Jamaica." Later, we hear that "Undine, unlike most of her fellow countrywoman, is well informed regarding her island home" (32), which conveniently allows her to conduct a guided tour and potted history of the island, pointing out its achievements and beauties with pride. Indeed, several narratives concur that "typical West Indians," although they criticize their own, none the less "place themselves as it were on a superior plane" (Cassin 1890: 61). So Morea revels in her own colorfully creole dress sense rather than "the horrible, stylish, uncomfortable thing" that her mother has "sent out for me from England" (40). In fact, dress serves as an appropriately "feminine" trope for a subtle critique of colonial mimicry, for English fashions are frequently represented as a torment for creole women. For example, in Bridges's memoir (1988: 157) the narrator's sister is dressed for the Debutantes' Ball held at Government House, where her mother hopes to contrive for her "the best possible match." Unfortunately Ruth's figure is ill-suited to "the [English] fashions of the day" and she must be squeezed and laced and corseted into the conventional ball dress. "I don't know how I shall be able to *dance!*" gasps Ruth, "I can hardly *breathe!*" (163; emphasis in original). Simulating an English complexion and wearing English fashions are, it appears in the texts, necessary but much resented prerequisites for the final goal of a woman: a good marriage. Femininity for the creole elite is *English* femininity. That this is indeed a masquerade is highlighted by whitening the creole's arms and shoulders with chalk and rouging her cheeks, since "a *soupçon* of colour will enhance Ruth's whole appearance! Remember . . . she hasn't just returned from England with fine rosy cheeks, and *vis-à-vis* the debutantes who have she will look pale and washed out" (Bridges 1988: 161). Dark enough to need whitening yet pale enough to need color, the white creole's indeterminate status is apparent; and like Ruth and Morea, she acquiesces only grudgingly in conformity to an imported ideal.

If some texts construct white creoles who resent English dictates and take pride in aspects of their West Indian culture, only rarely do we have a specifically local take on their surroundings, or an indication of what it means aesthetically to those who live and work it. Indeed, most probably shared the exasperation of the "discontented West Indian" encountered by Layard, who responds to the tourist's hyperbolic praise of the beauties of tropical nature with the retort: "Yes, but you cannot live on scenery!" (1887: 117). Napier's *A Flying Fish Whispered* (1938) is exceptional in the exquisite and clearly *informed* depiction of the Dominican landscape in all its specificity.[16] The intimacy of the creole protagonist with the beloved place, is revealed in precise details of observation: a roof is "rusted to the pale red colour of mango flowers" (16). By contrast, the expatriate Janet illustrates once again the tendency of foreign observers to project their own fantasies and fears on to the Caribbean landscape. For the threatened Janet, a "palm-tree quivered as though with fever" (58) and the river in flood is red "as though it carried blood into the sea" (61). The only space she feels to be safe (because similar to the British equivalent) is the orchard she has planted behind the house. Rivals in love, both creole and expatriate anthropomorphize the landscape in female terms: the forest is, for Janet, "a dark sinister woman, ready to crush her, ready to steal" (55). By contrast, creole Teresa loves it and fears its taming, much as she fears her own. Certainly Teresa acknowledges that in Dominica nature can be destructive (83) – floods and landslides, blight and disease take their toll – but her respect for and affinity with the feminized landscape indicates a projection of her own passionate sexuality. By contrast, other islands like the neighboring Barbados "with its green glaring flatness" are inferior (54), and "can only boast the flat monotony of their own virtue" (88).

Not all creole characters are portrayed as attached to and at home in their tropical world. Lynch's *Years Ago* (1865) is a good example of the ambivalence of the creole writer/character toward her West Indian home. Unlike Lynch's other homiletic and cloyingly pious texts, this is a lively account, purportedly the diary of a high-spirited Jamaican planter's daughter covering the years 1790–5. Doss is very much in the mold of Austen's Emma, indulged by her father, apt to think a little too well of herself, addicted to matchmaking for others but deluded about her own feelings for the older, wiser Hugh. From the opening page, she insists that West Indians are cultured, citing her father's scholarship, and is indignant that some reviews of his work express surprise at a West Indian writing so well. "I do not think this was very complimentary," Doss protests, "as the fact of being born under a tropical sun does not generally deaden the senses" (Lynch 1865: 1). Doss is also quick to record positive opinions of creole women. Hugh thinks educated Jamaican women have the sweetest voices in the world (so much for the Creole drawl) and make the best wives and mothers (13). Papa too considers his daughters more sophisticated than sheepish English girls who "come out" in London society (39), and her sister's beau prefers "her style of beauty, far more than that of the robust English lasses, with their ruddy cheeks" (86). So much for the "yellow" creole complexion that needs to be disguised with rouge! Sensitive to the beauty of her surroundings, Doss agrees with Hugh that English people cannot appreciate the "peculiar beauty of the sugar-field" (212). Neither does she favor the "aping of England's court life" at stiff King's House dinners, agreeing with Hugh's assessment of the more informal West Indian social gatherings as far more genial (52).

But despite her pride in West Indian landscape and society, Doss displays a fluid national allegiance. Itemizing provisions, she refers to "the common candles that *we* call dips in England" (33; my emphasis). Again, admiring a Jamaican sunset, she distinguishes it from "*our* English twilight" (172; my emphasis); some pages later she comments that "we West Indians are so foolishly attached to large houses" (197). And in a discussion of coins her use of the possessive pronoun is almost schizophrenic :

> I have seen the English pennies. Papa has some in his desk, with *our* good old king George's head stamped on them, which he keeps as a relic of his schoolboy days. *Our* smallest coin, according to the Spanish currency prevalent in this island, is five-pence, a small silver piece, equalling in value three English pence. Then *we* have the macaroni, the tenpence, the bit, and half-bit. Papa says this is quite unlike English money. The doubloon is the most beautiful of *our* golden coin.
>
> (233; my emphasis)

Who is "we" and *what* is "ours," what Jamaican and what English, and where does the speaker place herself? The dual allegiance suggested in the passage is a recurrent feature in texts written by, or featuring, creole women. Doss herself is aware of this odd relationship to the mother country (207–8):

> I, who have never set my foot on English ground, can be eager for the honor and welfare of my home and country, my dear ancestral land.
> It may seem like a paradox to call that distant land in the cold northern seas my home, but let me tell you, dear old journal, that I never look forward to the future, I never take a trip into dream-land, without England being my resting place, the haven after so much wandering.

The novel closes with a happily married Doss "wandering" only as far as Montego Bay on Jamaica's north coast, remaining quite content with her tropical home. England is relegated once more to "dream-land," a place of the imagination. Morea, in *With Silent Tread*, does go "home" to England from Antigua, but insists on distinguishing herself there *as West Indian*. The creole Madam de Souza in Fraser's novel *Lucilla* "made a point of never speaking of Europe as her home; whereas the other ladies, many of whom had never left the island in their life, spoke of England as 'home' constantly and aggressively" (1896a: 58–9). But

Madam de Souza, it is hinted, may have colored blood and so the affectation of claiming Europe is not for her; "my world," she tells her niece Liris, "is not London or Paris, but yours" (69).[17] White creole women are represented as ambivalently committed to the Caribbean as a true home, but there is no ambivalence concerning the pull of their native land felt by many who emigrate, and the depth of their joy on return. On the voyage back to Jamaica in *The Cotton-Tree*, Emily reflects with pleasure "how soon I should again see my native land, the home of my happy, happy childhood" (Lynch 1847: 85). "Through all the dour English winters" and "those long days of raw damp cold," Em in *Luminous Isle* dreams of the glorious Jamaican mountains (Bliss 1984: 85–6), although she finds much that disappoints her on her return.

What accounts for this disappointment, this disillusionment with a once loved place? In hindsight, flaws in the social order are more obvious: Bridges realizes how much the well-regulated household of her idealized creole childhood masked the ruthless, restrictive control of a mother who tyrannized servants, dominated her children and rushed daughters into loveless, but "good" marriages. No wonder she opts to transfer her loyalty to the wider possibilities of England, the "land of my fathers." More generally, creoles are portrayed complaining about the shortcomings of their island societies, especially in comparison with the amenities of England. Indeed, as one Antiguan lady comments in *With Silent Tread*, "the West Indies would certainly be endurable were it not for the West Indians" (Cassin 1890: 38). But such discontent has less to do with the native place than with the island's *colonial* status, with the imposition of English rule and all the trappings deemed necessary for its maintenance. In a few cases, like James's travelogue, British colonialism is directly indicted. Musing on "the colour question," James observes

> One's heart is with one's own kind, there is no doubt of that; but when it comes to a question of seeing the truth, one's sympathy goes assuredly to the negro. He has never seen justice, he has never since the beginning of things, *had* justice. The white man took him out of his own land whether he liked it or not. He dragged him away to a white man's world; he beat him, robbed him of his freedom, stole the reward of his labour and violated his women . . . And the [African] forest isn't theirs any longer, even if they wanted it. It's Ours.
>
> (1913: 139–41; emphasis in original)

This kind of plain speaking by an Englishwoman with regard to colonial guilt ("It's Ours") is rare. However in the twentieth century, *creole* writers like Bliss and the (self-identified) Dominican Napier lash out at English behavior in the colonies. In Bliss's *Luminous Isle*, Em is "frustrated and stifled" by the expatriate "garrison set" with "their golf, their tennis, their bridge, their vocabulary, and lack of it, their social code with its hypocrisy and hidden indecencies" (1984: 119). She is increasingly alienated by her family's investment in such petty concerns (81), and the loud, authoritarian posturing of army men like her father who has "something of the bully in him" (83). Additionally, as a woman she resents the policing of gender roles among the expatriate community where "narrow-eyed older married women [are] always on the look-out for some new scandal" (97). Em foregrounds her superiority to creole and expatriate whites in claiming that "colour prejudice is something I don't understand" (131).[18] In the end, it is such narrow-minded colonial ideology that spoils the island for her, and she leaves for "the future" abroad.

More forcefully than Em, the creole protagonist of Napier's *A Flying Fish Whispered* (1938) allies herself with the local population, black and white, against colonial expatriates. The plot of the novel concerns a doomed relationship between Teresa and a married white man. Derek comes to the island of St Celia (Dominica) from Parham Island (Antigua), known for its brutal plantocracy, and attempts to manage his new plantation along similar lines, which are in conflict with more communally minded local practices. The aim of his wife and himself "is to succeed financially as planters" whatever the cost in human misery to the islanders. Creole resentment of this exploitative sensibility is reinforced by unflattering judgements on expatriates in the Caribbean, particularly the much loathed type of "Englishmen whose slogan is 'the Empire for the English' " (Napier 1938: 167), and "English women in the West Indies [who] do their own cooking to economize on ingredients" but "keep servants for the sake of being able to write home with pride in their number" (25). Teresa and her brother unapologetically prefer "Creole cooking" to the insipid English food served at Government House (75), and dispense with English traditions: "thank God for no plum pudding, no snow, and no robins" (102). Her brother has a colored mistress, and Teresa herself contemplates an affair with a colored man but worries he may be suspicious of "the impertinence of whites": "It isn't that we dislike you . . . we distrust you," he tells her, and she replies, "*Et avec cause*" (75). Aware of the history of English racism and exploitation of blacks in the colonies, Teresa understands such distrust; likewise she loathes expatriate and colonial administrators who have no real commitment to the island beyond making money, and who construct a creole like herself as "a savage West Indian" (103).

Napier's text articulates a deep anger on the part of the creole for the damaging physical and psychological legacy of British rule in the West Indies. Greene's study (1987) of the development of a Barbadian identity among settlers in the seventeenth century emphasizes the role that British prejudice played in the formation of a distinct creole self-image. Faced with metropolitan contempt for what was perceived as the "degenerate life styles, indolence [and] wantonness" of these settlers (1987: 246), he argues that Barbadians reacted by stressing pride in their *own* societies. Watson (1998: 18) records that the distinctly creolized nature of Barbadian society "was noted and commented on by almost every eighteenth-century traveller's account," and sums up white creole patriotism in the words of a planter who boasted of Barbados that "tis to me the first country in the world." "This proto-nationalism," Watson continues, "manifested itself in many forms, amongst which was hostility expressed by local whites towards Englishmen who were considered to be snobbish and takers of the best positions available in the island" (18). More generally, West Indians resentment of burdensome British taxation and trade restrictions which fostered dependency, undermined ties to the mother country. So in *Cousin Stella*, when Jamaicans perceive British designs on their wealth, loyalty goes out the window: "we'd rather give ourselves to the Americans" (Jenkin 1859, vol. 2: 20). In Napier's novel, the disregard of England for the welfare and long-term development of her colonies and the construction of creoles as inferior, fosters a deep and abiding hostility for the center among the supposedly loyal subjects of empire in the West Indies. Alienated from the majority at home *and* in the Mother Country, defiantly creole and even proto-nationalistic yet referring to England as "home," passionately attached to the landscape of the tropics or socialized into a colonial condescension for the local, the creole woman's relationship to the West Indies in the early narratives is a peculiarly complex one. Problematic as their politics may be for modern readers, deCaires Narain (2002: viii) argues for reading such works "in the spirit of recognizing fully the hybrid 'origins' of Caribbean literary culture." Not all white creole women anguished over their in-betweenity, she argues, citing Allfrey's choice of title for her poetry collection, *Palm and Oak*. Like Bridges, Bliss, Lynch, Napier, Stephenson and Cassin, this title underscores a "sense of a dual cultural heritage and her insistence on claiming both" (30).

5   Narratives of tainted empire

The problematic "colonizing subject"

The first two chapters of this book focused on representations of white women in the West Indies, and the second two dealt with the region itself as constructed in a selection of writing by such women. In the last two chapters, I want to suggest some ways of *reading* these texts. Why read them at all? Well, according to Ashcroft et al., "the rereading and the rewriting of the European historical and fictional record is a vital and inescapable task at the heart of the postcolonial enterprise" (1989: 196). However, other critics worry that focusing on this record may distract from the more urgent need to recuperate the silenced and marginalized colonial subject. For example, Paxton (1992: 406) considers that "attention to the subjectivity of the colonizer can erase the subjection of the colonized."[1] Further, as Haggis notes, histories of white women in the colonies suggest that their accounts may be as guilty as those of their male counterparts in circulating "colonising and Euro-centric discourses" (1998: 45).

On the other hand, Donnell (1995a: 101–2) argues for relaxing such restrictions on what we may legitimately read, warning against the "homogenization of polit-ical intent" implicit in focusing only on the voices of the marginalized. Chrisman too suggests some disadvantages of banning imperial discourse from postcolonial study: denied self-representation, such discourse "remains, paradoxically, frozen in power, and repressed, an absent 'centre,' a hidden referent" (1990: 38). Further, she rightly reminds us to attend to differences within and between imperial prac-tices themselves, as well as to what these have in common. Chrisman's point is that within colonial discourse, complex and heterogeneous self-representations did exist, and awareness of these should govern analysis of the various narrative structures which in turn produce plural forms of native "Othering" (40). Imperial-ism, she writes, "even at its most basic is capable of constructing itself as a contradictory process, of commenting on its own self-mythologising, and eco-nomic, imperatives, while in the course of pursuing them" (41).

In this chapter I shall read texts of colonial discourse for just such "contradict-ory processes." To begin with, let us consider once more the narrative "I": the author and/or narrator who presumably, in writing the West Indies, also writes herself in relation to it as a "colonising subject," in David Trotter's terminology

(1990: 3). Trotter observes that in effect "the study of colonialism has become the study of the roles allocated by the colonisers to the colonised: 'representations of the colonial subject.'" Critics like Bhabha, JanMohamed and Spivak, he considers, have concentrated on ways of dismantling the signifying system of colonialism and showing how it silences and suppresses the colonial subject. But for him the drawback is that they

> propose to analyse that "signifying system" in and through its "operation," to its effects, its brutalising of "the colonial subject". When they speak of "the colonial subject," they mean the *colonised* subject only. In their view, colonialism is an encounter between a colonising machine or system, on one hand, and a colonised subject, on the other. The *colonising* subject has been elided, his or her subjectivity wished away.
>
> (Trotter 1990: 3; emphasis in original)

Just as JanMohamed's totalizes "the imperialist" or "the European" (always male), so the homogenization of the colonizing subject excludes any consideration of gender. For theorists like Said, Trotter claims, "the White Man is a code of regulations, a text without an author. Of the White Man's subjectivity, founded on the need to begin again [in the challenging East], and reinvented by each evaluation and gesture, he has little to say" (1990: 4). Of the white *woman's* subjectivity, even less. The universalized colonizing subject was normatively male and it was his version that was heard. Although it can be argued that the voice of the "massa" implicitly spoke for the mistress too, there is still a sense in which the *female* colonizing subject needs to be considered separately. Certainly feminists have objected to Said's formulation of Orientalism on the grounds that it takes for granted an entirely male conception of colonialism. Again, Haggis (1998: 45) argues that feminist historians have revealed "the gender biases of colonial writers such as Kipling, who helped concoct and popularize the stereotype [of the colonial white woman], and the male historians who have built on and continued the memsahib image, charging the white woman with the ruin and loss of empire." After all, as Shepherd et al. explain (1995: xiv), historical scholarship until recently "conceptually subsumed white . . . women to their male counterparts in assessments of . . . activities in colonial culture."

Catherine Hall too (1993: 9) is interested in interrogating colonial discourse concerning the valency of apparent "facts and presuppositions" about the colonizing subject, about colonization and indeed about the whole notion of "white identity." Hall argues that since "the histories of Britain and empire have been mutually dependent," then white British identity, like white (and non-white) West Indian identity, "has been made by the relations of empire, our identities constituted through our different relations to those hierarchies of power" (3). In addition, Hall attends to "the power relations that always operate between the sexes as well as between classes and . . . racialised groups" (9). Rather than conceiving analysis of "colonialist discourse" in terms of attention to one group or the other, Hall sees her project as complementary: that is, attending to the changing construction of blackness (particularly by abolitionists) in post-emancipation Jamaica reveals awareness of a changed understanding of whiteness by the English middle class. Hall's thesis emphasizes once again how a careful reading of colonial narratives (in this case, missionary reports and official documents) makes it possible to demonstrate the constructed nature of racialised/national identities, as well as to highlight the textual interdependence of the very notions of a colonized and colonizing subject.

White women were indeed involved in the project of colonialism, many even seeing the imperial enterprise as constitutive of their own agency; but most "related to it in different ways than their male counterparts did."[2] White women's place in the myth of imperial conquest and consolidation, as noted, was a strictly supportive one: "they performed the roles assigned to the 'incorporated wife,' serving as hostess, wife, and mother" (Paxton 1992: 392–3). Surely then, women writers would have been sensitive about claiming in their texts the power and agency of the normatively male "imperial I"? Certainly Nugent, occupying the highest official position a woman could hold in colonial Jamaica, never assumes the rhetoric of state power and indeed, on more than one occasion, mocks the pompous displays of authority associated with the ruling (male) elite. To assume the role of a colonizing subject in the public sphere was fraught for a woman, and attempts to insert herself into the master narrative of empire is sometimes accompanied by authorial discomfort with the conventional script. It is precisely because of her anomalous position – complicit in, yet marginal to colonialism proper – that the early narratives by white women offer a unique perspective within colonial discourse.

The ambivalent allegiances of the white colonial woman is evident in Gaunt's *Where the Twain Meet* (1922). She informs the reader that she was born in Australia and, moved by the slave forts of Guinea, refers to herself as "a woman from the South, the land of liberty" (85), clearly disassociating herself from British depreciation of Africa, as of Australia, as inherently savage (39). But like many colonials, she also refers to going to England as a young girl in terms of coming "home." Whitlock (1994: 92) observes that in *Reflection-in Jamaica*, Gaunt "identifies herself as 'colonial born' and identifies with the Jamaican view of life, in opposition to the English. Elsewhere generalizations based on race emphasize the narrator's difference and Britishness." While Whitlock stresses that this is part of Gaunt's packaging of the West Indian "Other" for Europe, I want to suggest that the strained assumption of "imperial eyes" by such narrators foregrounds a problematic relation to colonial discourse, and that this is even more so the case for West Indian creole writers.

A further difficulty in pinning down a female colonizing subject is where to put the white creole. White creole consciousness is naturalized by constructing black West Indians as Other, but in several texts it is clear that for European colonialists, the creole was herself the Other: the more creolized, the more "not quite white." As such, white creole women occupy an ambiguous place in colonial discourse. For Catherine Hall, Trotter, Gregg and Raiskin, the female colonizing subject comes in a variety of models. Perhaps this shifting positionality accounts for narrative variations on colonial themes by such women, several of which (I suggest) are deliberately or unconsciously ambivalent about the meaning of the colonial project and whose writing highlights its flaws and failures. This is hardly surprising since even in Said's outline of Orientalism, there is the implication "that colonial discourse is in fact fractured in its operations, aims and affective economy" (Moore-Gilbert 1997: 44). For example, by foregrounding Said's ambiguous distinctions between "latent" and "manifest" Orientalism, Moore-Gilbert can read Kipling's writing as both a universalist assertion of the Orientalist vision of colonial India and, because of the writer's unique personal style and vision, able to "question and even challenge the dominant ideologies of imperialism and received traditions of writing about empire" (43). This kind of dual reading of the colonial story, Moore-Gilbert feels (117) is further developed in Bhabha's concern with "the degree to which the colonizer's identity (and authority) is in fact fractured and destabilized by contradictory psychic responses to the colonized Other." So, as Gikandi concludes (1996: xiii), some white writers *did* generate narratives "that refused to fit into the hierarchies of colonial government and rule, narratives that dislocated the colonial project or called its central assumptions into question."

Looking at a cross-section of texts, it seems to me that women's role of "moral housekeeper" in the West Indies explains heightened sensitivity to some "dislocations" in imperial practice. In their representations of an empire in decline, decay is not represented as solely due to economic woes associated with the end of slavery, nor only to the shame of slavery itself, but also to an awareness of the pervasive moral degradation that is its legacy. However allied with the ruling ethos, some women writers voiced dismay at aspects of the social landscape, such as racial and moral contamination, so that – read from a postcolonial perspective – they locate *internal* flaws in colonial discourse, the presence of which suggest the precariousness of the edifice of empire. Accordingly, this chapter examines white women's constructions of the West Indies and suggests that – whatever the authorial intention – when such discomfort surfaces it serves to point up certain cracks in the imperial edifice. In particular, while direct criticism of colonial policy is rare in early narratives by women, the West Indies is frequently constructed as a corrupted paradise, a place that impacts negatively on the physical and moral fibre of white settlers. I want to go on to posit that textual emphasis on this corruption – physical degeneration and moral bankruptcy – can be read as suggesting deep unease about the validity of the colonial project.

The curse of slavery: miscegenation

"Conscience, sir . . . is apt to lie torpid in these climes. Are her active powers wont to be manifested in the white slave-holder; or in the black victim of cruelty and crime? or in the wretched mixture of the two, heir to the vices and miseries of each, the outcast of both, the isolated, insulted being whom your wanton caprice sometimes rears.

(Tonna 1827: 147)

Mary Prince's slave narrative offers a new twist on depictions of the West Indies as infernal. Sold to a Mr D——, Prince is sent to Turk's Island, no more than a large sandbank, to work in the salt ponds. There she and the other slaves labor

> through the heat of the day; the sun flaming upon our heads like fire, and raising salt blisters in those parts which were not completely covered. Our feet and legs, from standing in the salt water for so many hours, soon became full of dreadful boils, which eat down in some cases to the very bone, afflicting the sufferers with great torment . . . Work—work—work—Oh that Turk's Island was a horrible place! The people in England, I am sure, have never found out what is carried on there. Cruel, horrible place!
>
> (Prince 1987: 198–9)

There is true horror here in the desolate landscape, the insidious salt pickling human flesh and the sun converting the seaside scene into a place of torture. The elements conspire in a regime of human suffering, but the actual source of pain and dehumanization is the unnatural power relations of slavery. Far worse than the infernal climate, Prince's misery has a human cause which taints *all* landscapes. Overjoyed at leaving one cruel master, Prince finds "it was but going from one butcher to another" (198), and her experience of England is no better. The English climate inflames her painful rheumatism, but her main hardship is the inhumane rule of her owners. Legally free she might be in England, but with neither support network nor money, she must remain in the abusive household of a mistress who informs Prince that "she did not intend to treat me any better in England than in the West Indies—that I need not expect it. And she was as good as her word" (209).

For many white women and men writing in the nineteenth century, the system that could so use a human being was downright sinful for *all* involved. For example, Marli Weiner's study of elite women in the American South finds the institution articulated as a curse on themselves and their societies. One woman wrote in her journal in 1858, "God forgive *us*, but ours is a *monstrous* system & wrong & iniquity . . . [L]ike the patriarchs of old our men live all in one house with their wives & their concubines" (Weiner 1996: 288; emphasis in original). For this author, slavery degrades women of both races, "degrades the white man more than the Negro and oh exerts a most deleterious effect upon our children" (289). Patricia Morton (1996: 13) characterizes the representation of slavery in white women's writings as a poison, infecting the private lives of all, especially the family and the role of women therein: it was constructed as a *sexualized* conflict. While male writers also expressed abhorrence of slavery, outrage at specific abuses related to the domestic sphere – white men's licentiousness, their neglect of their colored offspring, and sexual abuse of female slaves – are a constant in narratives by women.

An example is Tonna's *The System; A Tale of the West Indies* (1827) by "Charlotte Elizabeth."[3] Ragatz (1932: 368) provides this synopsis:

An attack on slavery in narrative form. George Belmont had inherited property in the Caribbean while his brother, William, had fallen heir to a baronetcy in Great Britain. The former had originally been shocked at the conditions under which slavery existed in the sugar colonies, but had become accustomed to it through the course of years. A visit made by his brother William, who was greatly opposed to human bondage, is the means employed by the authoress to set forth her arguments against "the system" in telling style.

Ragatz neglects to mention the subplot involving Caesar, the colored son of a planter who returns to the West Indies after an English education. Spurned by the whites for his "taint of negro blood" and enraged by his sister's dishonor at the hands of a white man, Caesar leads a slave revolt against the barbarous plantocracy. *The System* reserves its most outspoken polemic for this latter group via Sir William, the author's mouthpiece, who tells a group of sugar planters (21):

> I look upon the system under which these islands are internally governed, as radically bad in all its bearings. I consider the negroes as a race aggrieved beyond all redress, while that system prevails: and I look upon you, my friends, as conniving at the secret but sure progress of a fatal mine that will eventually bury you in destruction.

Repeatedly, this sentiment is articulated in the text, usually by Sir William.[4] Slavery, for him, is England's "scandal and her curse" (194).

In Gaunt's travel narrative *Where the Twain Meet* (1922: 89), the narrator observes of nineteenth-century Jamaica that "on any land where was such slavery as this, there seems to have fallen a curse." Similarly, a poem in *Scenes in the West Indies* (1843: 6) by "Adeline" (Jane Sergeant) depicts the beauty of Jamaica darkened by the sin of slavery. The inscription of slavery as a curse recurs in Jenkin's *Cousin Stella* (1859). Set in the 1820s, the text brings Stella to Jamaica to keep house for her father, the Custos, and her stepmother. All her family perish by poisoning, and she is left to the guardianship of her planter cousin Louis, who shares her anti-slavery sentiments but worries that emancipation will lead to economic decline. A love relationship develops, threatened by misunderstandings and a violent black insurrection in which Louis is crippled. Stella marries him and tenderly nurses him as they travel around Europe. For Louis, emancipation may ruin the West Indies, but it is a ruin much deserved: "[t]he punishment of the children for the sins of the father is at hand" (Jenkin 1859, vol. 1: 255). "The infernal system of slavery" (vol. 2: 37) destroys goodness in women as well as men (vol. 2: 47), and the bloody uprising of the blacks who demand their liberty is acknowledged by Louis's doctor as divine judgement on slave holders: "Those who sow the whirlwind will reap the tempest – they and their children's children" (vol. 3: 202).

While these texts do not question white superiority or female submission – indeed, Stella positively revels in Louis's displays of authority over her (vol. 3: 12)[5]

– none the less the sexual ramifications of slavery, its exploitative, often brutal interracial congress, appalled the sensitivities of women writers. Lanaghan sums it up with delicacy: "the root of all West Indian misery is illicit love."[6] And the *products* of such "illicit love" – colored or mulatto offspring – are targeted for a variety of negative depictions in the narratives. Miscegenation, the visible proof that the categories of racial hierarchy were neither enforceable nor impermeable, is invariably censored. Fenwick, as we have seen, was incensed by white men who fathered children with slave women and then put *their own* children into the fields as slaves. Openly contemptuous of this dishonorable and hypocritical behavior, she voices "disgusted antipathy" concerning a mulatto boy acting as servant to his white half-sister. Fenwick speaks for several women writers when she pronounces "I am ready to hail the Slave and reject the Master" (1927: 169).

It appears that in the West Indies, physical and social surroundings conspire to deprave. Witness the opinion of the English captain in *The Jamaica Lady*:

> He enquired how she came into that cursed country, for he said none but mad people and fools, when possessed of a plentiful fortune or even a modest competency in England, in Paradise, would leave it to go to Jamaica, the sink of sin and receptacle of all manner of vices, a place so intolerably hot and suffocating that he swore there was only a brown paper betwixt it and hell.
>
> (W.P. 1963: 95)

For many commentators, something disturbing happened to white people in the tropics, particularly men, and it was rooted in slavery:

> The white man in tropical America was out of his habitat. Constant association with an inferior subject race blunted his moral fibres and he suffered marked demoralization. His transitory residence and the continued importation of Africans debased life. Miscegenation, so contrary to Anglo-Saxon nature, resulted in the rapid rise of a race of human hybrids. Planter society was based upon whites and blacks, removed to unfamiliar scenes, and their unhappy offspring.[7]

The stories of the American Mrs Schuyler Crowninshield (1898a), are set in the Spanish Caribbean but rehearse the same sentiments. Interracial sex is referred to as "pollution" (9–10), and miscegenation is viewed as horrific, but like Fenwick narrative sympathies lie more with the "unhappy offspring," the mulatto and octoroon characters than the villainous, bullying white masters, on whom exploited colored women frequently wreak revenge. Wilcox (1909: 223) delicately alludes to lust as somehow inherent in a hot climate:

> Morality, as we understand the word, and the Tropics are antagonistic terms in any part of the world. The equator is a girdle of Venus; and on her alters of pleasure, humanity is prone to offer up all its sterner principles. It may not be true that Martinique was the wickedest city in the world, as has been said;

but since through all West Indian cities, licentiousness stalks naked and unashamed (as he who passes through their thoroughfares for even a day cannot fail to know), it is a probable supposition that Mt. Pelee buried more vice than virtue under its boiling tons of lava.

More pointedly she censures its result, "the tragedy of mixed blood. When the Spanish race brought over the first African slaves, in 1509, miscegenation, the greatest evil which ever befell the black or white race, took root in the West Indies" (239).

An unhappy hybrid of immoral planter/slave liaisons, the colored or mulatto character appears as a tragic figure in many early narratives. One such is *Constance Mordaunt* (1862) by "E.J.W.," purporting to be the authentic "history of Constance Mordaunt's early life and her subsequent trials [which] were communicated to the Author by that lady herself, who furnished her [the Author] at the same time with the extraordinary documents to be found in the second part of this narrative" (iii). The story of Constance's creole childhood in St. Vincent, her experience of English boarding school, return to the island and various marital fortunes, is of tangential interest here. But the "extraordinary documents" appended to the second volume are centrally concerned with miscegenation. The first is the journal of Emma, Constance's friend from English boarding school, who discovers to her horror that the "dark nurse" vaguely remembered from childhood is in fact her own mother. On hearing the word "daughter" from the strange "fat, bleareyed woman, nearly black," Emma disgustedly recoils (E. J. W. 1862, vol. 2: 94). Ashamed of her behavior, she none the less insists that "[f]rom first to last I have thought of her with unmitigated repugnance" (95). Her English father admits his deceit, though "[n]o mention was ever made of the unhappy being whose presence had brought so much trouble on us" (vol. 2: 97): the black woman is the culprit, and is written out of the text. Emma passes for white, marries an Englishman, and reluctantly accompanies him to the West Indies, terrified that her secret will be discovered. And so it proves. She is approached by a colored man and is, predictably, stunned at the suggestion that he is her half-brother: " 'Good God!' I exclaimed, almost aloud, 'what can I have to do with this degraded being? Is the man mad?' " (vol. 2: 106–7). Presented with proof that like "this degraded being" she too is of mixed blood, and afraid to confess to her husband, Emma sickens and dies.

Why is this extraneous material included? Clearly, readers are meant to sympathize with the cruelly deceived Emma but also, as Joyce Walker Johnson notes (1994: 18), writings like these serve to normalize the racial hierarchy by portraying "a disreputable Negro community from which persons of mixed racial origins feel they must escape" by acknowledging only white connections. The "naturalness" of such ranking is internalized by coloreds and according to Wilcox (1909: 240–1),

it is a curious fact that the one race in the world which universally strives to conceal and deny itself when mixed with other bloods, is the African . . . In the effort at concealment continually being made in the West Indies by people descended from a mulatto, or an octoroon, or a still more remote type, lies the tragedy of the age.

To illustrate, Emma's journal itself contains another document, the story of Mary, wife to Emma's mulatto half-brother. As if to qualify the negative judgement of all mixed-race people, Mary is described as an excellent woman who is well aware of her place and duly deferential in the company of her betters. The daughter of a Scotsman who came to the West Indies "to try his fortune," and a mulatto mistress, Mary is brought up by a Scottish aunt on her father's death, which presumably explains her good-breeding. Back in the West Indies, she is pushed by her mother to seek the company of white men, is seduced and abandoned, pregnant, by an Irishman. As "my standard was greatly lowered," she settles for an unhappy marriage to Emma's intemperate and profligate half-brother. The interpolated narratives clearly serve a didactic purpose, demonstrating that the colored Emma, Mary and her husband all, in different ways, suffer for the sins of their fathers.

But in other texts, the colored characters appear to deserve their outcast status. "The right down and out negro is bearable perhaps," complains an overseer in Cassin's *With Silent Tread*, "but it's these chocolate coloured imitations that I can't stand; they are rascals . . . God may have made the black man and the white, but the devil made the mulatto" (1890: 102). Joyce Walker Johnson explains that the "diabolical nature ascribed to mulattoes is attributed to a keener sense of their degradation which, it is also suggested, makes them psychologically different from 'pure' Negroes" (1994: 4); the latter resent the condescension of coloreds as coloreds resent that of whites. In all cases, no good can come of racial mixing. Fraser's *Lucilla* (1896a), for example, details the ill-fated marriage of an English music mistress in the West Indian island of "San José," to a well-to-do quadroon. Heavy symbolism prefigures the doomed nature of the union: on her wedding day, "the dark wings of a rat bat brushing her white veil" suggest an "omen of evil" (34), and Lucilla is appalled at the "new and dusky world in which she found herself" (40). Her husband soon falls "back into the darker side of negro life" (330): he is superstitious (219), has an illegitimate colored daughter (185), eats with his fingers (195), associates with black servants who turn out to be his relations, strikes his wife (251) and, when an epidemic breaks out, deserts her like a "cowardly beast" (241). Sick at the discovery of his degradation (and hers by association), Lucilla flees the island and wanders around Europe bitterly regretting her folly. She cannot even bear to hear the rustle of palm trees for the memories that are awakened: "[t]he far-off West Indian island had graven its lessons on her heart well enough" (331–2).

What are these lessons? The plot of Fraser's *Lucilla* gives plenty of scope for fixating on racial hybridity, something the early narratives obsessively castigate as evidence of a hidden, shameful stain on a West Indian pedigree. As one colored character in Fraser's novel puts it, "a curse rests on us" (1896a: 108), for "[t]here is darkness and Africa on our mother's side; but our fathers, the old planters, were not particularly good specimens of Englishmen, and if these doctrines of heredity are true, we have all against us" (107). The trope of a corruption of blood endures into the early twentieth century. Bliss's narrator in *Luminous Isle* (published in 1934) refers to the colored Leila Mendez: "made to pay for the dark shadow that hung over her family name, she was ostracized by all except a few more independent spirits among the Island society" (1984: 118). The durability of the stigma continues well into the century, as evident in Esther Chapman's *Too Much Summer* (1953: 132). Here, an expatriate Englishwoman assures her mixed-race lover, "But Van, my darling Van, you are not a Negro, you are not a black man of repugnant physical type," to which he responds: "But I have Negro blood in my veins, and to some degree, to some extent the repugnance exists." One agrees with Birbalsingh's evaluation (1989: 75) that Van's "masochistic self-hatred seems theatrical, irrational, excessive," but the sentiments expressed are consistent with those ascribed to mulatto characters in narratives since the early nineteenth century. Bliss was a Jamaican and Chapman an Englishwoman long resident in the island,[8] and it is interesting to note how their "local" depictions concur with those of European women writers over a hundred years previously, who insist on investing people of mixed race with psychological trauma.

In the cosmology of these narratives, slavery is the crime and miscegenation its accursed legacy, punishing the innocent mulatto offspring of licentious planters. More, as Fraser's *Lucilla* (1896a: 92) reveals, it constitutes a threat to whites. Terrified of the taint of black blood that has infected their families, the novel describes West Indian whites attempting "to maintain the past dignity of their race" (93) by constant vigilance for signs of racial impurity. Joyce Walker Johnson (8) quotes from a British review of *Lucilla*, which disingenuously explains that

> Local feelings about colour [in the West Indies] in all its various degrees and kinds is extremely strong. Over there things are viewed from a widely different standpoint from ours. We are more ignorant about fine shades and distinctions in complexions. West Indians regard mixed marriages with feelings of contempt and horror.[9]

This reviewer, like Fenwick in her letters, pointedly distances himself from the West Indian obsession with color gradations: it is a *creole* problem, not a British one. Again, one can observe the sloughing off of disreputable aspects of colonialism on to local whites who are ridiculously obsessed with color and shade because they clearly have grounds for anxiety on the subject of their pedigrees. For example, in Jenkin's fiction (1859, vol. 1: 10) the heroine's "Spanish blood" from her Cuban mother, as well as the fact that she could dance the "comba" like the blacks when not yet 3 years old (vol. 2: 186), sound warning bells for her aunt who is well used to color gradations in the West Indies. Further, her dark complexion fuels suspicion that she is mixed: her stepmother's mother declares of the new addition to the family, "I won't have the care of any half-castes" (vol. 1: 229).

Crommelin's novel *A Daughter of England* (1902) is similarly pervaded with caste, race and color anxieties. The plot is simple. After a hard life, English orphan Alice discovers she is an heiress with West Indian connections, and that part of her fortune belongs by right to the colored family of an ancestor's mistress. Off she goes to Jamaica to make restitution. There she is warned by local whites not to describe her complexion as "brown" as this might suggest a drop of black blood which, she learns, *will* out: one fellow turns out to be colored "though he showed it so little that he even got an American, a poor governess, to marry him, but she was mad angry when she found it out" (213). His even "whiter" daughter is exposed by, of all things, her "bluish nails – I noticed them at once" (213), and her large feet that "cover up the ground" (251). Again, in Atherton's *Adventures of a Novelist* (1932), an apparently white girl is referred to "by the aristocracy, as a 'White Negress.' 'You can always tell them . . . They can't fool us. There's *something* about them that gives them away' " (338; emphasis in original). White, but not-quite: colored and creole are conflated here, both infected by the legacy of slavery.

I want to mention two final examples of this anxiety about miscegenation which, I am arguing, suggests anxiety about the very foundation of the colonial enterprise. The first is Gaunt's historical novel, *Harmony* (1933). Set at the end of the eighteenth century, it concerns the son of a white planter and a black slave woman. The mulatto youth is passed off as his father's heir when the legitimate white son dies in infancy, and educated in England. He returns to Jamaica in 1817 to take up his inheritance and marry a lovely English girl. But something is not quite right. Heavy-handed symbolism signals the incongruity of the match: "the scent of the flowers in the air, the salt tang of the sea, and also the odour of decay, for . . . all the débris, animal and vegetable litter . . . was swept just outside the area and there left to rot" (13); elsewhere, the smell of orange blossom, coffee blooms and jasmine is "mingled with the hot odours of vegetable decay that is typical of the Tropics" (25).[10] Soon all is revealed. Unmasked as the son of a slave, Roger is himself enslaved, escapes and hides out with other runaway slaves. Unable to shake off his in-group loyalty despite his mistreatment, Roger warns the planters of the slaves' planned insurrection. It is foiled, he is declared a hero but, still a slave in the West Indies, he must leave for a new life of freedom in England. There is much irony in this highly unlikely tale. The son of a black slave who thinks himself white and thus exempt "from the taint of mixed blood" (44), Roger feels English abolitionist sympathies to be misplaced and laughs at his father's humane treatment of his bondsmen. After all, he opines, "[w]hat else are these men fit for? Look at their faces. Beasts of the field" (94). When made aware of his own "taint of black blood" (159), he cannot stop thinking like a white man: so, sharing a cave with other runaway slaves, "he [still] felt his superiority, the superiority of the ruling race" (245), and "felt himself smirched" by close physical proximity to blacks (242).

For all its flaws, the novel is intriguing in its defamiliarization of race stereotypes. A slave hero who retains *white* characteristics might not be a difficult concept for the Australian author to entertain, I suppose, but is entirely anomalous in the context of the West Indian narratives. Despite his black blood he is painted as the handsome, cultivated, courageous and honorable English hero of romance. In short, his behavior remains "white" and his girl loves him despite her mother's outrage that a *slave* "had aspired to her daughter's hand" (194). Gaunt's text invites sympathy with the wronged slave and mockery of the ignorant planters who revert instantly to stereotypes: "a man with black blood in his veins is always ready to stick a knife into you, violate your—" (165), one Busha[11] declares. The narrative proves him entirely wrong, privileging nurture over nature and suggesting the flimsy basis of the racial hierarchy which grounds slavery and colonialist discourse.

Cassin's *With Silent Tread*[12] (1890) is a more subtle and powerful evocation of the horrific ramifications of interracial congress in the tropics. Lanaghan noted that "leprosy is a frequent disease among the negroes" of Antigua and much feared for its contagious nature (1844 vol. 1: 255), and Cassin's novel employs it to indicate the sickness of West Indian post-slavery society. Leprosy, the opening page informs us, is a terrible scourge that "often in secret, invades the circles of West Indian families" (Cassin 1890: 1); it affects both black and white, who are then "shut up" together (7). It is so infectious that people dare not buy chickens raised by lepers because they "use bread poultices on their sores, they throw them away afterwards – the fowls wander about and fatten on whatever they can find" (98). The opening scene graphically evokes an old black leper imploring his white former mistress for sustenance in his hour of need, being spurned by her and lashed by the carriage driver until he falls, a dusty heap, in the road. Along comes the mistress's little ones with their nurses, and in vengeful rage, the leper picks up and kisses one infant in a deliberate effort to spread his misery to the unfeeling white family. The text thus begins with an indictment of the former slave-owning class, who continue to sin against duty and human compassion in their relations with the descendants of slaves. It is compounded by another sin, that of revenge against an innocent. The incident is covered up and the action resumes many years later, when all this is ostensibly forgotten. But as the plot develops, more sins are revealed and an inexorable cycle of punishment comes to fulfilment.

The infant glimpsed in the opening scene has grown up into a fine creole girl, Morea, although it is noted that she is dark, "a quaint Eastern type of beauty" (Cassin 1890: 26). Cassin's narrative strategy is to bring an English cousin to the colony for a visit. The visitor asks questions about the new place, the locals answer, and the usual "manners and customs" portrayal of colonial life is thus integrated into the text. Yet the outsider's quest for the truth is constantly frustrated: Marion is "interested in the reality" not the "polite fictitious reason" with which she is generally fobbed off (98). The novel is full of hints and allusions to secrets, and the West Indian reality proves evasive. The ignorant visitor initially finds her tropical cousin "unaffected by a life which contained more dark corners than Marion at first suspected" (41), but Morea proves herself well attuned to such "dark corners" and intuits that visits from her old nurse are not innocent: "I believe she was a faithful servant and means well, and has a genuine interest in me, but she gives me a creepy presentiment of coming evil whenever she appears here, and I like to have little to do with her as possible" (54).

Another creole woman admits to Marion that "[t]here is a tragic side to West Indian life," but wonders whether this is not also true in England. Marion replies (85) with powerfully evocative metaphors:

But at home, at least, our dangers may claim to be open and above board, here they seem to run in little silent undercurrents seldom spoken of and dangerous to recognise. One might live out here for years and go home at last perfectly unconscious of any dangers lived through or of any dormant volcanoes under one's feet.

Much is shocking or downright incomprehensible to the English observer, because the shared social and cultural universe of West Indian blacks and whites is entirely outside her cosmology. None the less, Marion finally grasps that a shadow lies over Morea's life. Now in England, and happily engaged to be married, Morea strikes her cousin as doomed: "[s]ome strange subtle presentiment seemed to sweep over her . . . like a cold wind blown backwards over the ocean of time, and the sense of the relentless, the inevitable future that may not be entreated struck deep down in her heart" (111). And she is proved right. Days before the wedding, the truth is revealed: "the bride-elect is a leper" (149). Morea disappears to die in isolation, though not back in the West Indies (which is clearly the source of her contagion). Three years later her ex-fiancé marries the English Marion, a much safer choice in the circumstances.

A related subplot in *With Silent Tread* is another hidden West Indian contagion arising from forbidden black and white contact. For one of the dark corners of family history is the fate of Morea's elder sister Thekla, who has committed the unpardonable sin of marrying a colored man. Similar to Caesar in *The System*, the young man arrives from the continent, where he had been accepted by the best society, but

> better educated and of more refined tastes than half the lazy, loutish white young men out here, whose only recreations are smoking, playing tennis, or drinking cocktails, he found himself looked down upon as not fit to associate with them, and exposed at every chance to nasty under-hand slights and indignities from them.
>
> (Cassin 1890: 89)

Shocked at his "barefoot mother and his wooly headed father" (89), and without other resources, he is forced to take "some small clerkship" and dropped from "good" society. Thekla, however, is already in love and marries him. The "strict old-time ideas with regard to keeping colour at a distance, and all the abhorrence of a touch of the tar-brush" (90), causes mother to disown daughter, and Thekla's name is never spoken by her family.

To be a leper, Morea knows, is a terrible fate in the West Indies: "it meant separation, suffering, loneliness, death" (149). The same fate, the narrative suggests, awaits those who are tainted by miscegenation. It is significant that in both the Old and New Testaments, leprosy as a term – though actually referring to a number of unrelated physical conditions – was considered a punishment for sin; the victim was said to be in a state of defilement. Like the threat of infection, fear of *racial* contamination is heightened by the smallness of island society: "we're all cousins here more or less," Marion is told (21) and even the black cook claims her as "Ah-we new cousin" (79), which in the West Indian context is not unrealistic. Nevertheless, this forbidden hybridity is profoundly disturbing for creole whites anxious to preserve "purity of blood," and distasteful to English observers. In Rhys's *Wide Sargasso Sea*, Antoinette's husband thinks how much his wife resembles the brown servant Amélie: "Perhaps they are related, I thought. It's possible, even probable in this damned place" (1968: 105). Again, while the husband has no qualms about sleeping with Amélie, the result of such perverse relations – racially mixed people – are considered unnatural, and their conception sinful.

If miscegenation is slavery's curse on the white race, Cassin's novel suggests the tragic repercussions. For Morea's mother is clearly responsible for her innocent daughter's suffering: her callousness to her old servant led to his revenge on one daughter, and her prejudice against Thekla's colored husband endorsed the ostracization and penury of another. "For the sins of the Mothers" is her admission of guilt (156). And she too is punished. She contracts leprosy whilst caring for Morea, and is forced to return to the West Indies to the care of Thekla, whose husband has also expired from the disease. That it is to her spurned daughter whom the mother, now herself a contaminated outcast, must turn for charity is, she confesses, her judgement (158). It seems to me that this reading of "the old ways" as responsible for the tragedy of the innocent – white, black and colored, in leprosy or social disgrace they are all "shut up" together – marks a significant if subtle critique of colonial discourse in the narratives of the West Indies.

What such texts inadvertently suggest is that racial admixture is not in itself a recipe for moral degeneration; Emma and Mary in *Constance Mordaunt*, Thekla's husband in *With Silent Tread*, Roger in *Harmony* and Caesar in *The System* are all colored, but all retain fully human (white) morals and standards until their return to the West Indies. The European-educated Liris Morales in Fraser's *Lucilla* is unfailingly portrayed as excellent in all respects and treated as an equal in England. But because she refuses to marry white once back in the Caribbean and thus repudiate the "burden" of her race, white creole society rejects her entirely. Along with her equally respectable aunt, Liris is visiting an Irishwoman newly arrived in the island, when a number of local white women drop in. Their response is to render the colored guests invisible: "[l]ong habit had made them adept in the precise way to treat 'coloured people.' Madame de Souza and Liris were apparently simply nonexistent to their eyes" (1896a: 87–8). Newcomers are forced to choose between white or colored society; they may not access both. The bewildered Irishwoman sees the injustice of such a situation but, as in so many narratives, the outsider's standards cannot prevail over the set rules of white creole society.[13] Returned to the colonies, the contempt and social marginalization which colored characters must endure withers their spirit and drives them to despair and failure, like Liris, or like Caesar, turns them "bad."

Gaunt's *Where the Twain Meet* links the slave castles on the Guinea coast with the island of Jamaica, delicately suggesting that the "problem that they ['those grim old slavers'] started still remains, and has only been taken with blood and bitter tears to the other side of the Atlantic" (1922: 86). One of the painful legacies of the "problem" is miscegenation, and the most vigilant in rooting it out are white women. Again, this is not to suggest that male writers of the period ignore the issue, but that it is a persistent and stridently censured theme in the texts of women. I have suggested that this is in part due to white women's perceived role of moral housekeeper in the colonial period. The increasing and very visible presence of mulattos, it seems to me, was a public sign in their eyes of betrayal: betrayal by white men of the marriage contract, and indeed of the social contract. For under the paternalistic construction of slavery and colonialism, the white master was not just the superior but the *protector* of his chattels, women and slaves. The casual siring of illegitimate brown babies alongside legitimate white ones made a mockery of this protective role. Further, on an ethical level, imperial conquest could be justified to even the most squeamish European conscience as a civilizing mission, bringing Christianity to ignorant and childlike savages. White women invested a great deal in this project, but once more, the evidence of colored people pointed to the licentiousness of the very agents of Christian civilization and emphasized the degenerate nature of those superiors entrusted with teaching and ministering to a childlike race. Simply put, colored characters in the narratives are reminders of "the circumstances of their birth – circumstances in which, it was felt, considerations of caste and class had been overcome by an 'animal impulse' " (Joyce Walker Johnson 1992: 18). For if blacks were savages and whites superior, how could a white man actively seek sexual intimacy with his inferior? And when that black or mulatto favorite, or her child, publicly flaunted the connection and gained status thereby, surely the racial hierarchy and the notions of difference which sustained it, came into question? I am suggesting that such questions, undoubtedly motivated by outrage and insecurity among white women, foreground in their texts the flawed moral nature of the colonial social contract.

"They . . . become as the expression is, almost a white negro"[14]

If miscegenation was encoded as the curse of slavery on whites in the West Indies, the negative effects of slavery on black and white character is no less remarked in women's writing. After all, as a white creole woman observes, what can one expect if "[v]ices are engendered by the system, those of stealing and lying in particular" (E.J.W. 1862, vol. 1: 192). So in the novel, a slave woman accused of theft rebukes the white mistress:

> "Me no *tief* um; me *tak* um. 'Spose me tief self. Buckra no tief, so well lika nigger? You *ma*mie tief, you *da*die tief, eberybody tief sometime."
>
> "What can you mean, Joan?" said Laura, the colour mounting to her cheek; "what did my father and mother steal? I am sure they never took anything from you they did not pay for!"

"Hut tongue, pickney; da wha dem been gie me dat time dey bring me come na buckra country? Dem no tief me na neger country?"

(E.J.W. 1862, vol. 1: 196–7; emphasis in original)

Again, slavery is the matrix for all kinds of immoral practice, for white theft of black as well as black robbery of white. In several of Crowninshield's stories (1898), English whites are just as dishonest as blacks; in fact, the American author paints them as the very models of greed and deception. In "Paul's Orange Grove," for example, Don César ruminates, "The native is cleanly as to his person, though I fear as much cannot be said for his moral." The response of a local is, "Why blame the native, when the white man sets the pace?" (269).

As late as 1957, Fielding's *Romance in Jamaica* insists that the warped values of the slave system continue to exert a malign influence. The morally retrograde nature of the locals – race unspecified, but clearly non-white – reveals itself: "the inhabitants regard work as a curse, not a blessing" (65), and this character weakness is traced directly "back to the terrible days of slavery" (67). Eschewing sympathy for history's victims, however, Fielding assumes the imperial "I" with its assumption that "we" know what is best for "them"(68):

Jamaicans should be proud of being Jamaicans and of being members of our truly glorious Commonwealth. They should be taught that in school—we would soon get rid of the useless politicians who do more harm than good. Fancy making a fuss over using the "cat" in cases of praedial larceny, a crime that is a danger in a civilised land.

More sympathetic (though no less condescending), the creole heroine of Napier's *A Flying Fish Whispered* (1938: 169–70) rails against the persistence of a "slave mentality" in the island:

A hundred years of freedom have not eradicated the characteristics of irresponsibility from a people, who, for generations, were allowed to make no decision, to have no independence of thought or action, so that now they seek always for help outside themselves. "The Government must do this, the Big House will give that." And above all they go to law . . .

What the narrator is describing is less a "slave mentality" than a colonial mentality, but the connection between slavery and continuing dependency is acknowledged, as are the detrimental consequences.

Slavery then, is the cause of continued flaws in "the negro character," and it is over-association with blacks that, some narratives suggest, has corrupted whites in the West Indies. Yet slavery hugely benefitted whites in England and the colonies; further, the narratives also indicate that immoral conduct among blacks is clearly modeled on white example! Again, the tortured logic enshrined in colonialist discourse highlights its inherent contradictions. Even Carmichael, the apologist for slavery, seems aware of the distortion when she insists that "I never heard the slave-trade mentioned with half the horror in Britain than I have heard it spoken of in the West Indies: and never let it be forgotten that Britain began the slave trade, – not the colonists" (1969, vol.1: 300). The rupture in any concept of a homogeneous white/colonial identity is evident in the shifting ascription of blame: wicked West Indian planters versus noble English abolitionists, or poor benighted colonists versus greedy metropolitan exploiters?

For many writers, the worst aspect of deterioration in the tropics had to do, like miscegenation, with the blurring of racial boundaries: that is, whites behaving like blacks. Let us survey a sample of textual descriptions, following a roughly chronological line. Carmichael's description of lower order white men learning bad habits from their black concubines and becoming "white negroes," is but one manifestation.[15] The English language, for example, is considered debased as a result of contact with African and creole languages. Lalla and D'Costa provide evidence that in the mid-eighteenth century "JC [Jamaican Creole] was commonly spoken as a first language by white as well as black Jamaicans" (1990: 131), as in the example of a white planter family at Prospect Penn in Jamaica. Carmichael notes the widespread use of "negro language" among the white population in St. Vincent, adding that creole children "have it almost as bad as the blacks" (1969, vol. 1: 76–7). Similarly, Lynch admits that "although my mother had taken pains to keep me from what is called, amongst West Indians, 'talking negro,' yet there was a langour and drawl in my manner of speaking, which drew from her the most cutting sarcasms" (1847: 17–18). In Jenkin's novel, when the heroine joins her father in Jamaica, she is shocked to find him prone to drink and showing signs of "talking negro": "[n]ebber, nebber say die," he insists (1859, vol. 2: 36). Yet in 1902, in Crommelin's *A Daughter of England*, local whites repeat Jamaican proverbs in Creole without any sense of embarrassment, referring to them as "ours": "Lizzard nebber plant corn but him hab plenty. We have no end of these sayings here" (265). Nugent's children, as we have seen, learn to speak in Jamaica and amuse British relations with their "little funny talk, and Creole ideas and ways" (1966: 259), as do the creole girls in *Constance Mordaunt* at school in England. The latter have not only acquired the language of the blacks at home, but also their songs and dances; and white creoles exhibited a taste for local dishes: "a good hot duckanoe, just out of the pot and still smoking, is the delight of all West Indian children be they black, white or coloured" (Drummond 1911: xviii).

For language is only one, if *the* most important and visible, site of creolization. In Chapter 2, I referred to Brodber's claim that creolization gradually eroded polarities between European and non-European in the West Indies, between white-skinned people and others, until by the end of legal slavery the region was producing Caribbean cultural forms. Even earlier, Greene's survey of eighteenth century historical accounts of Barbados (1987: 244) notes

> casual references to what was obviously a brisk sexual commerce between masters and slave women and complaints that continuing association with blacks was producing an Africanization of white language provided evidence

of powerful cultural influences of blacks upon whites and illustrated the extent to which white Britons in Barbados were coming to terms with slavery and with the black majority among whom they lived.

As already observed, the intimate, ongoing contact between black and white women (and children) in the domestic sphere was especially favorable to interculturation. However, from the perspective of many commentators, this translated as contamination. Even the gentle Nugent cannot forbear commenting on Lord Balcarres, who has clearly "gone native" as evidenced by his keeping a colored mistress and maintaining standards of cleanliness and manners in common with the "poor blackies." He lives in conditions of "dirt and discomfort" (1966: 15) in his country house, and his etiquette at table disgusts Nugent. Long before Fraser's Lucilla looks askance at her quadroon husband eating with his fingers, Nugent recoils from the white ex-governor "for the black edges of his nails really make me sick. He has, besides, an extraordinary propensity to dip his fingers into every dish. Yesterday he absolutely helped himself to some fricassée with his dirty finger and thumb" (Nugent 1966: 11). As for *creole* whites, they strike her as immoral, profane, unhealthy, with "yellow wrinkled faces" (10), speaking abominably and lacking in taste.

What incenses Nugent about Jamaica, as we have seen in the previous chapter, is "the immediate effect that the climate and habit of living in this country have upon the minds and manners, particularly of the lower orders" (98) of new arrivals from Britain. They soon succumb to the "creole" vices of sloth, overindulgence, tyranny toward servants, and – as noted in chapter one – "the influence of the black and yellow women" (12). Lanaghan too sees the "lower orders" as most susceptible to contamination, but Jenkin seems to suggest that creolization permeates all levels of society. In *Cousin Stella* the elderly white aunt of a coffee planter is described as a white negro in appearance, with "a stick under her arm, a thick bandana tied over her ears, a man's hat over that, exactly the costume often adopted by negro men and women" (1859, vol. 2: 79). Apart from the exceptional Louis, planters in this text are an unsavory lot, "slave-holders, men for the most part filled with new rum, wallowing in the slough of ignorance, lording it over a race degraded to the same levels as the mules" (vol. 2: 256). Indeed, Stella's own father and stepmother are unmercifully mocked. At home on their rural estate, they are "addicted to solitude, dressing-gowns, and the society of their slaves" who serve up "[a]ll the vulgar scandal of their estate." When the master and mistress bestir themselves to go out for a ride, their pretensions to grandeur are laughable in the excess of livery and decoration and the number of attendants needed for show (vol. 2: 100–1). Everywhere degeneracy, excess and savagery threaten to seduce the newcomer. Louis worries whether Stella can transcend the "drunkenness, luxury, superstition" that surround her (vol. 2: 85), and she herself comes to see "the terrible effects of slavery, not on the blacks alone, but on the whites" (88).

If whites are not speaking, eating, dancing and conducting sexual relations like blacks, their behavior is still a direct consequence of living among them in a slave or ex-slave society. Fenwick for example, is dismayed at the moral turpitude of

West Indian society and fears for her son lest "the practices of severity, which are really essential in the Government of Negroes, may chill and close his heart against those general sympathies which appear to me essential to the excellence of character" (1927: 169–70). In addition, she worries that he may acquire some of the vices common to young men in Barbados, where ladies live to a ripe old age but "men shorten their period by intemperance and sensuality" (171). Indeed, her "great uneasiness & misery lest he should acquire a habit of drinking" (173) does not appear groundless since "when we first arrived, he was cautioned against the water of the island" and so, in company with the other men, now "dashes his glass of water with a very small portion of rum"; women, she caustically observes, drink the water unadulterated with no ill effects and wonders how it "can be solely injurious to the male community" (173).

The cruelty and tyranny bred in whites as a result of unlimited power over blacks appalled many women writers. As noted, several viewed with horror the physical and verbal punishment of black servants by white mistresses. Some, like Fenwick and Nugent, dislike the creole socialization of children: indulged by servants over whom they have disproportionate power, white children become utterly spoilt and dictatorial. Nugent frets about her own son that "in this country, it will be difficult to prevent him from thinking himself a little king at least, and then will come arrogance, I fear, and all the petty vices of little tyrants" (1966: 146). The disadvantages of a West Indian upbringing then, include a "haughty and domineering" manner to underlings, and "the Creole drawl, so grating to the ears of Europeans and so difficult to be got rid of" (E.J.W. 1862: 72). Both failings are entirely due to contact with and the "servility of the slaves" (198). Whatever about the accent, a "haughty and domineering" manner was hardly appropriate in young white women. The spirited Doss, in Lynch's *Years Ago* (1865), is forced to agree with her chastened sister that "[w]e West Indian girls have such a foolish family pride instilled into us, that we begin almost from our cradles to think ourselves better than those who very often are far superior to us. Colonial life is calculated to make one narrow-minded" (255). In an effort to counter this socialization (or contamination), the proud little creole girls in *Constance Mordaunt* are sent off to an English boarding school, there to learn the "order, obedience, self-control and self-denial" appropriate to their gender (E. J. W. 1862: 66).

Lynch's *Years Ago* (1865), set in Jamaica of the 1790s, portrays the island as a place where religion has dried up (16), planters feast drunkenly and the piety of even the best of them is "blotted out by the iniquity surrounding him in this island" (79). Slavery is a sin that taints all involved, and so naturally the West Indies is a place where Europeans deteriorate: "[w]hite people rather go to pieces in Jamaica. It's the climate, I suppose, and the sickness" (Long 1936: 237). Long's novel is set in 1865, and constructs post-abolition Jamaica as a hotbed of physical and moral infection. In the wake of a peasant revolt and the brutal white backlash, sickness is rife. Noting the festering sores of people "round the door of the lazar-house" the heroine reflects that "[d]eath comes here easily" (312). A Scottish doctor talks casually of maggots, lice and leprosy at the hospital where he treats those who survived the rebellion; "It is the infernal Island," he muttered, "The infernal Island" (321). This physical contagion is paralleled by the degradation of conventional morals. In the text, indulgence in sexual exploitation across racial divides, permitted sensual excess, cruelty and unbridled greed, are all accepted and Angelica too must slough off her sensitive and delicate English persona and accommodate herself to the moral climate. Unable to endure her husband's promiscuity and appropriation of her fortune, she responds to his murder of her colored lover by arranging to have him poisoned. On the colonial margins, such savage behavior is possible, even commonplace. *The Golden Violet* is interesting for its ambivalent attitude to this scenario. In this tale of passion and cruelty breeding passion and cruelty there are no likable characters, but neither are there easy moral judgements. Angelica is ridiculous in her role of romance heroine, and a sinister creature in her new role of plotting poisoner. The latter, however, is victorious, for she avenges her lover's murder, regains her own money, dispatches a nasty husband and gets away with all of it. Is the narrative endorsing her transformation or deploring her degradation? In either case, the inscription of West Indian ex-slave society as pathologically corrupted is of a piece with the earlier texts discussed.

This construction prevails well into the twentieth century. Chapman's *Too Much Summer* (1953) tells the story of a white expatriate woman who "rather goes to pieces" in the colonies, becoming over fond of sex and alcohol and dispensing with accepted moral codes in her pursuit of escapist pleasures. And consider this synopsis of Lucille Iremonger's novel *Creole* (1950):[16]

> The story of the economic and moral decline of a Jamaican creole family seen primarily from the perspective of a young Oxford graduate who is manipulated into marrying the family's young daughter. An example of the theme of the corruption of the white population in the tropics prevalent in Jamaican literature until the 1950s.
>
> (Paravisini-Gebert and Torres-Seda 1993: 178)

According to the novel's dust jacket, Iremonger "breaks new territory in describing a Jamaica which has never been treated before – the real Jamaica underlying the glamourized blue Caribbean paradise of the tourist and the island of riots and religion of the political writers." Indeed, the portrayal of a degenerate white family of old stock who have acculturated to "the queer world of the back streets of Kingston," might be unusual in West Indian fiction of the 1950s; but it draws on a long tradition of women's narrative fascination with the "white negro."

Just as striking is Ada Quayle's *The Mistress* (1957),[17] linked by Anthony Boxill (1966) to deLisser's *The White Witch of Rosehall* (1929) and John Hearne's *Stranger at the Gate* (1956) in its concern with white creole plantation life in Jamaica. In Quayle's text, this life is chaotic and brutal. The protagonist is the white mistress of a rundown estate, caught between snobbish and brutal white society and the hostile and uncooperative blacks with whom they live in uneasy intimacy. The story demonstrates, yet again, how the violent interracial encounters and dysfunctional gender relations of the slave past survive into the twentieth century and continue to corrupt generations of white and black creoles.

I want to conclude by mentioning one further aspect of colonial society which is indicted in the early narratives. In *Cousin Stella*, a philosophy of unbridled avariciousness has utterly debilitated the white elite. A representative gathering of the plantocracy is illustrative:

> Surely those twelve persons there assembled were odd specimens of the creation. Men, the purple of whose faces, their misty eyes and sodden features, found an explanation in the long tenpenny nail hanging as a badge at their buttonhole; that nail measuring the depth of the rum in each tumbler drained many times a day. Men who could not sign their names until one or two such draughts had been swallowed. Others, lean, yellow, with red-rimmed, sunken eyes, above their leathery lantern jaws: these were the cruelest; the men striving to make money, honestly if they could, but money at any rate.
>
> (Jenkin 1859, vol. 3: 118)

Drunkenness, ignorance, cruelty and, above all, rapacious greed dominate the portrait, and such stereotypes inform the construction of West Indian planters and administrators in text after text. Fenwick observes that Barbados is a gambler's paradise, and the colonial ethos of risk taking encourages "speculations."[18] Her son-in-law is one of its casualties. Substantial losses, coupled with dipsomania, lead to the breakdown of his marriage and Mr Rutherford's abandonment of his family. Another perspective is provided by Nancy Prince. Commenting on the hard lot of the emancipated slaves in Jamaica, Prince describes them working for a pittance and exploited shamefully: "even religious teaching is bartered for their hard earnings" (1850: 47). Both publicly and privately she experiences the venal nature of ministers, preachers and Christian organizations, concluding that

> It is not surprising that this people are full of deceit and lies, this is the fruit of slavery, it makes master and slaves knaves. It is the rule where slavery exists to swell the churches with numbers, and hold out such doctrines, as *obedience to tyrants* is a duty to God.
>
> (Prince 1850: 56; emphasis in original)

In her estimation, "most of the people . . . seem blinded to every thing but money" (57) and she herself is nearly shot in an attempted robbery by old missionary associates! The prevalence of corruption, even in religious institutions, is squarely blamed on a history of slavery and the rampant greed enshrined in the discourse of imperial expansion.

In the early twentieth century, the same exploitative ethos is castigated in Napier's *A Flying Fish Whispered* (1938) as a survival of the carelessly greedy colonial philosophy. the novel refers to this mindset as "Parham Island ways," referring to the nearby island (Antigua)[19] where ghosts of unfree slaves seem to roam and indeed, conditions reminiscent of slavery still operate. Here, landless peasants are totally in the power of "the planters, the factory manager, [and] the merchants," the new masters who control wages and even where workers must spend their paltry wage (139). In Parham, the heroine is struck by the callousness of British neglect of a once-valued possession, as she observes a "sluggish stream oozing from the courtyard of what, three hundred years ago, had been the treasury building of the island's capital" (149), and the ruined wharves and fortifications of the port. " 'So much these islands mattered to us once,' the General said. 'And now so little' " (147). Back in her own island, Teresa reflects on a similarly careless disregard for ecological issues on the part of the British government representative charged with important decisions. After all, "he would never see the island again, nor care, after his departure, if it were networked with concrete highways, or left in pristine innocence" (257). Worse still, the same ethos is imported anew by a Parham Islander and his Scottish wife, new imperialists who proclaim their beach and their fallen coconuts off limits. If the fishermen and local peasants who have always enjoyed right of way and grazing rights will starve in consequence, "that would be their business, not ours" (64). In the hands of such people, St. Celia will become like Parham Island, sucked dry and abandoned to poverty and dereliction. There is little difference between Napier's new imperialists, their British colonial predecessors, Jenkin's degenerate planters, or Nancy Prince's corrupt religious leaders: making money, whatever the consequences, is all that matters. And then and now, their response to the Caribbean as a resource to be plundered and discarded, is deeply resented by the local community, black and white.

Greene explains that the "image makers" of Barbados in the late seventeenth century "portrayed the society created by the winners in the sugar lottery as extravagant, loose, morally and culturally debased, and riddled with fears of social revolt" (1987: 26). Nearly 200 years later, in 1850, Nancy Prince's account of conditions in Jamaica chronicles the widespread feeling in the colony that the bleeding dry of people and natural resources by "the winners in the sugar lottery" cannot continue. Prince records a local white predicting that continuing British exploitation will defeat expatraite and creole whites, as well as colored West Indians, so that "The negroes . . . will have the Island in spite of the—" (48). Such a sentiment, generally expressed with trepidation, recurs throughout the narratives. Brereton (1993) notes a sense of fear in the accounts of Nugent, Carmichael and Fenwick – who wrote of the last three turbulent decades of British colonial slavery – the consequence of living among an alien and increasingly hostile black majority that was prepared to fight for freedom. Wilfully blind to the failings of her precious plantocracy, Carmichael bemoans insubordination and threatened violence on the part of the slaves in the last years of the system (1969, vol. 2: 217–18), which made for the planter's "total want of personal security for himself and his family . . . surrounded on all sides by negroes" (vol. 1: 56–7). Eventually, seeing that the slaves now "shewed in their every action that they looked upon me, being *their proprietor*, as *necessarily* their enemy" (vol. 1: 244; emphasis in original), she is forced to acknowledge that the planter/slave bond "is for the present generation destroyed" (vol. 2: 276). The family determine to leave, sparing hardly a backward glance at "the negroes" for whom she has claimed such concern, and who weep to see her go. In truth, of course, the decision to abandon the West Indies is a strictly pragmatic one since "the best intended efforts all failed, either for the improvement of the people, or the benefit of the estate" (vol. 2: 334–5). The "improvement of the people" is but rhetoric; her primary concern is the "benefit of the estate," epitomizing the baldly materialistic self-interest that was the ultimate motivation for the colonial project in the first place. As many of the early narratives suggest, it inevitably corrupted the societies it spawned; as the twentieth-century texts corroborate, the new masters are no better than the old.

Narrative after narrative constructs the colonial project as fatally compromised by the iniquitous system of slavery. So Jenkin in *Cousin Stella* reduces the slave/ master relationship to one of "cunning and fear, in presence of drunkenness and absolute power" (1859, vol. 2: 142). This soon gives way to armed revolt (vol. 3: 177) that results in death and destruction for black and white alike, and the crippling of Stella's beloved Louis. Louis's disability is the logical narrative outcome of slavery's curse on a family who, however ambivalent their responses, benefitted from complicity in its maintenance. Louis had hoped to relieve Stella from involvement in slave owning, "the actual possession of many fellow creatures." It is this very "fatality which has pursued our families" with its curse, one he trusts the pure and pious (and importantly, English) Stella will be able to break (vol. 3: 268). His paralysis is a metaphorical admission that even the best-intentioned white man cannot remain unsullied within the parameters of the slave system: all are, in some way, tainted; all are corrupted; all are, in various ways, doomed by their participation.[20]

To be a colonizing subject in the West Indies, then, is to court degeneration if not damnation. Several texts, such as Carmichael's, construct the West Indies itself as the source of evil, only tangentially acknowledging that the imperial center is finally responsible for the forces now loosed without hope of containment. So in *The System*, the best of English manhood is

> sent here as a proffered sacrifice to every ill that human nature can encounter – to be familiarized with vice in all its forms, and danger in all its varieties – a prize for the fang of pestilence, the rage of the hurricane, the wasting progress of debauch, the soul-destroying example of avaricious tyranny and wanton oppression. Thus does England immolate the choicest of her flock, to support a system that is her scandal and her curse.
>
> (Tonna 1827: 194)

Apart from natural disasters, miscegenation, "debauch," "avaricious tyranny and wanton oppression" are vices which have their roots in slavery, a system that benefitted a few but is finally portrayed as poisoning the society as a whole. Europeans in the tropics who seek in this apparent El Dorado unlimited possibilities for personal and financial success, pay the price of irreversible corruption. Enraged, they blame the place, blame even that cursed malevolent planet which predominates in that island and so changes the constitution of its inhabitants that if a woman land there as chaste as a vestal, she becomes in forty-eight hours a perfect Messalina, and that 'tis as impossible for a woman to live at Jamaica and preserve her virtue as for a man to make a journey to Ireland and bring back his honesty.

(W.P. 1963: 110)

Repeatedly, women writers remark snidely on the language, the manners, taste, appearance and morals of creole and resident whites, who appear to have been contaminated by the climate, by the casual brutality of the plantation economy, and by "creolization," so that they have mutated into that most unnatural of species: Carmichael's "white negro." Some, like Jenkin, Nancy Prince and Napier, are equally damning about the corrupting effects of slavery and colonialist exploitation on the evolution of West Indian societies.

Attention to schisms within the supposed community of female colonizing subjects, suggests that white identity in the colonial context is complex, if not conflicted. The same can be said for the supposed unquestioning acquiescence of white women in the colonial ethos. The narratives suggest a more nuanced set of attitudes. Accordingly, I read recurrent articulations of reservations about and anger against the mother country and its representatives in the region, along with the textual inscription of moral and spiritual degeneration of whites in the tropics in consequence of slavery and its aftermath, as indicating some level of awareness of damaging cracks in the veneer of the imperial project.

6 Colonial discourse and the subaltern's voice

"White" texts on black subjectivity: the specular gaze

Ultimately, any suggestion about ways to read these early narratives will involve responding to the question: "why bother to read them?" What possible relevance can they have for contemporary West Indian women (and men) like the students I teach, the majority of whom are from non-white, non-elite backgrounds? I have always been puzzled by the term, "a usable past," suggesting as it does that some aspects of history can be tossed out as useless, and others carefully preserved according to some agreed agenda. Yet in a sense, as I have suggested in my introduction, this is precisely the thinking, implicit or not, which relegated most of these early texts to obscurity. So far, I have been arguing that *all* of our past is "usable," including these forgotten narratives. I have suggested their value in terms of representations and self-representations of white women in the region; as constructions of the interrelationship of black and white women in a variety of domestic situations; and as a resource for mapping narrative and ideological positioning in relation to the contemporary physical and social landscape.

In this chapter I want to address some of the original questions that motivated my study: I want to read the texts of white, elite women for possible traces of the *other* women. For example, is it possible to find any constructions of non-white women that evade the dominant stereotypes of the period? Do any of the texts invest non-white women with subjectivity, thus challenging the process of Othering which typified colonialist discourse? In what ways do the narratives "speak for" or to the experience of "native" women? Do any represent the voices of non-white women – however mediated – in a manner that might suggest access to an alternative, even counter-discursive, construction of the colonial Caribbean? Is it only experience of oppression that confers jurisdiction over the right to speak about that oppression, or can a text speak by analogy, for example between patriarchal subjugation on the part of white women and racial subjugation on the part of black women?[1] While not proposing definitive answers to these questions, exploring them seems to me a fitting way to end this study.

I have situated my textual analysis within a broadly feminist and postcolonial framework, and have referred to female authors/characters in the early texts in terms of "colonising subjects" operating within the parameters of colonial discourse. At the same time, I qualify such terms with reservations about over-rigid categorization. Indeed, in the previous chapter I called attention to ways in which apparently "colonialist" texts none the less reflect awareness of fractures and dissonances in the West Indian social order. I continue in this vein here, in light of the questions raised above. I do not believe that there are such things as essentially "female" or "white" or "black" experience which can authenticate a narrative as "true" of that particular experience, and I acknowledge that "the subject" is a textual production first and last. But I *also* acknowledge that for me, these texts allow some sense of access to life as it might have been experienced by representative women of the past.

In this chapter, I discuss texts already cited (James's 1913 *The Mulberry Tree*), as well as others mentioned only in passing: Fraser's novel *A Study in Colour* (1894) and short story, "Margaret: A Sketch in Black and White" (1896b); May Harvey Drummond's *The Story of Quamin, a Tale of the Tropics* (1911); and Alice Durie's *One Jamaica Gal* (1939). James's narrative persona has been sketched in Chapter 3, but what of Fraser, Drummond and Durie? *A Study in Colour* is a loose, anecdotal novel – what the author calls "these little stories" – written by an Englishwoman who accompanied her husband, a government official, to Jamaica in the late nineteenth century. On her return to England, she published two West Indian fictions, *A Study in Colour* and *Lucilla, an Experiment* (set in "Creolia" and "San Jose" respectively).[2] Along with "Margaret," the novels are obsessively concerned with the race/class hierarchy in the colony, mostly from the perspective of native women. Fraser (1894: 8) explains the impetus for writing *A Study in Colour*. Conjecturing about the lives of the negro inhabitants, she

> began to regard with a new interest the dusky servants that came and went about the house. The servant question is to the full as engrossing a topic in the West Indies as at home, but it was not from a domestic, but from a human point of view that I was considering them.
>
> Gradually I made friends with them; I found they were only too willing to talk about themselves, when once their first constraint was over, and they realised that I was truly interested in their histories; and as they talked there broke on me glimpses of a life so strange and fantastic, that at first I could hardly realize its existence.

Clearly, the focus here is the exotic ("a life so strange and fantastic"). But Fraser also insists on the veracity of her narrative, claiming that "I used to read what I had written, with, of course, certain reservations, to some of the servants" who were given leave "to criticise most freely, and tell me where I had made mistakes and how I was to alter them." Finally, "[w]hen it was right and they were satisfied they used to be so pleased and say, 'Dat quite right 'last, Missus, dat 'xactly de way we lib.' Then I felt proud, even though my audience consisted of but my brown nurse and a . . . cleaner-in-general to the household" (8–9).

Fraser's claims for her text are intriguing. On the one hand, she represents the narrative as transparent, a near transcription of the servants' accounts, subject to their corrections and rendered in (her version of) their Jamaican Creole; on the other, she calls attention to her editorial authority, reading back their words "with, of course, certain reservations." Ultimately the specular gaze of the fascinated tourist predominates, governed by a desire to familiarize the exotic for a "home" audience. This is the acknowledged aim of Drummond's novel. Like Fraser, Drummond – who was either born or raised in Jamaica[3] – modestly deprecates her text as having "no higher aim than the telling of a story and the occupation of an idle hour" (1911: v). However, she goes on to explain that *The Story of Quamin* relates "the life of a negro boy from infancy to maturity," with the secondary aim of "preserving the folk-lore of Jamaica." Clearly targeting an English audience, she begins her account (v) with

> a preface setting forth the point of view and intent with which it was written, explaining unfamiliar allusions and answering beforehand questions as to faithfulness to type, etc., which are likely to arise in the mind of the average reader, accustomed only to the more advanced negro of the Southern United States.

Drummond's agenda is the vindication of the basic decency of "the Jamaican negroes." "Decency" here translates into knowing their place. According to Drummond, black Jamaicans "are much better behaved than their brethren of the United States," and hence "outrages such as lynching and burning at the stake are unheard of" in the island. This is because "the crimes leading to these methods of punishment never occur in the British West Indies." And such crimes are not committed because "the negroes of these islands know that British law recognises no difference between the Governor himself and the humblest black man, and this knowledge makes them not only law-abiding citizens, but loyal subjects of the British Crown" (xix). "Jamaican negroes" are treated well because since they know British law judges them fairly, they do not commit the offences which merit the barbaric punishments meted out in the United States. The breathtaking manipulation of logic here is an ironic testament to the "compliance" of the Jamaican blacks! Drummond adopts a distanced, patronizing tone towards her subject matter, stating (vi) her intention

> to portray the childlike and fanciful imagination of the negro as we find him in the country parts of the island before the hand of civilisation has fallen too heavily upon him.
>
> It is true that this type is passing and in this fact lies an excuse for wishing to preserve some record of it, though no claim is here made of having sounded the depths or climbed to the heights of the negro nature.

Despite the disclaimer, much of the preface does attempt to "sound the depths" of an essentialized "negro nature." For example, notwithstanding attempts to cozily familiarize quaint beliefs – so Anancy translates into "the mischief-loving elf" (xvii) – blacks are represented as tenaciously clinging to "the supernatural, and obeahism . . . which has a tremendous influence for evil upon its devotees" (vi). Confidently, Drummond launches into a potted etymology of obeah, its practices and practitioners ("impostors"), along with selected manifestations "of African superstition" such as the "Roaring Calf" [sic] and "Duppies." Again, the casual pronouncements on local folklore speak to a superior knowledge: "[n]o intelligent argument has ever been brought forward as to the reason of the folk-tales . . . being called 'Anancy stories' " (xiv). Of course, this ignores the obvious, which all locals know: the tales *feature* Anancy.[4]

Preconceptions thus filter and distort her viewpoint, and textual reports are used to support preconceptions. Accordingly, since one cannot hope to encounter an "authentic" representation of West Indians via this kind of colonialist narra-tive, a more useful practice is to read for the *self-construction* of the (colonizing) tourist, noting the power relations inherent in these purportedly objective accounts. The dominant stance of these works, as in the texts discussed in Chap-ter 3, is the pose of the tour guide: knowledgeable but uninvolved, and concerned to fix the native (place and population) within a certain context, for the entertain-ment and education of a home audience. The "I" of Drummond's preface answers this description, although it is somewhat effaced in her tale: the central figures (into whose consciousness we are permitted to enter) are a black woman, Nana Dreckett, and her grandson, the eponymous Quamin, whose development forms the loose plot of the book. But despite their centrality, there is a recurring disparity between the overblown style and sentimental, frequently moralizing tone of the standard English reportage and the Jamaican Creole speech of the char-acters. This incongruity is most obvious in intrusive, inappropriate asides: witness, for example, the grief of the family at the death of grandfather Dreckett "creating a scene not unlike that of the lost souls in Hades pictured by Goethe in his Faust" (Drummond 1911: 126).

Fraser's gaze is more complex. Initially, the omniscient third-person narrative is mediated via the consciousness of "The Missus," through whose eyes a fascinating parade of native female servants is introduced. In asides and explanations the disjunction between their world and that of the (ideal) English reader is apparent: "[m]orals, as generally understood at home, were of the slightest, yet in their irregular domestic arrangements they were often most strangely and touchingly true to each other" (Fraser 1894: 19). After the sudden death of her child the Missus leaves Creolia, and the narrative excuse for insight into the feelings and thoughts of the black women ceases to hold. Perhaps this is explained by the same impulse that leads Fraser to use a pseudonym and to rename the site of her tale (from Jamaica to "Creolia"): that is, the desire to strengthen the illusion of ver-acity by downplaying her own involvement in the recording and shaping of the account. Such distancing ostensibly renders the narrative more transparent, more plausible. On her departure, the servant Justina becomes not only the protagonist, but the central consciousness of the text: it becomes *her* story, counterpointed with the tragic history of Elita, and the tone of tour guide is greatly muted. Only the odd essentializing comment – "like all true Creoles" (171) – calls attention to the Otherness of authorial voice.

Durie's *One Jamaica Gal*[5] brings this survey much nearer the West Indian present. Yet despite its social realism and the centrality of the black working-class women, to which few of the earlier narratives attend, Durie's representation of their consciousness is as problematic as any of the earlier texts because a similar narrative distancing obtains. The frequently condescending authorial voice here is removed from the social class of those described. The gap between standard English narrative and the (well-reproduced) creole of the characters, reinforces that between the sensibility of the author and the class of people she writes about: "most of the Jamaican peasantry" (1939: 16), we are told, are of a different breed. When Icilda's white employer discusses the servant problem with a friend, this class distancing is evident: "You can't expect a girl like Phoebe to feel about these things the way you do. Haven't you a hundred interests where she has only two or three?" (25).

Published in 1939, the novel is set in Jamaica and like H.G. deLisser's *Jane's Career* (1914), catalogues Icilda's progress up the social ladder from poor country girl, to Busha's mistress, to domestic servant in Kingston, to dentist's assistant, to respectable married woman. But her happiness is short-lived; her husband's death leaves Icilda penniless, and she drifts into a life of prostitution until she eventually finds her niche as head of a balm yard[6] in the slums. Her career suffers a setback when she is framed for holding counterfeit money. She is granted bail, only to meet an untimely death soon after as a random victim in a clash between rioting workers and the police.

Where the "I" persona intrudes in these accounts, it is usually to make moral judgements, as in Drummond's censure of the irrational and "tragical" practice of obeah. Durie peppers her novel with comments of the sort, "she should have been a wholesome peasant woman, working in the fields and mother of a brood of children" (1939: 58). Similarly, Fraser inserts herself into the last lines of her novel with an ambivalent disclaimer. Justina has ended up, successfully to her peers, as the mistress of a white man and the narrator comments, "[f]or my own part, I do not presume to offer an opinion on such a delicate question" (1894: 214). Despite the disclaimer, Fraser's text (like most of the others) most certainly does "offer an opinion" on the culture it purports to render mimetically. Thus, the role of these narratives in the naturalization of imperial rule appears straightforward. But critical studies of colonial discourse have demonstrated that alternative readings *are* possible and rewarding in that they can yield insights at odds with the apparent agenda of the writers.

Colonial discourse: "disparate projects"

Within postcolonial studies over the last twenty years, there have been varied critical positions on colonial discourse as articulated in literary texts of the eighteenth and nineteenth centuries. Some have reservations about the validity of critical engagement with such texts. Parry (1987) is one of the most outspoken, and a useful synopsis of her stance is provided by Maxwell (1991) in her essay, "The Debate on Current Theories of Colonial Discourse." To contextualize:

Maxwell situates debates about theories of colonial discourse around two kinds of contending claims concerning subjectivity. On the one hand, some – like Parry – hold that "the postcolonial intellectual should be engaged in the attempt to recover an autonomous form of subjectivity for the Others of Europe that will allow them to 'speak for themselves' " (1987: 81). Critics of this persuasion concentrate on "articulating the margins," that is, recuperating elements of traditional native culture which Parry considers resources to be called upon as an alternative representational framework in the fashioning of a combatant subjectivity. Such a project is more politically valid than the purely negative task of deconstructing the texts of colonialism. This seems to be the line taken by Hoving (2001: 352) in her discussion of women's writing from the Caribbean: avoiding a definition of colonial discourse, she privileges reading for "the postcolonial strategies that subvert [it]."

On the other hand, Maxwell explains (1991: 81–2), there are those – like Spivak and Bhabha – who consider that

> the theorizing of an autonomous subject for the colonized ministers to the desire of First World intellectuals to know and thereby control the Other of the West. Faced with this prospect, the most that postcolonial intellectuals can hope to do is to continue critiquing the subject of the West.

Gikandi (1996: 8) offers a sensible middle way between such polarized positions, insisting that when we engage with early texts,

> we cannot operate outside the colonial episteme and its institutions, [so] our challenge is not to transcend it but to inhabit its central categories, to understand the histories and functions of these categories, to come to terms with their effects, and to deconstruct their authority.

This may be a daunting remit, and perhaps inhabiting the "central categories" of colonial discourse is not even possible for modern readers. However, it is also a useful reminder that writers are the product of their own times and that their texts can hardly elude the hegemonic discourse which, in the nineteenth and early twentieth centuries, assumed the superiority of English culture and civilization. At the same time, Gikandi's thesis is that colonial cultures were *central* to the transformation of English identities even though colonialism as a political system circulated in its literary productions a marginalized view of the colonial world.

Of course I am grossly oversimplifying the complex nature of the theoretical debate, but it emerges clearly that colonial discourse analysis is informed by quite disparate projects. Rather than attempting to endorse any one perspective, I want to appropriate specific aspects of *several* theoretical positions in my own experiments with reading women's texts of the colonial period. Accordingly, in what follows I discuss selected texts in light of orientations suggested by JanMohamed, Parry, Bhabha and Spivak.

A *"manichean" reading*

The key tenets of JanMohamed's critical project, particularly his stance on colonialist literature, are outlined in "The Economy of Manichean Allegory" (1986). For JanMohamed "colonialist fiction is generated predominantly by the ideological machinery of the manichean allegory" (102), and functions to articulate and justify the moral authority of the colonizer by positing the inferiority of the native as a metaphysical fact, working on an axis of "diverse yet interchangeable oppositions between white and black, good and evil, superiority and inferiority," and so on (82). This system of unequally loaded binary oppositions holds despite contradictory textual images/stereotypes of the native – as in the coexistent representations of the "pathetic half-breed" and the "vengeful mulatto," noted in the previous chapter – hence the *economy* of the manichean allegory. The colonialist text then, is primarily narcissistic: its pleasure in the superiority of "Us" (for "author" and like-minded reader) resides in the simultaneous denigrating of "Them." Attention to this central power relation leads to an overtly political reading of the literature, one rooted in "the dense history of the material conflict between Europeans and natives" (79). Any pretense at genuine or objective representation of the "racial Other" is thus exposed (100). Despite reservations about his almost total lack of attention to the role of gender and non-African contexts,[7] JanMohamed's manichean allegory is appealingly straightforward and I have implicitly coopted his methodology in reading some (previously discussed) texts. I want now to briefly consider Drummond's and Fraser's novels in light of his contention (88) that the colonialist text ethnocentrically constructs the native as mirror for the colonist's morally superior self-image, a construction which involves "complicity between reader and author."

A prime example of this complicity is the particular humor of much colonialist fiction: local ways are described in such a manner as to stress their absurdity to "Us." Many narrators find amusing the native "imitation-to-excess" of English habits, as in Drummond's mockery of servants dressing themselves for special occasions in inappropriate cast-offs (1911: 21ff). In Fraser's *A Study in Colour* (1894: 15), an account of black women's church outfits evinces a subtle manipulation of "objective," even sympathetic description for the narcissistic consolidation of European taste over that of the native:

> Fortunately, like most of us poor mortals, they were sublimely unconscious of their own deficiencies, for in each other's eyes (which, after all, is where our standard of taste is to be sought for) their faintly colored flowered prints and white Gainsborough hats, over-burdened with feathers and mock pearls, looked very correct, and what they themselves termed "stylish," even although they surmounted a collection of tightly plaited wooly locks.

Ostensibly, this comment pretends to social leveling: for *all* of "us poor mortals," beauty is in the eye of the beholder. In fact though, the narrative gaze focuses on the aesthetic "deficiencies" of these women, their "over-burdened" millinery sense, and the incongruity of the epithet "stylish" for *anything* that sits atop "tightly plaited wooly locks," much less "feathers and mock pearls." Implicitly, the reader is invited to share the Missus's smile along with her "regretful glance."

Humor at the expense of "quaint" native practices is facilitated by an essentializing narrative taxonomy. So in *A Study in Colour*, "negro servants" are all picturesque, if lazy; "affectionate as children"; steal "with a frank-hearted enjoyment of their cleverness," and so on (Fraser 1894: 19). James too, in her breezy tour guide manner, mentions that "the Jamaican negro" is lazy but charming (1913: 39) and refers casually to "the senseless, brainless cackle that is the peculiar property of negroes" (40). In Durie's novel (1939: 17), the black rural working class are also homogenized into a generic group, as in "the peasants had a way of working out their hate in such wise." Repeatedly, the narrative places Icilda and her ilk within the mould of the primitive and innocent: she is "a child of nature and like her kind, lived in the present with an intensity of enjoyment that forbade dwelling on the possible chagrins of tomorrow" (56).

Such essentializing facilitates a racialized agenda within these texts: a justification of white paternalism. More insidious, the texts represent black women internalizing the idea of their own inferiority. Fraser's novel does attempt to depict the closeness of women across race and culture – in grief, and in "womanly fears" (1894: 78), Justina and the Missus draw "very near together" (146) – but the inexorability of racial hierachy is never in question. Justina, we are told, confesses that "I nebber could lub a black little chile same as I do de white" (58) and is resigned to the fact that even in the afterlife, whites will occupy a different mansion in heaven (147). Additionally, Fraser's stories of Justina and Elita deal with black women's desire to "improve their colour" by liaisons with light-skinned men.[8]

Durie's *One Jamaica Gal* also rehearses the fine color distinctions and prejudices familiar from earlier narrative constructions of West Indian society. Here they are ventriloquized not by white observers but by black and white *Jamaicans*. Selected as Busha's "housekeeper" (mistress), Icilda is puffed up with pride at the economic and social status this confers, and her father is delighted at the prospect of "a yellow grandchild." Busha's mother accepts the interracial union with equanimity as "a custom handed down from slave days": indeed, her own "grandfather, father and husband had all produced 'outside' families with comely brown paramours" (1939: 12). After Busha leaves the island, Icilda is determined to find another white employer because, she declares, "White man treat black man bes'. Brown man, him too uppish" (19). Given the internalization of white privilege, and its repetitive reinforcement in the narratives, it is a short leap to conflate racial and moral characteristics. Despite the Missus innocently wondering at negroes confusing "fairness of skin with excellence of character" (Fraser 1894: 133), her narrative casually attributes Sambo Samuel's "singular steadfastness for a negro" to his "irregular Scotch extraction": "He was very dark . . . but otherwise a rather good sort of fellow" (124).[9]

Conventional [European] morality is foreign to the simple Icilda who could quite understand the cause for people stealing and she did not blame them, on occasions; she also comprehended the urge of the flesh and took it for granted that most girls would have sexual experience, and one baby, and probably many more, without benefit of clergy. That there was a strong economic reason for marriage, besides a religious one, she did not comprehend. She never sat down to figure out the menace which under-nourished, indisciplined children are to society, nor did she ponder over the fact that promiscuity breeds disease.

(Durie 1939: 33)

Like Fraser's Missus, Durie's narrative tone is mildly judgmental, but resigned to the fact that such "children of nature" know no better (8). Like children, black Jamaicans are represented as governed by their instincts. Jealous rage prompts Busha's cook to give Icilda "a butt in the pit of the stomach . . . and tear out her hair in handfuls" (10), and loyalty is rare: Icilda "had been brought up without moral ideals and had been trained to take advantage of any weakness in a superior" (26). Fine distinctions are beyond her, so that once married respectability ceases to provide financial security she drifts into prostitution with no qualms, for "prostitution was as easy a way to live life as any other" (55).

Working-class women are represented then, as living according to an alternative set of codes. Fraser's text acknowledges a quite distinct value system among such women, with but a thin veneer of "English ideas"; however, there is no question of equivalence between their values and English ones. Among black and colored women the "social ethics at Creolia are not all that could be wished" (1894: 53). Moral failings then, become a matter of black *nature*. For example, "black mothers are often very cruel to their own little ones, although they make the best of nurses to white children . . . in this, as in many other ways, they appear to defy and contradict all natural expectations" (69). In terms of sexual fidelity, modesty, sensitivity to their partners, gentleness, honesty and "respectability," black women are represented as lacking in comparison to the ladies "at home." Hence the construction of the gendered racial Other serves as a flattering testament to the inherently superior white woman. In at least one instance, however, Fraser savagely undercuts the smug ignorance of English *male* pronouncements about native women. Justina's shock at her husband's death in jail, is interpreted by the warder (for whom she works) as evidence of callousness. "Even the best of them have really no feelings," he concludes. To which the corrective, and ironically insightful, narrative commentary is: "He had not known her life, and judged it only from his own scanty information. He admitted, however, that as a washerwoman, she possessed distinct merits" (207–8). In the end, a lack of sensitivity weighs less in the scheme of things than her excellence as a washerwoman.

Inherently flawed natures can never really be civilized, it seems: even the exemplary English schoolmaster, so "gentle in dealing with his dusky little scholars," is "a pure pessimist at heart about the permanent advancement of the negro race" (Fraser 1894: 181). In fact, *A Study in Colour* suggests that such "advancement" is not entirely desirable. For example, Justina's embracing white "airs" and values leads to alienation from her peers: her pride and sexual reticence are considered "mad ways" learned "from dat Buckra Missus" (198), and ultimately do her no good. Similarly, in *One Jamaica Gal*, Icilda's one consistent motivation, and the cause of her downfall, is aspiration to the class of her white and brown employers. After her promotion to Busha's mistress, she flaunts her prosperity and "[t]he envy and wrath which she knew her suddenly exalted state had awakened in the bosoms of her friends made her feel strangely elated" (Durie 1939: 3). Eventually her pride and the jealousy of those she leaves behind cause her misfortune, and this cycle continues throughout the novel. As the Jamaican proverb has it, "the higher monkey climb, the more he expose."

Too "advanced" to "go back to a primitive mode of life in her parents' hut" (19), Icilda heads for the city. There she learns more refined ways from her mistress, whom she strives to emulate, again exciting resentment. Her imitative behavior is questioned by her sister: "Wha' a nager gal lak you wan' wi' such mincing ways?" (27). The text implicitly critiques the spiritual bankruptcy of the rising brown middle class, whom Icilda must ape to rise socially. But her own efforts to "better herself" (38), climbing up the social ladder until "she had risen many grades higher" than her origins (43), although they pay off temporarily, end in failure. "[A]nxious to break away from any ties which might jeopardize her new social position" (45), Icilda invites envy and ill will which result inevitably in her humiliation. Widowed, diseased and destitute, "her self-esteem humbled," she ends up living in a tenement yard and dying on the street. Accidentally shot during a riot, an observer who knew her in her "respectable" days recognizes the body: "It's Icilda Green, one of our church members . . . I used to know her . . . Lawd, how she come here?" The reader asks the same question. Hardly a subject invested with agency, Icilda's character is *acted upon* in the narrative and, betrayed, misled and powerless, she drifts towards a useless, arbitrary death.

Fraser's Justina is luckier. She not only survives, but ends up the mistress of a dipsomaniac Irishman. From her neighbors' "point of view and her own," we are told, she "is a most respectable and prosperous woman"; the narrator, as we have seen, does "not presume to offer an opinion on such a delicate question" (1894: 214). The point is, of course, that there is no *need* to do so. Like Durie's, Fraser's text implicitly makes the point that even the best of native women eventually reverts to type, thus reinforcing the "naturalness" of the moral superiority of European womanhood, and the hegemony of colonialist values. JanMohamed's contention that colonialist fiction is generated by the ideological machinery of the "manichean allegory," helps to highlight textual strategies whereby black women are essentialized and totalized in the service of the self-consolidation of European female taste and values. However, reading strictly within the taxonomy of colonialist and colonized seems to me to trap all representations of a complex West Indian past within simplistic binary opposition. Yes, all relations can ultimately be reduced to power relations; but having said that, is there no other reason to read these narratives? Accordingly, I want to pick up on previously discussed features of narrative ambivalence (or possible self-contradiction) and of interculturation through the enforced intimacy of black and white women, in order to suggest other reading strategies that can, perhaps, discover traces of West Indian culture that *refuse* to be appropriated by colonialist discourse.

An oppositional reading: obeah as "alter/native tradition"

Parry's (1987) injunction is to locate counter-discursive sites in the margins of colonial discourse, particularly elements of traditional native culture which serve as alternative representational fields for the colonized's redefinition of self as agent. At first glance, Durie's *One Jamaica Gal* appears to suit this project. Certainly, the novel is far more insightful about the materialist context of the Jamaican underclass than most earlier narratives. Life is hard on the land as peasants struggle to make "a living from the land which was baked by the sun or scoured by the rains" (1939: 6). Similarly, conditions of city squalor are detailed including the infamous "Dungle" (a wretched collection of shacks thrown up on a garbage dump outside Kingston), which is portrayed as "a fester [sic] sore of crime in the vicinity of West Street" (75). *One Jamaica Gal* clearly reflects the island's political history, its social and racial inequalities and the simmering civic anger at an insensitive and exploitative colonial government, which led to industrial action and the growth of nationalism in the years that followed its publication. Durie's narrative exposes "the sad state of things in Jamaica—rapidly increasing population, filthy housing conditions, illegitimacy, venereal diseases, hookworm, yaws, tuberculosis, illiteracy" (69). Popular unrest is mercilessly exploited by opportunistic politicians who are caricatured throughout the novel: Horatio Briggs, for example, is portrayed drunkenly declaiming on "his distorted idea of self-government" (46), which translates into "Jamaica for Jamaicans and . . . my own kind in every office in the government" (47). At the same time, Briggs's critique of colonial rule (47) is astute:

> What do all these white officials know about us when they come here? And by the time they do know something, off they go again. None of them give a damn for us or this little island. All they're thinking about is getting on the easiest way and having a good fat pension in the end.

Again, the text fits Parry's preferred focus on concrete socio-political issues and on representing the potentially counter-discursive inscription of indigenous cultural practice, in this case the African-derived belief system of the balm yard where Icilda, like many others, finds an empowering community. But while Durie's novel acknowledges the social problems resulting from unequal power relations, it also subverts the kind of revolutionary impulse from the margins that Parry advocates. For example, the text mockingly refers to the nascent pan-African popular movement as a "cult" which "preached the annihilation of all the white men in the island" (61):

> The white man! Yes, he was the cause of all the trouble, low wages, lack of work, drought, Panama disease, and all the rest. And after him the yellow

man and the brown man came close seconds. When the purge began there would be no more pale skins in Jamaica, only black ones, and the negro would rule the land and despoil all those who owned property.

Just as the narrative implicitly critiques Icilda for attempts to rise out of her station, so the prospect of black self-rule is ridiculed by equation with mob rule.

And while Durie portrays the power of syncretic creole spiritual practices, the text undermines their validity by brutally reducing the balm yard rituals to mindless barbarism. Hence the scene at Mother Divine's funeral (1939: 64): "Sweating, straining, gasping, swearing, the multitude trampled each other . . . The high smell of unwashed bodies in dirty clothing cut the air with acrid pungency. Here was a free show for all and the rabble demanded due enjoyment of it." Indeed, the text employs the same language of savagery as, for example, some of Fielding's short stories, and are specifically constructed in terms of African primitivism: the drum rhythms "breathed of the jungle" (64). At the Naomi Balm Yard, "where those of more primitive instincts could find emotional relief in nightly shoutings and dancing" (59), a tone of fascinated disgust dominates the evocation of the brethren who "uttered babblings in unknown tongues" as their dancing "became more frenzied" and whose "red tongues lolled out, teeth flashed and blood-shot eyes glistened" (66). The derogatory, even racist selection of detail renders them no different from the mob of strikers and looters in whose midst Icilda meets a random death (78).

Durie's portrayal of working-class protest and indigenous religious ritual proves bankrupt, and the counter-discursive potential of a marginalized but clearly influential cultural praxis is utterly discredited. In the end, the specificity of Jamaican cultural variants is coopted for a political agenda: at the very least, the story suggests that the different races/classes should continue to know and maintain their places. Similarly, Drummond's *Quamin* (1911), despite its "objective" tourist gaze and simple romance storyline, can also be read as consolidating the colonial status quo. Quamin, the "good black," is hardworking, pious and properly respectful of the law and is paired with the similarly "good" – if somewhat more spirited – Quasheba. In direct opposition is the mulatto Harry (211); the mixed-race Harry is the only character to bear a non-African or non-biblical name, possibly hinting at his alienation from the black community. Certainly Harry, like the mulattoes discussed in Chapter 5, is unhappy with his servile lot, seeks material and social status and achieves this at Quamin's expense through deceit and trickery, particularly the manipulation of obeah.

Harry's female partner is the colored Cubenna, a "yallah snake" (207). Quamin falls under their bad influence, and is framed by them for their murder of a white sailor. He flees for his life but all comes right in the end. The villains are dispatched by a natural disaster; Quamin is cleared, reunited with Quasheba and lives happily ever after. Drummond's tale portrays the black figures as childlike throughout, and works on one level to minimize and finally eliminate the threat of the aberrant (racially mixed) Other (the kind that kills a white man), legitimizing instead the values of the good, law-abiding Jamaican negro of her preface. None the less, on another level the text can be read in Parry's terms as counter-discursive in ascribing power to that which it denigrates: that is, faith in the force of obeah. For *Quamin* is also a "cautionary tale" in its handling of obeah. Part of Drummond's agenda, spelt out in her preface, is to discredit obeah as fraudulent superstition. Much is made of the extortionate nature of obeah men who demand payment for what the dismissive narrator assures us are simply childish tricks (62), a familiar colonialist strategy for demystifying alien cultures and rendering them "safe."

However, like Durie's balm yard, obeah is a pervasive and significant force in the lives of the Jamaican peasantry. Their profound belief in its efficacy and the respect due its practitioners (Drummond 1911: 59, 208) counter narrative attempts to render them farcical, and the portrayal of the obeah man's very real power suggests the force of an "alternative native culture" that resists dismissal. In other words, the "quaint" becomes strange and somewhat frightening because the text is forced to confront the *power* of such cultural systems. Ferguson points out that "African people's distinct cultures and religions scarcely counted or registered" in official accounts (1992: 65), and where they do infiltrate "Christian" colonial culture, are denigrated as "connected with devils, superstition, fetish, idolatry, and savagery" (59). Yet such demonization can serve to *foreground* non-official beliefs and practices by revealing just how threatening they are to the dominant order.

What Drummond's text does, despite itself, is to demonstrate two very different, but equally self-validating epistemologies. Quamin and James actually *see* the "Rowlin' Calf . . . a four-legged animal dragging a heavy chain" (72), even though the text suggests that it is only an illusion orchestrated by Harry. Again, the certainty of the black people that Quamin's injury is supernaturally inflicted is directly in contrast to the white doctor's diagnosis of knife-wound: "Samuel shook his head and cast a despairing glance at his neighbours in protest at the 'Bockra's' incredulity" (87). In a story appended to the text, "Busha' Chicken," a similar conflict of belief systems is evident: the white doctor's diagnosis and treatment, and that of an old black woman originate in two quite discrete discourses, and clash without possibility of compromise. "Go 'bout your business and don't bother me with your nonsense," says the doctor, to which the woman's response is: "Me no talkin' nonsense! you bockra . . . nebber t'ink say neager know anyt'ing but w'en de pick'ney dead you will be sorry you wouldn't lissen" (299).

In her preface, Drummond recognizes but cannot comprehend the "contradictory" nature of negro spirituality, that syncretic capacity to patronize divergent religious rituals (Christian and obeah). While she grants the medicinal basis of the obeahman's wisdom (1911: viii), these anomalies signal a lack of rational "proportion." I would suggest that in representing this aspect of indigenous Jamaican culture, her attempt to privilege the European over the native perspective fails. The tactic of demonstrating how credulous blacks are duped by the illusion of obeah, bounces back – like obeah itself – on the perpetrator: if Harry harms Quamin by misappropriating to himself the power of the supernatural, in effect "call[ing] obeahman name in vain" (59), the evil ricochets, and

Harry and Cubenna perish as a result of a parallel sham-obeah staged by Quasheba (205ff). Similarly, Drummond's marginalization of an important African cultural survival can be read as turning back on *her text*. Her intention is to bring obeah and "superstition" into disrepute. The narrative not only fails to invalidate this alternative spiritual belief system, but indeed demonstrates this other knowledge as a vital native practice.

An analogous internal fracture – what might be called counter-discursive insurgency within the colonialist text – occurs in Fraser's novel, where again obeah is sneered at (1894: 192): "I do not believe that a dead roach and two sheep's teeth in a bottle can produce such tragical results . . . it seems rather incongruous to think of such things taking place in this enlightened nineteenth century under British rule." Nevertheless, as the narrative chillingly attests, they *do*. The text records incidences of the power of obeah (113, 183ff), particularly convincing in the vivid detailing of Elita's deterioration and death. In a sense Elita's case, presumably cited to discredit such practices, ends up affirming their power and testifying to their tenacity in the Caribbean. The efficacy of obeah, a historically recorded mode of resistance to colonial hegemony, is consolidated in Fraser's text when a spurned suitor curses the scientific reasoning of "all de white trash" and chooses a far more potent means of revenge: old Joe's arcane knowledge (183).

It is tempting to speculate whether what I have called an internal fracture, might result from an unconsciously ambivalent positionality on the part of these partially acculturated writers. Obviously, Durie, Drummond and Fraser are steeped in African-Jamaican culture which, however they profess to despise it, is recognized and even "normalized" in their texts. Acknowledgment *and* denigration of obeah and related folk-wisdom is part of the inheritance of a creole upbringing which, as discussed at the end of Chapter 4, familiarizes the white child with aspects of "native" culture that, as a member of the elite, she is gradually socialized to repudiate. Yet some texts testify to the indubitable penetration of the "little tradition," and the marginal/local can be said to "talk back" to official discourse. Accordingly, following Parry, I suggest that in these narratives the reluctant concession of power to alternative cosmologies invests believers (female and male) with a means to agency. Instead of JanMohamed's predictably monolithic colonialist discourse, what emerges in this reading is more heterogeneous, an ambivalent and even self-contradictory representation of West Indian culture. In the following section, I explore this focus on ambivalence and self-contradiction in Bhabha's colonial discourse analysis.

Reading for "ambivalence": stereotyping as self-revelation

In what Moore-Gilbert (1997: 116) calls the "first phase" of Bhabha's thinking, covering the period 1980–1988, Bhabha is more interested to "emphasize the mutualities and negotiations across the colonial divide" than in the project of redressing native stereotypes. Bhabha sees such stereotypes as evidence of the degree to which his psychic responses to the colonized Other fractures and destabilizes the colonizer's identity (like JanMohamed, the colonizer/colonized is normatively a "he").[10] For Bhabha (1985), colonial discourse is ambivalent, refracting the subjectivity of both colonizer and colonized, and textual analysis discovers a certain "play" between the two. Influenced by psychoanalytic theory, particularly Lacan's radical revision of Freud, Bhabha considers such discourse to be marked by a simultaneous recognition and disavowal of difference analogous to "the mirror stage" in Lacan's conceptualization of the Imaginary. For Bhabha the complex, contradictory and ambivalent modes of representation of the Other in colonial discourse suggest that the "authority of colonial power was not straightforwardly possessed by the colonizer" (Young 1990: 145); in short, the taking up of a subject position (for colonized *and* colonizer) is always problematic and fraught with underlying contradictions and anxieties.

This is particularly the case in native "mimicry" of the master, which puts into question the apparently solid ground of colonial discourse (Bhabha 1994): mimicry "at once enables power and produces the loss of agency" (Young 1990: 147). For the native, mimicry is a form of defensive camouflage, and thus a means of potential resistance, re-turning "the gaze of the discriminated back upon the eye of power" (Moore-Gilbert 1997: 131).[11] I want to focus here on Bhabha's notion of the ambivalence at the heart of colonial discourse, and of mimicry as an unsettling of power relations between colonized and colonizer, indeed as unsettling the whole notion of identity. In the texts discussed, I maintain that it is possible to read into contradictory narrative stereotyping of black women, a certain ambivalence in the white female's *self*-representation. In other words, this stereotyping indicates less a reinforcement of the self/other gulf than a repressed exploration of the otherness inherent in the white woman's slippery place in a patriarchal system.

Like many of the early writers, Fraser, James and Drummond recognize at different points in their texts the strength, independence and pragmatism of the black women they purport to represent. Apart from Quamin, the "agents" in Drummond's story are all women, and it is the resourceful Quasheba who saves Quamin's neck. And again, with the exception of Quamin, all the men are easily manipulated by women. Similarly, Fraser portrays Justina as resilient and tenacious (1894: 159) despite grinding poverty. Motherhood spurs her on to work even harder: "she could not afford to be lazy, now that she had another to work for besides herself" (169). But this resilience is also characterized as a racial trait: "[t]he day after its [her baby's] arrival found her again at her wash-tub, for Nature does not deal hardly with the women of her race and clime" (168). Narrative stereotyping thus approves the black woman's independent determination to support herself and her child, while also justifying her servitude by the "fact" that she is naturally fitted for labor.

A positive response is encoded in this multiple stereotyping of the cliched "strong black woman," but there is also a certain defensiveness on the part of the narrative observer about attributes she herself obviously does not possess. Witness, for example, Maclean (1910: 48) claiming that in Jamaica female subservience is a relic of the African past since "in all savage races there is the idea that women are intended to be the slaves of men." The statement baldly contradicts accounts which testify to black West Indian women's fierce resentment of male domestic tyranny, and their single-minded pursuit of economic independence. Additionally, the implicit conclusion is that women in recently-heathen Jamaica are the slaves of men, therefore women in civilized Christian England are – what? Surely, at least, their equals? Yet considering the legal and economic context of Britain in 1910, this is patently not the case.

So early textual reactions to the independence of black West Indian women are rarely straightforward. James (1913: 137) purports to enjoy the company of Jamaican market-women, particularly in contrast to their English class-equivalents. But her admiration is tempered with unease at their casual appropriation of her space. These ebullient higglers will not "conform for the sake of the general good or the general comfort" on a tram (138):

> fifteen market women with fifteen baskets clamber up and struggle to find their places. There may be fifteen places for them, but there are not five for the baskets; but still they have to go somewhere, and with scant courtesy they are shoved under you and in front of you and beside you until you have no more room to move in than has a brick in a wall . . . No one makes room for you or tries to adjust the baskets. They are not insolent, they are simply indifferent to your existence.

They refuse, in Bhabha's terms, to acknowledge or return the colonizer's gaze or to be interpellated as "good" natives. Indeed, they protest vigorously at any infringement of their self-defined rights in the matter of public transportation. The point is not so much one of *conflicting* attitudinal sets, but that the English woman recognizes her values simply have no currency in this context, and finds this deeply unsettling. Far from being self-consolidating mirrors for her narcissistic Eurocentrism, the native women render her invisible.

On the other hand, James is as feminist as any higgler in her views on gender relations and rails against English notions of marriage, which she regards as a "business contract" that "tie[s] together two comparative strangers so inextricably that they have either to remain most hideously bound or else wade in the mud to get free" (1913: 104). She vociferously champions divorce as a means of escape from domestic misery, arguing that teaching a young woman "it is as unholy to sell her body in a church as in a street . . . will emaciate your divorce list very considerably" (108). Even more radical is her claim that the "attitude of mind of the Jamaican negress with regard to marriage is a distinctly advanced one" (103). Black women, she explains, are aware of losing financial and personal independence in matrimony, and sensibly prefer cohabitation. "[I]t would seem as if there were many lessons to be learned from the negroes in their domestic relationship," she concludes (104). James's comments have the effect of unsettling and rendering ambivalent the value weighting of two supposedly unequal moral systems, and in fact valorizing that of Jamaican women in this context.

Grudging awareness of native women's progressive attitudes surfaces even earlier in Jenkin's *Cousin Stella* (1859, vol. 3: 285), where the maid Rebecca offers Stella insight on men in the West Indies: "all bad, white man, black man, not a pin to choose 'tween em." The smitten Stella is blind to any faults in her Louis, yet Rebecca's impudence in comparing across racial lines is not rebuked or commented on. The black woman's view is represented as more pragmatic and, as it turns out, more accurate than that of the romantic Stella. The Missus, in Fraser's *A Study in Colour*, is equally uncensorious when representing black women's businesslike dealings with men: Rosa sees them primarily in terms of monetary support, and when her "baby father" is no longer useful in this respect, she is anxious to get rid of him (1894: 139). In Durie's novel too, Icilda's union with Busha is an economic arrangement, and is accepted as such by all. Similarly, her marriage to a "respectable" brown man is clearly motivated on his part by a desire for "a strong young woman to look after him and his house" (1939: 42). For her, it is a means to increased status as she conforms to the paradigm of a "veil and a white dress and herself leaning on a strong man's arm, like the brides she saw in the newspapers!" (38–9). There are no illusions about love between them, and Icilda does not regret his death.

While few writers approve black women's pragmatic approach to sexual matters as outspokenly as does James, many appear sympathetic to their rather cynical regard for men in general. In recognizing the necessary existence of an alternative gender politics in the West Indian context, rather than simply promoting the superiority of an ideal British model, the texts leave open the possibility of comparing the two, and not necessarily to the detriment of the former. For James anyway, male control of female sexuality is reprehensible cross-culturally: "the preservation of chastity in his women is as much an instinct with the savage as with the white man . . . it grew out of the desire of the male to *pre*serve and *con*serve [women] for his own particular use" (1913: 140; emphasis in original). She is unapologetically critical of white male exploitation of black women during slavery: "He took the creatures he despised, and bred from his honourable body and their despicable ones a swarm of outcasts . . . at the same time he demanded honour for himself while he treated as worthless that which he had of himself created" (140). In Fraser's text, all the black women are financially independent, and view marriage as an unpleasant social restriction notwithstanding the status it confers. Hence Justina chafes against its limitations (1894: 53), concluding – like Icilda – that "[m]arriage hab teeth" (155). And when her worthless husband is imprisoned, "Aunt Maria and her acquaintances were loud in their congratulations. Justina had fine luck, they said openly. She would now, they all agreed, enjoy her liberty to the full" (156). While the narrator's archness on the subject of native morality is not exactly approving, there is also recognition of Justina's triumph over male abuse, and perhaps even a guarded gesture of support.

While the representation of non-white women in these narratives participates in the conflation of "different" with "exotic," this does not always imply inferiority. For example, certain essential features of place are projected onto black women. As noted, the New World is depicted in terms of the uncharted, and thus challenging female body, as a sensual paradise *and* a source of wealth. But in several of the early texts, there is a kind of fascination with this embodiment of tropical excess. For Fraser, black women like Justina (1894: 60) exhibit traits very much of a piece with the Caribbean setting:

> their emotions succeed each other with a rapidity that is unknown to more northern races, and they in consequence can only be compared to the luxuriant tropical vegetation of their own soil, which springs up, flourishes, and passes away before a self-respecting English oak would be aught but a sapling.

While this is, of course, stereotyping of a most deterministic kind, it also situates these women as fully integrated into their landscape and at ease with their own emotion/sensuality. In such constructions lie the germ of the idealized black female character that appears in later fiction by white West Indian writers (Bliss, Rhys, Allfrey), one who embodies the physical, sexual and emotional freedom denied to white "ladies" by virtue of their class and race. For these features are precisely those forbidden to women raised to aspire to the "cult of pure womanhood," and to privilege the civilized, rational intellect embodied in the colonial male ideal. What is notable is the *complex* of characteristics employed in the representative process. In addition to vanity, superstition, and dubious morals, the texts also highlight black women's strength, resourcefulness, independence, pragmatism in gender relations, and frank enjoyment of their own sexuality. From a feminist perspective then, we can read here a subtle shifting in the weight given to values ascribed to women of both races. Certainly awareness that among other racial and cultural groups, women had a certain degree of control over their bodies *vis-a-vis* men of their own group and could profit from their labor, in however limited a way, led to a questioning of their *own* gender politics on the part of some white writers/readers. Perhaps the colonial context heightened women's awareness of their own subordinate status under patriarchy, by foregrounding their inferior gender positioning within a discourse that assumed their racial superiority. Following Bhabha, then, one can read these early texts for ambivalence concerning the necessary "rightness" of the narrator's home culture, which in effect points up the ambivalence of colonial discourse itself.

Bhabha's comments on the transgressive nature of inappropriate native "mimicry" are also useful here. While such mimicry is sometimes grounds for narrative humor it is also, as we have seen, grounds for discomfort. For Newton (1897: 19), such mimicry spoils the quaintness of the tropics, since "[u]nfortunately the European style of dress has seriously interfered with the picturesque appearance of the people." In stronger terms, James opines that the Jamaican peasant in his/her own environment is all very well, but the "semi-civilized negro of the towns is an unpleasant person" (1913: 141). The more the native conforms to the "norm" laid down by the English master, the uglier is the mirror reflection for the master: hence James's reference to the black man who "has been taught to steal by seeing his master steal from him" (ibid.). Even as she is unsettled by such mimicry, James is forced to concede that it highlights similarities between center and margin. After all, she concludes, "[t]here may be neglect and desertion and promiscuity among them [the blacks], but is there no neglect and desertion and promiscuity among us?" (104). A black servant "will lie to you whenever his need for lying arises. But a parallel can be found for that among the white-skinned rulers that come across the Battersea Bridge to dominate your home in Chelsea" (39). Religious fundamentalism is, for her, as abhorrent in white practice as in black: there is the "same terrified barter of this world for the next, the same frantic rush for shares in as estate that none had ever seen" (49). She concedes that "Vaudoux"(voodoo) sacrifice is indeed ghastly, yet observes how "we read quite calmly the twenty-second chapter of Genesis" (178). Fraser also makes cross-cultural comparisons, observing that practice does not always accord with preaching and "[t]his is the way of society, irrespective of shade or clime" (1894: 155).

Crucially, such comparisons highlight the relativity of moral judgements, which leads to a potential interrogation of the inherent authority of the colonial gaze. Illustrating her conclusion that natives are "born mimics," James relates an incident where a stolid, impassive black butler is transformed through "the most vivid, unselfconscious acting I've ever seen" (116), into an exact imitation of his master, complete with appropriate gesture, intonation and accent. This makes her wonder "what *we* look like [to those] in the kitchen" (116; emphasis in original). Recognition that she has misconstrued the butler as irredeemably stolid, suggests awareness that misconceptions, misunderstandings and preconceptions may dominate colonialist inscriptions of the native. As the butler parodies the master, so James's gaze turns inward, if briefly, to speculate on the *mutuality* of stereotyping in the colonial context.

Such recognition opens up a space beyond oppositionality, a site of hybridity in subject construction. These accounts by white women can be seen as textually mimicking black women, who are in turn represented as mimicking white behavior, sometimes prompting self-interrogation on the part of the colonizing subject. Indeed Gates (1991: 460) posits the hybrid nature of the colonial text. When he refers to "the disruptive articulations of the colonized as inscribed in colonial discourse," he emphasizes that this discourse contains *within* it an awareness of other viewpoints, other ways of thinking, other repressed dissenting voices. While postcolonial criticism has amply demonstrated the vital role of "literary documents" in the circulation of official ideology, Bhabha's point about the essential ambivalence of colonial discourse provides a useful reading strategy for such documents. Again, his concept of mimicry as a wilfully distorting mirror that fractures any monolithic identity assumed by the colonizer, suggests useful avenues of approach to my project of locating "disruptive articulations" of the colonized inscribed in the colonialist text. In the narratives cited, black women are shown to articulate – sometimes verbally but also, more importantly, in their assumption of sexual and economic agency – a challenge to dominant European notions of femininity and, indeed, to reinforce textual ambivalence on the part of women writers towards the normative patriarchal inscription of gender roles.

Reading for the "Other's" voice

For all her recognition of similarities across racial lines, James's narrative voice is the privileged one. Even as she acknowledges that the native may have a specific discursive position from which to speak and judge, this position is dependent upon *her* narrative for its articulation. Her text may suggest tolerance for other discourses, but in a sense this grounds her own narrative's hegemonic authority by lending it the impression of "objectivity." The echo of the native voice is heard, but only in so far as James's text can accommodate it. And this leads to consideration of Spivak's argument that in colonial discourse, the gendered subaltern *cannot* speak for nor represent herself. Like Bhabha and Said, Spivak firmly discredits appeals to an authentic or originary identity for either colonizer *or* native. To read the colonial text for the recuperation of the colonized subject/ Other, serves only to "conserve the subject of the West" and to continue the imperial project's constitution of this subject as "subaltern." Posing her famous question, "Can the Subaltern Speak?" (1988), Spivak answers in the negative; and "the subaltern as female is even more deeply in shadow" (287). She can only be spoken *for*.

The native subject is "muted as a result of imperialist praxis," clarifies Maxwell (1991: 77), in that the subaltern is constructed ("worlded") as a self-consolidating and silent Other within hegemonic European discourse and so, by definition, can only be known, represented or spoken for in a necessarily distorted or "interested" fashion within that discourse (Moore-Gilbert 1997: 80–1). Despite the desire of postcolonial feminists to imagine subaltern voices, within Spivak's paradigm we simply cannot access any "pure" or essential or originary subaltern consciousness, because "subaltern consciousness" cannot be reached independently of the colonial discourses and practices which have in fact constructed that subject-position. While female subalterns do, of course, speak, Spivak's point seems to be that such voices can never be heard in colonial discourse as an expression of their "true selves." Rather, since the native is always read as that which consolidates the sovereign subject of the West, she suggests a critical program of uncovering textual strategies by which this "worlding" is achieved. So, in her reading, the "colonial texts" *Jane Eyre* and *Wide Sargasso Sea* exhibit for Spivak (1985) certain imperialist tendencies towards the subaltern woman. Privileging European women's access to individualism again constructs native woman as Other for the narcissistic Western woman (creole Bertha for English Jane Eyre; ex-slave Christophine for planter's daughter Antoinette). For Spivak, "considering the 'native' as object for enthusiastic information retrieval" or "being driven by a nostalgia for lost origins" to seek an original, authentic native self-representation, is to forget that such a "native" is "an inaccessible blankness" staged by the narrativization of history (1985: 245).

In terms of the questions I posed at the outset of this chapter, Spivak's finality is daunting. There is no point in reading early texts by white women, situated as they are within colonial discourse, for any echoes of black West Indian articulations of subjectivity. But Spivak is sometimes guilty of what she censures in critical practice. For example, consistently refusing homogenization, she seems to me to unquestioningly homogenize "the West," a category ascribed to West Indian creole writers like Rhys, and subsumes the fictional creole Antoinette under a discussion of the practice of *sati* in colonial India. And some dissenting voices do question "Spivak's deliberated deafness to the native voice where it is to be heard" (Parry 1987: 39). For example, Parry maintains that the ex-slave Christophine in Rhys's text "subverts the Creole address that would constitute her as a domesticated Other, and asserts herself as an articulate antagonist of patriarchal, settler and imperialist law" (38). Not only does the subaltern speak in Rhys's text, but for Parry her defiance constitutes a counter-discourse. Gregg also points out that the "silenced" subaltern Christophine,

> *through the narrative structure* [of Rhys's novel] effectively gains access to the husband's thoughts and feelings and articulates them (*WSS*, 152–9). This textual strategy inverts one of the classic tropes of colonialist discourse, that of the imperial I/eye who positions, explains, and speaks for the "native."
>
> (Gregg 1995: 42; emphasis in original)

Again, Gail Hershatter (1993: 119) argues

> that in some measure subalterns both literally speak (that is, make utterances which enter the historical record as texts recorded by others) and represent themselves (that is, craft their explanations of their own experiences and activities in particular ways, in order to secure what advantages they can).

The example of Mary Prince immediately springs to mind. Yes, Prince's voice is constrained by the generic and gender contexts within which she wrote, but is this equivalent to being silenced? I will return to this narrative in the final section of the chapter. As for the texts by white women, there are of course immense difficulties in attempting to recuperate within them the "true" experience of the marginalized. Yet even in colonialist narratives, Moore-Gilbert wryly notes (1997: 107), "dominant discourse records the subaltern's resistance to a far greater degree than Spivak's own work, albeit that such resistance may be encoded in all kinds of negative terms."[12] Indeed the resistance of subaltern women – including laziness, dishonesty, surliness, truculence and deceitfulness – has always been acknowledged in colonial discourse.

Finally, Spivak's odd construction of the white creole woman seems to me to complicate the whole notion of subalternity. For as Parry's critique implicitly suggests (1987: 37), Antoinette also participates in subaltern status *vis-a-vis* colonial discourse. Rhys's narrative is written entirely from the perspective of the West Indian woman, and intended – according to Rhys herself – to give a voice to the degraded native/creole, the silenced and imprisoned subaltern, in Brontë's English text. Further, Antoinette is represented as sharing with the black Christophine a Creole language from which the white English male is excluded. And as Ferguson (1992: 238) points out, "a different language augments political strength and the possibility of numberless viewpoints." How then to accommodate in Spivak's schematic dictum a white creole author (part colonizing subject, part colonized native) rendering Dominican patois (the subaltern's language, erased from the colonialist record) to speak "as" Christophine, an oppressed but articulate and defiant black woman? Is she in fact speaking "for" the subaltern, but in the subaltern's own tongue? And if that tongue is *shared* by Antoinette, the white creole who acts as colonized native to the imperialist husband, does this suggest that Antoinette too is a subaltern who speaks authoritatively in the local, creole text but is silenced in Brontë's English one that appropriates her?

I want to conclude by suggesting some ways in which the complex linguistic situation in the Caribbean qualifies Spivak's silencing of the native woman, as well as prescriptions about who can/does speak for whom in colonial discourse. For several of the early texts by women *do* attempt to articulate native voices in native language. Where texts employ standard English, the gap between Creole speaker and the voice that speaks *for* her is jarring. Fraser tries to explain this awkwardness by claiming that the Missus has no choice but to speak for the servant who cannot "define her own sensations" (1894: 44); the subtext here is that the Missus is well aware that the failing is not Justina's, but her own. Fraser is well able to reproduce Justina's Creole vernacular, and does so for most of the novel. Justina can and does "define her own sensations"; so the Missus's intrusive interpretations clearly flags the one-sidedness of the colonial account. Although sometimes little more than a caricatured version of broken English with "funny" pronunciation, the rendering of Creole is generally adequate. Granted, it is often glossed or clarified by word pairs for the European reader, but this was also the case with most attempts by twentieth-century West Indian authors. Perhaps then, we can conceive of the "subaltern position" as that which cannot speak because denied access to the language of the colonial text, that is, the published, "literary" English book. Creole and English, which encode different world-views, are unequal in the literary work given that the subaltern's Creole accounts, if recorded at all, are collected and mediated (for anthropological interest, for local color) *through* that text.

Nevertheless, Creoles are syncretic, hybrid languages, born out of culture contact and not to be confused with any notion of a "pure," ancestral tongue, which (like the "real native") is impossible of recall. And by the nineteenth century, West Indian cultures were also creolized, hybrid entities: as noted, the white doctor in "Busha' Chicken" slips into a mesolectal register of Jamaican Creole when angry (Drummond 1911: 299). Above all, the engagement with Creole speech – if not orthographically accurate – which these writers demonstrate for extensive sections of their texts to express a wide range of issues and responses, presumes a certain amount of bilingualism on their part, if not situating them firmly within the Creole continuum. By the nineteenth and early twentieth centuries, Creoles had long succeeded pidgin languages in the West Indies, and there is ample evidence that natives of all races had competence in some registers of the language. Therefore, texts which extensively utilize Creole in effect undermine any simplified equation of non-English speaker with inferiority. When the "colonialist text" is fractured – as in the case of Rhys's rewriting of *Jane Eyre* – by the native Rhys "re-articulating it in broken English," this necessarily "perverts the meaning and message of the English book . . . and therefore makes an absolute exercise of power impossible" (Parry 1987: 42).

In several of the texts mentioned, the language of the master (English/the narrative) does become a site of hybridity (Jamaican Creole/multiple discourses) and in this, I think, we encounter a problematizing of the very terms I have been casually using, "native" and "colonial." "Quasheba, you is a nasty pick'ney . . . look here, Godpa, she jus done bite off de bullfrog toe" (Drummond 1911: 34). This is written by an elite white woman ventriloquizing a subaltern's voice; but it is certainly the voice of a *native* speaker, despite the clumsy rendering of the Creole. Indeed, it is no more clumsy and no less accurate than early attempts to render the vernacular in mid-twentieth century West Indian literature. The colonial text, in these instances, represents a *blurring* of voices. If Drummond speaks for Quamin, in Quamin's "native tongue," is this not also Drummond's tongue *within the narrative context?* Fraser's linguistic fluency is evident in capturing not just the deliberately stylized approximation of formal English adopted by a colored social climber – "MY BELOVED MAMA, – This is to acquaint you that I return to you as the prodigal son did from the Swine" (Fraser 1894: 132) – but *also* the subtle nuances that speak to creole interference in the standard. Whose "tongue" is speaking/being spoken here?

Such "doubleness of enunciation" also characterizes several of Fielding's short stories (1915). The representation of Jamaican Creole is meticulous and the orthographic accommodations to pronunciation are accurate ("seeam" for same; "togyedda" for together), but more importantly, the Creole *takes over* the rather stilted standard English of the narrative. In "Crop Over Day," for example, a resident Irishman describes an old-time celebration in Jamaica. As he talks, his narrative segues into that of the characters in his tale, Jamaican peasants who speak through him in an excellent approximation of the Creole language. The English narrator and the Irish storyteller are effaced, and a rich continuum of Jamaican speech, song, proverb, quoted verse and dialogue is represented with no apparent mediation. The speaker is complimented on his ability to "speak nigger" (30), a skill shared by characters and narrators in other stories who also slip in and out of Creole speech with facility. Patterson in "Jacob Wake," for example, convincingly assumes the voice of a local spirit and warns his co-conspirator that "Bush habe ease, and wall habe eye" (59). Farquhar similarly compliments the accurate reproduction of Antiguan Creole in Cassin's novel (1981: 32–3):

> When the black characters speak . . . there is little of the awkwardness of the non-West Indian writer trying to create local colour but whose ears are not attuned to the non-standard, little of the inconsistency on the part of some West Indian writers who, although quite familiar with popular speech, lapse into a kind of self-consciousness when they transfer their characters' utterances to the printed page.

Like Fielding, Cassin describes white West Indians moving easily in and out of Creole. Describing Mammy's day in court, Morea seamlessly shifts between reported and direct speech: "[s]he said afterwards it was as good as a mock-a-jumby show at Xmas time, to see 'de big jedge on de box, and all the little jedges sitting round de table' " (50).

Napier's *A Flying Fish Whispered* (1938) evinces equal facility with diglossia or code-switching, to the extent that the narrative moves from the consciousness of the white creole protagonist into that of black characters: one chapter, for example, is set entirely among the peasant Rosalie's family and neighbors and the white protagonist is only mentioned in passing, while elsewhere the reader is given access to the conversation and thoughts of the unemployed in Parham Island or an ex-postmistress, in their own words and with no reference to the central consciousness. Despite the "objective" perspective adopted by the narrators of many early texts, issues of linguistic complexity and competence suggests that the West Indian situation does not easily support oversimplified positioning of black and white in terms of articulate colonial and silenced subaltern.

Finally, one can argue that black West Indian women "speak" in these texts in their roles as interpreters and translators. Certainly, white women like Fraser's Missus arrive in the colonies with preconceptions; but residence in and growing familiarity with the region lead, in several texts, to a certain questioning of pre-conceived notions and a reliance on black women as interpreters of what proves to be a different culture that *resists* European pre-scriptions. In the travel narratives of Nugent, Fenwick and James, care is taken to detail the persona's interpersonal relations with black and white locals, investing native women with another kind of authority: that of translator. For just as James acknowledges the erroneous nature of several of her preconceptions, so many of the white female narrators/ characters in the early fictions are faced with a strange new world in the colonies and need help interpreting it. Here, black domestics often feature, playing roles which destabilize to some extent the "truth value" of the colonial account and offer another as complementary knowledge. Like Emily in Phillips's *Cambridge* (1991), European women find in the colonies new epistemologies and cosmologies which they are unable to read without assistance, and are forced to rely on their servants to explain. For example, as noted previously, newcomers to the West Indies are unable to distinguish the fine distinctions of racial admixture that operate. In Fraser's "Margaret: A Sketch in Black and White" (1896b), an Englishwoman learns from a colored nanny about such distinctions, as well as the interracial unions which give rise to them. In Jenkin's *Cousin Stella*, the young arrivant from England is *expected* to be taught about West Indian culture by servants: after Stella is frightened by the sound of a whip, her father rebukes the maid, "Why didn't you tell your young mistress that it was only the signal to bring up grass, you ninny?" (1859: 63). And indeed, it is Rebecca who answers Stella's litany of questions about domestic and social affairs (72–3), while her father and stepmother garner the neighborhood gossip from their slaves (101).

Here the authority of the colonizing subject's inscription of the West Indies is in part revised and translated as a result of the input of native women as interpreters of the local. I suggest that the texts' assignation of such crucial roles to black and brown women, whose insights are represented (with varying degrees of fluency) in approximations of Creole vernacular, *can* enable imaginative evocations of these women as subjects, not entirely circumscribed by stereotyping or a mirroring role as "self-consolidating Other." For me, the voices of the Justinas and Elitas and Nana Drecketts, mediated to be sure and sometimes falsified, are still recognizable across the centuries, and still have something to tell us.

Will the real subaltern please speak

It is appropriate to end this chapter with reference to the texts of the few "subaltern" women who have left written records, although it needs to be said that while such texts provide insights unavailable in those of white women, neither Prince's account nor those of the Hart sisters or Mary Seacole provides unproblematic access to the "authentic" voice of black West Indian women of the period. Constrained within the conventions of the slave narrative, "the circumstances governing the textual production of Mary Prince's narrative unquestionably altered her individual voice" (Pouchet Paquet 1992b: 131). The expectations of the Moravian mission, as well as the form of the slave narrative as a vehicle, all shaped the final text. Further, as Ferguson maintains (1992: 283), the editor's

> use of footnotes to "explain," "decipher," and "elaborate" on Mary Prince's autobiographical narration certifies his desire to present and produce her narrative as emancipationist evidence in 1831 of the "civilizing mission" – to "Europeanize" people of African descent "for their own good." Her testimony corroborates (is) his authority and vindicates his values – or superficially seems to do so. Thus Pringle mediates between Mary Prince and the public, refracting her oral narrative according to several considerations.

One consideration is the virtual silence regarding her sexual relationships, whether forced or freely entered into, since such explicit content was frowned on socially especially by religious institutions, and the interests of the Anti-Slavery Society lay in presenting the female slave as a wronged victim not a sexually active woman. Again, Midgely (1998: 89–90) suggests that Susannah Strickland, the secretary of the Anti-Slavery Society who transcribed Prince's story, may have omitted or downplayed instances of Mary's rebellion against and retaliations for abuse. Editor Pringle is certainly a thorough censor, and in his lengthy summary he examines and weighs Prince's own self-representation alongside representations of her by other (almost entirely white male) testimonials, including his own. At times it seems that the authority which gives credence to Prince's account is finally to be granted only by these arbiters.[13] In the text as a whole, then, there are *several* Mary Princes: constructed by Strickland; by Pringle; by the Woods; by other "character witnesses"; by the abolitionist lobby; and by her own self-censored construct. Observing correspondences between the slave narrative and the picaresque tale, Cesareo (2001) calls attention to similar survival strategies of dissembling, masking and role-playing, which Prince also uses in her narrative. Layer after layer separates the reader form the "real" Mary Prince.

Despite his insistence on the accuracy of the narrative, Pringle is ultimately forced to leave judgement to the reader: the "facts there stated must necessarily rest entirely, – since we have no collateral evidence, – upon their intrinsic claims to probability, and upon the reliance the reader may feel disposed, after perusing the foregoing pages, to place on her veracity" (Prince 1987: 233). And for many readers, the controlled emotion and the power of Prince's testimony *do* prevail over concerns about veracity, omissions and editorial interference. While acknowledging the forces which shape and control her voice, Ferguson (1992: 283) considers that "Mary Prince does not . . . readily surrender her narrative to editorial rule," in that the narrative insists on constructing her as an agent who *resists* the degradation she endures. Her economic efforts at self-determination (she works "on the side" wherever possible to earn money for her manumission), her physical acts of resistance (she runs away, answers back, refuses certain conditions, and even fights off the drunken Mr D—), her articulation of her life story and her insistence on her right to liberty, effectively refashion the conventional abolitionist stereotype of the slave woman as passive subject. As Pouchet Paquet puts it (1992b: 138), in Prince's account "[t]he victim of the slave auction . . . recasts herself as witness, judge, and evaluator" of the entire system of plantation slavery. Indeed, she contradicts the "master narrative" of colonial authority by resource to the evidence of silenced slaves:

> I have been a slave myself—and I know what slaves feel—I can tell by myself what other slaves feel, and by what they have told me. The man that says slaves be quite happy in slavery—that they don't want to be free—that man is either ignorant or a lying person. I never heard a slave say so. I never heard a Buckra man say so, till I heard tell of it in England. Such people ought to be ashamed of themselves.
>
> (Prince 1987: 214)

It is important, I think, to attend to traces of an oral Creole account in the scribal text, as when Prince interrupts her tale with "emotive and evocative apostrophes, philosophical reflections, and moral lessons," (Pouchet Paquet, 1992b: 137). She boasts how she verbally opposes her owners on several occasions (Prince 1987: 203, 208, 209) and significantly, when she chooses freedom in England, she insists with dignity on having the last word at their expense (212). West Indian readers familiar with the socio-linguistic ritual of "tracing"[14] or "throwing word," will pick up cues in the narrative and recognize the performative aspects of her behavior as she seizes the opportunity to publicly denounce her unjust employers. Listening with an educated ear, one can read into this episode the physical gestures which accompany the ritualized humiliation of her tormentors: the turning on her heel to address the household, the apparently spontaneous but carefully timed peremptory instruction to put down her trunk while she speaks, the arms akimbo in a gesture of aggression even as her words bespeak the wounded victim, and so on. Encoded in her narrative, in the master's book, are cues to what she is saying: within a genre that constructs her as passive, she incorporates examples of her agency in the kind of doublespeak that served as a crucial survival strategy for slaves. Helen Thomas (1999: 5–6) notes of slave and ex-slave narratives, that for those who survived the middle passage and for their descendants, "their subjectivities and citizenships had become problematized and, in many respects, negated"; none the less

> despite this oceanic unmaking, the work of Wheatley et al. appears to unsettle Gayatri Spivak's claim that there was 'no space from where the subaltern (sexed) subject' could speak or that the 'subaltern as female' was a figure who remained unread or unheard . . . Wheatley's position as a female slave in the households of eighteenth-century Britain and its New England colony, was not too dissimilar to that of the 'doubly-oppressed native woman.' As the publication of her poetical works demonstrates, Wheatley is not the 'historically-muted subject' defined by Spivak's thesis; neither is Equiano or Sancho or Gronniosaw [nor, indeed, Mary Prince].

At the same time, Pouchet Paquet explains that the writings of the Harts, Prince and Seacole are all "circumscribed by generic function and circumstances of publication" and far from homogeneous (1994: 279). There is *always* a certain ambivalence in the self-construction of non-white women within colonial discourse, as Spivak's argument makes clear. Let us look briefly at the example of the Harts' narratives. As part of the religious and cultural intelligentsia in Antigua, these women achieved a certain measure of protection from whites by virtue of their status, education and marriage to white men of influence, but as coloreds and Methodists were never part of the status quo and thus were trusted by the non-white community whose betterment they sought. They openly challenged racial inequality, the supposed superiority of the plantocracy and, to some extent, patriarchy. As mission statements by respectable colored women, the Harts' narratives are counter-hegemonic in insisting on the equality of all races under God, and the legal and social rights of blacks to freedom. And they stand out among the other early narratives in their insistence on the need for female education, not merely for economic self-sufficiency but to a level of social mobility and respectability which the sisters themselves enjoyed.

However, their insistence on racial equality does not involve an interrogation of *social* stratification. Ferguson observes that "Elizabeth Hart Thwaites's ambivalence – her conflictual attitudes concerning the equality of all African Caribbeans, the pre-eminence of the free colored population, and white prejudice— infuses the text" (1993: 41). And Pouchet Paquet notes that Anne Hart Gilbert's "stalwart Methodism is not without its downside," for her text suggests that "even if the African convert was the equal of the European in the new religious order, ancestral Africa and African-derived customs were rejected as signs of ungodliness, ignorance, superstition and sin" (1994: 283). So the Hart sisters do not speak so much *as* subalterns, but *for* them: the experiences of black women and slaves are included and indeed championed in their histories, but the Harts' privileged status, and their belief that educated coloreds such as themselves are "better informed" and thus more fitted to lead, makes for a distinction between them and their flock.

My point is that the Hart sisters' accounts – like *all* the narratives discussed in this study – are constrained by the contexts of their class, their involvement in a specifically gendered role within the evangelical movement and the conventions of their narrative genres. Empowered as women who could actively teach and preach their revolutionary ideas, they had also to maintain religious humility and docility as respectable wives. Fighting for the rights of enslaved black and colored Antiguans, they allied themselves with a powerful metropolitan institutional base, and took for granted that it was people like themselves who were most fitted to guide and train that group. Writing their lives as individual agents, they stay within the guidelines of the conversion narrative and excise all that is not strictly relevant to the Methodist cause.

I want to end this chapter, and its project of reading for buried voices or non-stereotypical representations of black West Indian women and *their* constructions of the West Indies, with the elusive Mrs Seacole. For the narrative persona created in this work is itself a fascinatingly hybrid and ambivalent, multilayered text, incorporating tensions and even contradictions: one minute a strong-willed feminist, the next coyly feminine; a proud West Indian creole who unashamedly calls England "home"; outspoken about her racial pride yet ready to use racial stereotypes for "inferior" blacks; endorsing empire yet subtly critiquing English manners and mean spiritedness.

The issue of *direct*, rather than contextual, mediation is less important in Seacole's autobiographical narrative, for her voice is unmistakably her own. Craig (1984) notes its particular stylistic qualities: direct address to the reader whom she flatters and flirts with; endearing self-mockery; vivid thumbnail sketches; a dual role as recorder and reflective commentator; the tendency to switch to present tense to suggest heightened excitement; and a good ear for accents and idiosyncratic speech habits in dialogue. To this we might add her clever use of irony and pathos, eloquence in times of emotion or horror, and the amazing energy of the narrative which bustles along at a pace reflective of its author. Despite the conventional apologia – "I am fully aware that I have jumbled up events strangely" – Seacole knows what she is doing, and insists on the validity of her narrative choice: "unless I am allowed to tell the story of my life in my own way, I cannot tell it at all" (Seacole 1984: 185). The account has its own distinctive style, but this is not to say it is a critically unproblematic textual representation of "the black woman's voice." In fact, her narrative is less a comprehensive autobiography than what the title proclaims (an account of wonderful adventures) and more: the deliberate construction of the public Mrs Seacole.

Unlike Prince's, Seacole's narrative is not part of the anti-slavery tradition. Slavery is only mentioned in the section set in Central America (1984: 67), where she lashes out at Americans:

I have a few shades of deeper brown upon my skin which shows me related—and I am proud of the relationship—to those poor mortals whom you once held enslaved, and whose bodies America still owns. And having this bond, and knowing what slavery is; having seen with my eyes and heard with my ears proof positive enough of its horrors—let others affect to doubt them if they will—is it surprising that I should be somewhat impatient of the airs of superiority which many Americans have endeavoured to assume over me?

But while Seacole affirms pride in her race and admires the free blacks in New Grenada, she distinguishes herself – as the Harts do, in effect – from working-class blacks such as the "excited nigger cooks" of Cruces (73) or her servant Francis, one of "the good-for-nothing black cooks" (180) who is depicted somewhat stereotypically, with "his eyes rolling angrily, and his white teeth gleaming" (158).

Neither does Seacole's narrative concern itself with constructions of the West Indies. A brief sketch of her parentage, childhood and young womanhood in Jamaica takes up the first one and a half chapters and then, apart from an eight-month sojourn in the island in 1853, the entire narrative is set abroad. Pouchet Paquet (1992a: 656) concludes that while Seacole places herself as Jamaican, this "does not suggest belonging in the sense of nation, home, or community"; the center is "not located in a Jamaican social reality, but 'at home' in post-Crimean England. Seacole's roots may be in Jamaica, but her narrative is rooted in England." In this, she is hardly singular: while proud of their origins, neither the Harts nor Prince trumpet their specifically Antiguan or Bermudan identities. Like many of the early white creole writers, and indeed many West Indian writers today, the location of "home" for the products of colonialism and migration is always complex. As deCaires Narain observes (2002: 46), well into the early twentieth century "the ambivalence with regard to [self-] location inside and outside the region" is one which marks white and black West Indian writers, problematizing the categories of "native" and "outsider." At times, Seacole longs for "my pleasant home in Kingston" (1984: 73) and avers that "our West Indian dishes" are a match for those of Europe's finest chef (187). On the other hand, the final section of Seacole's last chapter, titled "Home," refers unambiguously to England. In common with other colonial writers, she disingenuously elides the contradiction in claiming both: for her, to be Jamaican was also to be British. As Whitlock puts it (2000: 83), "what we might now represent as a 'national' or 'regional' identity is spelt out through a version of imperial supremacy."

None of the other early travel writers discussed come close to Seacole in transgressing "proper" female behavior and appropriating a predominantly male vehicle for self-promotion, even to heroic status. In this alone, her narrative exploits – as I argue in Chapter 3 – are radically feminist. Indeed, as a woman who appropriates the expansionist colonial spirit as part of her own cultural inheritance, and stakes her claim in both the New World *and* in Europe, she is outstandingly so. Seacole travels as "an unprotected female" by *choice* – she is clear on this – through all kinds of hazardous situations: she opens and runs businesses at home and in frontier territory; she manages servants, sometimes with the aid of a horsewhip (196); she attends to cholera and yellow fever cases at home and abroad, even performing a covert autopsy to find out more about the disease; she braves cannon fire and musket shot to tend the wounded on the battlefields of the Crimea.

At the same time, Seacole stresses her gentle heart and feminine nurturing qualities quite as much as her aggressively adventurous nature and cold-eyed business sense. Pouchet Paquet highlights this ambivalence, observing "discernable contradictions in Mrs. Seacole's narrative and her commitment to 'English values' "; on the one hand, she defines herself in action as the equal of any man, and on the other "embraces conventions of Victorian womanhood when writing about herself" (1992a: 654). Seacole is insistent on her motherly qualities and the soothing nature of women's hands which "are moulded for this work" of healing (1984: 146). Her dress sense is emphasized (66), her decorum under trying conditions insisted upon, and her self-sacrificial virtues in the service of men frequently paraded: "I love to be of service to those who need a woman's help" (78). Indeed, she emphasizes that her economic interests "are not allowed to interfere in any way with the main object of my journey," which is to minister to her sick or wounded "sons" (128).[15]

Seacole's text produces a complex and often contradictory figure, to whom critical response has been divided. Pouchet Paquet (1992b: 659), for example, finds Seacole's "colonial psychology" poles apart from the (critically privileged) "peasant consciousness" of Mary Prince. Alexander and Dewjee, editors of the 1984 edition of *Wonderful Adventures*, reluctantly acknowledge Seacole's "snobbery and coyness," her disparaging of other ethnic groups and her "contradictory feelings about her status as a black woman" as "unacceptable today" (9). "Seacole's representation of self as model of Victorian womanhood and [her] erasure of race issues" have, as Hippolyte points out (1996: 3), been simplistically equated with "alliance and cooperation with British imperial and racial ideology." For Hippolyte, Seacole's contradictions, repressions and silences are designed to circumvent charges of unfeminine conduct, and avoid confirming constructed images of the black woman as "Other," in order to shape a textual persona that is both proud of her difference *and* acceptable to the white British audience at whom her book is targeted. As Whitlock notes (2000: 90), Seacole is quite the tactician in finding room to manoeuver within her quest for British patronage.

Writing her text, observes Gikandi (1996: 127), is a means of affiliation with Englishness and in her account she stresses her *British* genealogical and cultural connections, leaving the rest vague. Gikandi claims that Seacole exemplifies the "ways in which the colonized subject fashioned itself by questioning and appropriating the civilizational authority of Englishness"; hers is *not* a discourse of resistance *nor* "a narrative of self-vindication in the field of empire," but *both* (xiv). How then, he asks (122), are we to read the texts of such women, "who seem to write their narratives – and their identities – in the service of empire even when they exist at its margins"? Basically, he argues that such an ambivalent location within colonial representation sets up a "complicity/resistance" dialectic, which is evident in Seacole's living "in and out of Englishness, attracted by its culture and civilizational authority but haunted by its exclusive racialism" (126). Her solution is to place herself firmly within a mid-Victorian *ideal* of Englishness by valorizing its codes – self-help, bravery, hard work, moral restraint, public duty – qualities which, her text makes clear, she herself embodies. Further, her adventures – struggling in Central America and the Crimea against the forces of barbarism and savagery – align her with European civilization (133); hence her stress on the contrast between her prim dress and maternal air, and the alien wilderness against which she must prove herself. For Gikandi, Seacole's writing bravely claims a place for this brown woman in the drama of imperial culture (142).

What Seacole is doing in her text constitutes an "unfixing" of self from stereo-typical pre-scriptions, and this is nowhere more evident than in her refusal of the "lazy Creole" label. Craig's review of *Wonderful Adventures* begins with a survey of early textual representations of the denigrated figure of the seductive, indolent, ignorant and self-satisfied mulatto woman. One variation on this figure is even more relevant to Seacole's text. In Jenkin's *Cousin Stella*, the heroine arrives in Jamaica and is taken to the lodging house of a "tall, fat, brown woman, dressed in a loose, short, white bedgown and a white petticoat" (1859, vol. 2: 30). Miss Hawkes, with "a high-pitched drawling voice" orders her maids around from her chair, and has only harsh words for "dem 'bominable lazy blacks" from whom she distinguishes herself by virtue of the fact that "I hab jist fust-rate English blood in my veins" (vol. 2: 39). A similar caricature of a colored proprietor occurs in *Constance Mordaunt* in the person of Miss Freeman, described as "a pretty fair specimen of the indolence and impudence of her class" (E.J.W. 1862, vol. 2: 156). And in the opinion of local and expatriate whites,

> A lodging even in Europe is a comfortless place for a man of domestic habits, and what must it be in the West? They are always kept by women of colour, and these are so afraid of being mistaken for slaves, that they will do nothing themselves. I never pass Miss Freeman's that I do not see her slipshod, seated in an open gallery, balancing herself backwards and forwards on a chair, screaming out her orders in the tone of a macaw in a shower of rain.
>
> (ibid.)

Given that Seacole followed in her mother's footsteps in running just such a boarding house, it is imperative that she refute such stereotypes in *her* self-construction as an energetic, sophisticated, groomed and cultivated career woman with a motherly concern for the sons of empire. As Gikandi notes (1996: 136), the emphasis on femininity also counters "the masculinized image of black women which dominates traditional imperial discourse."

Reading Seacole's text within certain models of colonial discourse analysis proves difficult. On which side of the manichean opposition would JanMohamed place her? Clearly not a subaltern, is she then a "colonising subject"? If she can only speak through the text of the dominant discourse, does she not also turn the tables in self-consciously reflecting a pleasing "Englishness" back to the English, who pay for the privilege? Her text provides ample evidence for counter-discursive resistance via "native" culture, but would Parry approve of her syco-phantic attitude to the colonial center? Indeed, as Gikandi claims (1996: 121), "students of colonial discourse and postcolonial theory do not know what to do with the women of empire – whether these women are European or native."

In the end, response to Seacole's narrative persona is subjective. Pringle admit-ted Mary Prince's "considerable share of natural pride and self-importance" (Prince 1987: 230), and Mary Seacole too "always conveys a positive self-image. She likes and approves of herself and engages the reader" (Craig 1984: 44), while refusing anyone's condescension. Within the contexts of their time, and despite the mediation of their narratives by direct editorial or other restrictions of genre and convention, the three autobiographical voices discussed above are anything but "subaltern" in their articulation of consciousness. Their texts demonstrate aspects of regional society and culture and provide access to female voices in ways unavailable to the white writers. Arguing the case for attending to such accounts, Beckles (1998b: 154) admits the important factors of contextual, generic and indeed, editorial mediation. At the same time, he insists that we should try "to 'feel' the texture, and hear the tone, of their indirect or engineered voices."

The disparate early narratives I have been surveying, loosely grouped here under the category of colonial discourse, illustrate the complexities of mediation and the dangers of a transparent model of the literary text. Further, rigid adher-ence to the problematic concept of "the subaltern's voice" and overly restrictive binary constructions of female "colonising subjects"/ "subalterns," would seem to limit the more heterogeneous and exploratory reading strategies outlined in this study. It is the utility of existing categorization that I have queried throughout, suggesting finally that it is less profitable to talk about subaltern voices in terms of who *speaks*, than who *hears* and why.

Afterword

The diaspora experience as I intend it here is defined, not by essence or purity, but by the recognition of a necessary heterogeneity and diversity; by a conception of "identity" which lives with and through, not despite, difference; by *hybridity*.

(Stuart Hall 1993: 401–2)

Reading through this sample of women's writing from the West Indies of the nineteenth and early twentieth century reinforces, for me, the *centrality* of what Hall (above) refers to as "the diaspora experience" to the history of the region, and indeed to all kinds of records of this history, including the literary. The narratives of Fraser, Cassin, Lynch and Nugent, as much as those by Seacole and Mary Prince, have their matrix in the *transcultural* engagements of women. However, if there is any general conclusion about the various accounts of these engagements, it is simply that no one narrative version adequately conveys the complexity – the heterogeneity, diversity and hybridity – of what the West Indies meant for those who wrote and read it.

Who now reads these accounts? Certainly some texts have served as resources for "facts and figures," providing useful data to support arguments in studies of the colonial period: a linguistic analysis of features of nineteenth-century Creole languages, perhaps, or a historical comparison of reproductive statistics pre- and post-slavery. But not many readers approach these early works as *narratives*, as stories, as constructed productions; not many read them with an awareness that no matter how located they are within the context of their time, they do not constitute transparent mirrors on a the past. Part of what I have tried to do in this survey is to suggest that the way we read such narratives has much to do with how we choose to shape and reshape our history. I also image this book as a kind of necessary ground clearing exercise, with all of the tedious and mundane remit involved, as well as the rather patchy terrain that results. The landscape gardeners will come after; indeed, while I have mostly resisted the temptation to detour into close readings of particular texts or focused discussion on specific issues within a group of narratives, I know of several enthusiastic readers even now engaged in mapping the territory in new and exciting ways. For those new to the field let me conclude by briefly summarizing what my digging uncovered, and why I consider these narratives worth reading. Finally, to belabor the gardening metaphor, I want to outline one or two possible plots that might yield fruit: some aspects of the texts which I found intriguing and which bear further investigation

My initial focus is on the figure of the white woman in West Indian plantation society, a subject until recently paid scant attention by Caribbean history in its colonial and postcolonial manifestations. These mostly privileged women, the authors and subjects of a diverse collection of epistolary, documentary, auto-biographical, fictional and travel narratives, resist – like their texts – easy summary. Constructions of the ministering angel, the white witch, the self-sacrificing plantation wife/worker, the degenerate creole, are circulated in one text only to be contradicted in others, or even within the same account. Representations and self-representations are further complicated in texts which differentiate between *kinds* of white women, such as creoles and British, residents and tourists, elites and indentured servants. In the second chapter I discuss works which focus on the domestic sphere, and in particular those which deal with relationships between black, colored and white women. Despite the racially stratified nature of plantation society, the world of the household was an intimate one and the texts admit of a surprising level of interdependence between these groups. This suggests to me that however neatly maintained in theory, women's power relations on an everyday level were anything but stable, and that hierarchies and boundaries were constantly being negotiated and transgressed.

The next three chapters turn to representations of the West Indies and narrative/ideological positioning in relation to this construct. I survey examples of women's travel writing – another problematic generic category for female practitioners – for ways in which possession of the tropical landscape is narrativized around the polarized tropes of paradise/hell. The region itself is evoked in terms of a contradictory amalgam of myths and facts, fantasy projections and "scientific" data, and is filtered through a bewildering array of preconceived constructs. The trope of El Dorado is one such projection, which I interpret in terms of women's efforts to achieve fulfillment via adventure or security (but always some kind of independence outside of Europe), ultimately domesticating the frontier and achieving a "home" of their own. Chapter 5 extrapolates from textual representations of the West Indies as a place of disease and degeneration to suggest pervasive reservations amongst writers about the legitimacy of the colonial project. I posit that despite the powerful circulation of imperialist ideology, colonial discourse in these literary manifestations emerges as fractured in that while the rhetoric of discovery postulates a "virgin territory" to be conquered, the female-authored accounts reveal a moral and spiritual void at the core of the colonial project in the West Indies. Accordingly, I read these inscriptions – and the homogenized "colonising subject" who writes/enacts the processes of colonial discourse – as ambivalent and contradictory. The contested place of white creole women authors within such discourse further complicates easy conclusions about the society they depict.

My final chapter investigates aspects of several theoretical models as tools for reading these accounts. The chapter analyzes the specular gaze in texts by white women, and the extent to which such texts can or do invest black women with subjectivity. I also consider the mediation of "native" women's voices in the narratives, as well as issues involved in "speaking for" these Others within the constraints of genre, gender and the socio-historical conventions of the period. The role of non-white women as interpreters and translators of the local is considered, as well as the extent to which their input destabilizes the "truth value" of colonial discourse and offers another, complementary knowledge. I end with the few historical "subaltern" women who *did* leave written records, discovering that these too are as circumscribed by gender expectations, generic function and the publication process as those of the white writers. None the less, albeit in sometimes conflicted ways, they do serve as sites of resistance, "answering back" to representations of patriarchal and colonialist discourse, and articulating perspectives unavailable to white women.

Ultimately, I argue that these narratives are worth reading precisely *for*, not despite, their heterogeneity, and because they enable "a different sense of our relationship to the past, and thus a different way of thinking about cultural identity" (Stuart Hall 1993: 402). While Hall's concept of diaspora experience as central to any conceptualization of West Indian identity is indisputable, the significance of the colonial encounter requires *ongoing* reassessment. Of course this reassessment is hedged about with difficulties, not least being the view in some Caribbean circles that only *some* relationships to the past are valid, only *some* versions of historical reconstruction are "usable." I reiterate here the crucial value of attending to *all* voices and versions, in an effort to revisit restrictive notions of identity and push back the boundaries of what constitutes West Indian literary history. For Pouchet Paquet (1999: 21–2), reading early texts by white creole women demonstrates, among other things,

> the difficulty of maintaining exclusivist paradigms in respect to identity for-
> mation in the Caribbean, even within the narrow confines of a common
> colonial settler/creole experience within a specific discursive form. Their
> narratives confirm that nothing is fixed or monolithic in a multiply centered
> diaspora network like the Caribbean . . . To use their race/color as the cul-
> tural/political sign of inferiority or degeneracy is to devalue their contribu-
> tion on the basis of race and perpetuate their legacy of skin color as a "visible
> and natural" object of discrimination.

This seems to me even more important when we consider that current networks of Caribbean community are even *more* complex, and new permutations of national and regional identity are still evolving. The resultant multiplicity of cultural affiliations, hybrid identities and cultural forms, has fostered a critical climate in which it is now possible to review the early literary record without adhering to rigid boundaries of "relevance" and "authenticity." For example, as deCaires Narain points out (2002: 220), competing definitions of what constitutes "the" Caribbean woman writer are still being aired, complicated now by issues of residence: that is, critical disagreement over the importance of locatedness *within* the region, as opposed to broader, more diasporic identities (221). In discussing women's writing from the West Indies, now as then, Pouchet Paquet's assertion that "nothing is fixed or monolithic in a multiply centered diaspora network like the Caribbean" is as relevant as ever, and the maintenance of "exclusivist paradigms" of West Indian identity is less than helpful for situating writers or narratives. In effect then, this study foregrounds the heterogeneity, ambivalence and instability of early textual constructions of women in the West Indies and representations of the West Indies by women. I suggest that the narratives loosely grouped in this study contribute to the range of literary representations of the region, highlight the importance of considering a gendered perspective and context, broaden our understanding of the different myths and stories, as well as the different voices, that wrote the West Indies, and *why* they were important to writers and readers of the period. Theoretically, too, I have emphasized the value of paradigms which address the significance of difference, plurality and syncretism – processes crucial to the development of a creole culture – in an effort to qualify totalizing accounts of history, as well as our understanding of those who made and wrote it.

While I maintain that the early writings do have a place in a West Indian literary tradition, this is not to argue for any filiative connection. With few exceptions, the early authors can hardly be termed literary foremothers to current West Indian women writers. Yet it is also true that many writers now are partially motivated by the task of deconstructing *precisely* those representations circulated by the earlier works.[1] Thus, some of the texts I discuss might be seen as precursors to what postcolonial theory calls "writing back to the canon": Seacole rewrites negative stereotypes of colored creole women in her own positive self-construction, just as Rhys restores the white creole marginalized in *Jane Eyre* to centrality in *Wide Sargasso Sea*. I want to conclude by pointing to an avenue of further investigation suggested by this intertextuality: possible parallels and/or continuities between the texts surveyed and more recent writing by regional women.

Certainly there are borrowings between the early narratives. In Chapter 2, for example, I mention James echoing Nugent's *Journal*. Though unacknowledged, Nugent is also a source for Gaunt's fiction: the creole Marse Septimus in *Harmony* is said to have "drunk like a cormorant" (1933: 89–90), recalling Nugent's disparaging description of Jamaican planters who "eat like porpoises and drink like cormorants" (1966: 81). Again, Campbell notes parallels in the twentieth-century Dominican novels of Napier and Rhys, although according to her (1982: 92), Napier wrote to Alec Waugh in 1939 asking "who is Jean Rhys? I must try and read her . . . None of us have ever heard of her." Rhys left Dominica around 1907, while Napier only arrived in the 1930s. Yet Campbell notes echoes of images central to *Wide Sargasso Sea* (first published in 1966) in Napier's earlier *A Flying Fish Whispered*, including a woman's red dress on fire (1938: 114), the mirroring of the white woman in the black (118), the reclamation by the forest of a house associated with white privilege (124) and the depiction of a wild tropical landscape beloved of the white creole female protagonist but distrusted by her British lover who prefers "a tamed and ordered Nature" (43).

But there are also reverberations of earlier writing in more recent work by Caribbean women. Abruna (1991) discusses resemblances between Rhys and Kincaid; similarly, Allfrey's depiction of a white creole woman who deliberately situates herself within the struggle for black political liberation in *The Orchid House* (first published 1953), is a theme central to Michele Cliff's *No Telephone to Heaven* (1987). More generally, narratives by white creole women like Lynch, Bridges, Napier, Bliss, Rhys and Allfrey share thematic continuities. Specifically, they all detail the deep attachment of the creole woman for her tropical landscape, which exercises a powerful influence. Compare for instance Rhys's Antoinette – and Rhys herself prostrate and kissing the earth in *Smile Please* (1979) – with the white creole protagonist's craving the Dominican landscape in Napier's *Duet in Discord* (1936: 8–9) with a "love that has something almost physical about it, so that in moments of pain I have quite literally lain down full length and drawn solace from the ground." Or indeed, consider the portrait in Bliss's *Saraband* (first published in 1931) of the "lonely, unhappy, frightened" Louie, who avoids the adult world and takes solace from the tropical earth that she too physically embraces (1986: 35). Other recurring issues in the texts of creoles are the gaps between various cultural groups that must be delicately negotiated; the problematic pull between mother country and island home; and the intimate yet fraught relationship of black and white women in the domestic realm.

In terms of genre too, the travel account, appropriated and adapted by early writers like Gaunt, James, Atherton, Crommelin and Seacole to reflect in part their "feminine" concerns, is further reworked by current authors like Kincaid and Joan Riley, whose fictions detail gendered voyages of discovery. Dealing now with the journey from periphery *to* center, their narratives expand on Cassin's and Seacole's nineteenth-century exploration of the complexity of the migration experience for the colonial-born woman. Further, the "unhomeliness" of white creole women in the West Indies mentioned in Chapter 4, resonates with a different twist in modern "diaspora" writing, where migration and remigration are configured as reinterpretations of the myth of the uncharted New World (Kincaid's *Lucy*) or via a pervasive sense of unbelonging in metropolitan center as well as in the now-distant West Indian homeland (Leone Ross's *All the Blood is Red*).

Obviously, the Caribbean focus makes for textual commonalities: certain images in the earlier works crop up in recent West Indian women's writing,[2] as do race and class inflections in portrayals of women.[3] Again, one notes the continuity of oscillating depictions of West Indian landscape as both a paradise, particularly in rural districts, and a nightmare of poverty and oppressive social forces inherited from a history of slavery and colonialism.[4] The ambivalent conception of "home" by the creole writer who must engage with her landscape in terms of its already-scripted identity as a "tourist paradise" of projected desires, is a subtext in the writing of Symmonett and Lynch, prefiguring a similar problematic in Rhys's West Indian novels as well as Kincaid's *Lucy* and *A Small Place*.

For me, this survey of early constructions of the West Indies and its people offers mixed blessings, not least because of the variable quality, diverse narrative forms and perspectives, but also because of subject matter. The narratives *do* tell ugly stories, stories of exploitation, violence, racism and corruption; and yet it is possible to find representations of selfless generosity and courageous, even heroic endurance and resistance. They include loving testaments to the natural beauty of the tropical paradise, as well as almost wilful blindness to the impoverished lives of most of the people who live there. They incorporate querulous pleas on the part of the elite for the maintenance of privilege, yet inadvertently expose this privilege as inherently unjust and ultimately untenable. They demonstrate intermittent glimpses of human connection in an inhumane social order, and a subtle, even unconscious, interrogation of the system in which the very production of their texts is implicated. They articulate condescension towards a stereotyped Other at the same time as evincing recognition of dependence *on* that Other, and take for granted the "naturalness" of privilege which the questionable nature of their authority as women actually belies.

They evidence alternative Caribbean systems of knowledge resisting textual containment, and inscribe normative race/class/nationality hierarchies which come undone in the very exempla cited as illustration. They demonstrate elevated "literary" language foundering under the weight of responses to the contradictory, disturbing allure of the West Indies. They anxiously display a "feminine" sensibility whilst appropriating "masculine" subjects and forms. They complicate simplistic assumptions of who speaks for whom and in what language, within an evolving creole continuum, and demonstrate the fluidity of identity formation in a creolized social order. They attempt to transform a lived tropical home, via an imposed map of pre-scriptions, into a commodity for sale to the metropolitan home readership and, in so doing, inadvertently reveal the fraught nature of such a project. In summary, then, the texts serve to demonstrate within the specifics of the Caribbean colonial situation, the irreducibly *multiple* constructions of the West Indies, of women's placing in colonial discourse, and of received notions of West Indian literature and identity. These often contradictory impulses, I would maintain, can still be observed informing women's writing of the region today.

Notes

Introduction

1 By West Indian, I mean the Anglophone Caribbean territories. While acknowledging the extensive field of other Caribbean literatures by women, my own linguistic limitations impose the Anglophone focus.
2 See Moira Ferguson's 1993 edition, *The Hart Sisters: Early African Caribbean Writers, Evangelicals, and Radicals*. Anne Hart Gilbert (1773–1834) and Elizabeth Hart Thwaites (1772–1833) were educated colored women born into a network of small but powerful and propertied mixed-race families in Antigua. Their father had himself been a slave owner, albeit a humane one, but the women, who converted to Methodism in 1786, were staunch opponents of slavery. Methodism, as Ferguson elaborates in her introduction, was firmly established in Antigua by the 1760s and, unlike the Anglican Church to which most whites belonged, aimed at converting blacks and coloreds. Perhaps as a result, it was openly abolitionist, if not uniformly emancipationist. The Hart sisters, particularly Elizabeth, outspokenly promoted emancipation and were among the first educators of slaves and free blacks in Antigua. They were arguably the first non-white women of letters in the West Indies, and championed the provision of education for all women.

Ferguson's edition includes letters, hymns and verse by Elizabeth Hart Thwaites, and Anne Hart Gilbert's co-authored biography of her husband. But the central texts are the sisters' identically titled histories of Methodism in Antigua. Written in the epistolary mode, and at the request of a senior church official, these are brief documents (eighteen pages from Anne and seven from Elizabeth) which Pouchet Paquet categorizes with "nineteenth-century African-American spiritual or conversion narratives" (1994: 283). For her, Anne's *History* is more concerned with the public and historical development of Methodism in the island, and with a denunciation of slavery and the plantocracy. Anne's chronological account insists on the contribution of non-white women to the faith, and indeed mentions specific individuals. By contrast, Elizabeth's narrative is more personal, detailing the circumstances of her birth and parentage and dwelling on the intimate details of her spiritual life, although she too speaks out against slavery and racial inequality.
3 *History of Mary Prince, a West Indian Slave, Related by Herself* (1987; first published 1831). Moira Ferguson maintains that "no African-Caribbean slave women are known to have written before the publication of Mary Prince's narrative in 1831" (1992: 26). However, I have seen a photocopied extract of "Memoirs of the Life of Florence Hall" (catalogued by the Library Company of Philadelphia and the Historical Society of Pennsylvania as "Autobiographical Memoir of the life of this Ibo slave in Jamaica describing her capture and trip to Jamaica *ca* 1820"). Of the four short handwritten pages, only the last few lines deal with arrival in Jamaica, the loss of her "Ebon" name and her bewilderment at "another name – a strange language, & a new master."

Prince's account details in about twenty-eight pages the life of a woman born into slavery in Bermuda around 1788, who was sold away from her family and subsequently worked for four different owners in Bermuda, the Turks Islands and Antigua, before accompanying a family to Britain in 1828. "In London, she walked out of slavery and made contact with the Anti-Slavery Society" (Brereton 1995: 64). Its secretary, Thomas Pringle, eventually employed her in his home where she dictated her story to Susanna Strickland. The story, published in 1831, is bracketed between editor Pringle's preface and an extensive supplement, the latter containing a number of letters, character references and other documents which authenticate Prince's good character against the charges of her last owner. The text is a classic slave narrative following the conventions of the genre, articulating the cruelty suffered at the hands of masters and mistresses, the unending labor, the severing of the bonds of family or marriage, and the denial of control over her woman's body.

4 *The Wonderful Adventures of Mary Seacole in Many Lands* (1984). Mary Jane Seacole née Grant was born in 1805 in Jamaica (then still a slave colony), the mixed-race daughter of a Scottish officer and a free black woman who owned and operated a successful boarding house cum nursing home for British officers. On her mother's death, Seacole operated and expanded the business and formed a lasting attachment to the British military establishment. Following in her mother's footsteps as a "doctress," she was in much demand at home and abroad during outbreaks of yellow fever, cholera and other epidemics. In addition, Seacole engaged in various business enterprises which necessitated much traveling, something she thoroughly enjoyed and indeed came to crave. She married, was widowed soon after and, at the age of 45, traveled to Central America where she initiated and ran several businesses, and later to England to offer her medical services in the Crimean War effort. Official permission proving elusive, she made her own way there in 1854 and set up the British Hotel near Balaclava which combined the amenities of a hotel for officers, a canteen for ordinary ranks, and a dispensary for the medicines she herself administered to the sick and wounded at the front.

When the war ended abruptly, she had to close her operations at a loss and returned impoverished to England. There her reputation as Mother Seacole, minister to the troops, earned her recognition, gratitude and official sponsorship. To capitalize on the military's campaign to help her, Seacole published her *Wonderful Adventures*, an account of her travels and wartime adventures. The book was a success. Honored by the public and supported by friends in the military, even decorated, she lived comfortably at the heart of Empire where she died in 1881.

5 Una Marson (1905–65), daughter of a Baptist minister and his wife, was educated on scholarship at Hampton High School, a boarding school for elite girls, and went on to become one of Jamaica's pioneering journalists, editing the *Jamaica Critic* and, from 1928 to 1931, her own publication, *The Cosmopolitan*, in which "Sojourn" appeared. A poet and playwright, and a champion of women's rights, she traveled to Britain in the 1930s where she became a social activist within the League of Coloured Peoples and, in 1935, took a post at the League of Nations in Geneva where she subsequently acted as secretary to Emperor Haile Selassie in his dealings with the League. In 1941 she was appointed a BBC commentator, coordinating the series "Calling the West Indies" until her return to Jamaica in 1945. Her four collections of poetry were well received and her plays were performed to some acclaim both in Jamaica and in London. For a comprehensive biography, see Jarrett-Macauley (1998).

Because of its brevity, I mention Marson's story only in passing. Like many of the longer fictions I will discuss, "Sojourn" is concerned with racial demarcations and, secondarily, with gender roles in middle-class Jamaican society of the period. A young Englishman comes to the island on business, and learns about its landscape and culture from the colored family with whom he lodges. The daughter of the family, darker than the others, is attracted to him but is inhibited by her knowledge of his prior attachment in Britain and, more importantly, by her sensitivity to English prejudice toward "coloured blood." They become close, but he is called back home by the illness of his mother, and his departure marks the end of the story.

6 Most were educated in the colonies, and by the beginning of the nineteenth century, schools for the free non-white population existed in a number of islands. By 1821, Wolmers School in Jamaica had a majority of free colored students; again, however, this was a boy's school.

7 William Dickson referred in his *Letters on Slavery* (1789: 73) to a "black teacher who is employed by several white families in Bridgetown [and] writes a variety of hands elegantly." It is clear from Dickson's account that this teacher was male.

8 For example, the Barbados Archives contain wills and letters written by several individuals, such as Jane Lane who, in 1813, wrote to her master to request the freedom of her two sons (MS. 523/690). Watson (2000) reproduces correspondence between slave women on the Newton estate in Barbados and their absentee master, and E.B. Underhill's *The West Indies* (1862) refers to Maria Jones in the post-emancipation period, who learned to read and write at the age of 60 in an evening class conducted by a teacher of the Mico Charity in Trinidad.

9 *Report of the Mitchinson Commission on Education* (1857), housed in Barbados Archives. Cited in Sybil Leslie (1984: 1).

10 A rare few – like the James Hill Literary Society in Clarendon, of which Claude McKay was the secretary, and the Readers and Writers Club, founded by Una Marson in 1936 – tried to promote local writing.

11 Engber's *Caribbean Fiction and Poetry* (1970: 5) purports to be a compilation of "fiction and poetry by Caribbean authors published in the United States and Great Britain since 1900." In fact, the list is very partial and contains inaccuracies (Paule Marshall is said to hail from Jamaica) that cast some doubt on the usefulness of the work as a bibliography. Of the entries for the Anglophone Caribbean, under the headings "short stories" and "novels" there are only a few by women writers, all of whom are quite well known. An exception is Mary Lockett's *Christopher* (1902). According to Virginia Blain et al. (1990: 667), Lockett – who contributed to the first *Treasury of Jamaican Poetry* – was "one of Jamaica's first novelists and poets. Very little is known of her." *Christopher* is referred to as her "odd religious-didactic novel" but is, I discovered, only tangentially concerned with the Caribbean, and even then not the Anglophone Caribbean. After Lockett, Engber's list jumps to the 1950s, mentioning the work of Ada Quayle and Esther Chapman (both of Jamaica). Generally speaking, it is a disappointing source for discovering "many unknown women writers."

12 Alison Donnell (1998: 1) also queries the critical disavowal of some early West Indian poetry by women, work ignored or dismissed as "embarrassing and undesirable, often imitative and usually dependant on colonial forms and ideologies."

13 Phyllis Shand Allfrey (1908–86) was born in Dominica, the second daughter of the English Crown Attorney and his wife, of French Caribbean stock. Educated at home, she lived in England during the 1930s and 40s, where she and her husband were actively involved with the Fabian Society and the British Labour Party before returning to Dominica and co-founding the Dominica Labor Party. In 1958, she was elected Minister of Labor and Social Affairs in the West Indies Federation government. After the collapse of the Federation, she and her husband ran the *Dominica Herald* and later the weekly *Star* newspaper until the 1980s. As well as poetry, short stories, a novel and essays, she also wrote an unfinished political novel. For a comprehensive biography, see Paravisini-Gebert (1996).

14 The term is difficult to pin down, so in this study, I use "colonialist discourse" (including literature) to refer to textual productions which endorse and normalize the type of racially inflected and unequal power relations described in JanMohamed's model (1986). "Colonial discourse" (including literature) is used as a blanket term to refer to texts produced during the colonial period and does not necessarily indicate the clearly imperial/racist ideological slant of the former term. This seems to follow

JanMohamed (79) in his polarization of "colonialist" texts (which encode an oppos   itional material conflict between European colonizer and native subject) and texts of "colonial discourse" (as the term is used by Bhabha: that is, the discourse of the dominators and the dominated). Where JanMohamed uses "colonialist" he deliberately suggests a critical reading that focuses on its ideological function; where "colonial" is used, the critical interpretation seems less ideologically loaded and turns rather on the textual representation of the colonial contact. However, it should be noted that the distinction is not always clear given that JanMohamed occasionally uses the two terms interchangeably, and with variable use of inverted commas.

15 See also Ashcroft *et al.* (1989: 5).

16 See Brathwaite (1969: 270).

17 Peter Hulme (1994) attempts such a revision by opening up the very category of "West Indian" in his reassessment of the place of Rhys's *Wide Sargasso Sea*. Surveying nearly forty years of critical work on the novel, Hulme includes and comments on the problems inherent in Brathwaite's position.

18 Responding to Hulme, Brathwaite (1995) claims that the former has made "an utter travesty of what I say in CO ['Contradictory Omens,' 1974] & what I represent"; the travesty has been repeated by many other postcolonial critics "& I guess that I'll always be attacked on this by those who don't want a blk [black] norm for the Caribb[ean]" (70). Brathwaite goes on to reiterate and expand on some of his earlier comments on the racial derivation of authors and critics, but he also acknowledges the political context of the period in which they were made, "since in the 60s we were so race-consciously fragmented, some of us at least fought over the importance/value/ significance" of *Wide Sargasso Sea*.' He locates his 1974 monograph as "part of those uncivil wars w/in Caribb culture" (75).

19 This seems tacitly taken for granted, for instance, in Nasta's edited collection of essays, *Motherlands* (1991), which includes white writers under the subhead "Black Women's Writing from Africa, the Caribbean and South Asia."

20 The year-by-year bibliography in Ramchand's *The West Indian Novel and its Background* (1972: 282–6), lists Durie as the only woman writer up to 1939, and no others are cited until Allfrey in 1953.

21 Although more women began to publish fiction in the late 1940s in regional "little magazines" like *Bim*, gender imbalances in literary production remained. See also deCaires Narain (1995: 25) on the low profile of gender issues within this emergent nationalist literature.

22 I have argued elsewhere (1993a: 6) that these are also features of contemporary West Indian writing by women.

23 See Kirsten Holst Peterson and Anna Rutherford (1986).

24 Mary Anne Stewart (1830/2–1911) was born in Spanish Town, and sent to England at a young age to be schooled. She married George Barker, an officer knighted for military service in India, and went with him to Bengal. On his death, she returned to England and married Frederick Napier Broome. They lived in New Zealand, running a sheep farm for some years. She also continued to travel, including to the West Indies, and to write about her experiences of these places.

25 The first women's national anti-slavery society – known as the Birmingham Ladies' Society for the Relief of Negro Slaves – was instituted at the home of Lucy Townsend, wife of an Anglican minister, on April 8, 1825.

26 Lynch's novel *Years Ago* (1865) explores this important subtext, and merits a brief digression here because the novel is as much concerned with writing as it is with the ostensible romance plot. Claimed by the author to be a "real" diary, found years after its composition, the narrator is a young white Jamaican of the plantocracy, encouraged by her father to keep a journal. She has long wanted to write a book of her own, but has been kept busy copying out her Papa's manuscript. The choice of narrative vehicle, as the opening pages emphasize, is imposed by the patriarch and Doss worries that her

inclusion of "trivia" may undermine his expectations of the enterprise (9). But very soon, *his* expectations are subsumed by her own shaping narrative and the "trivial" domestic drama she records is acknowledged as being very much like "a scene in a novel" (89). As she imposes her own form on the material, Doss refers to her text as "half novel, . . . half history – a kind of attempt at writing a book" (107). From transcribing the words of the father, to accepting his choice of medium for her own text, the girl finds her own preferred genre and subject matter, and produces the book *she* wants to write. Writing is explicitly linked with *power* to change the world (209). However, as Doss enters womanhood, self-censorship becomes evident: what, she wonders, would pious Aunt Ellie think if she were to look into the book (161); or indeed Papa (107), or Mama (139)? A shaping adult/masculine imperative once more regains control of the text as Doss, engaged and subsequently married to Hugh, records with increasing frequency not her own interpretations and impressions, but what her husband says, does, and tells her is the case. Once more, her authorship is clearly directed at fulfilling male approval.

27 I am grateful to Stephen Slemon for suggesting this idea, and recommending readings.

28 In Caryl Phillips's novel *Cambridge* (1991), set on a West Indian plantation in the slavery period, the narrator Emily, an English spinster, conceives of this "space outside" as a fantasy of escape from the confinements of home and an arranged marriage: as she is about to leave England for her father's estate in the unnamed island, she acknowledges that "she was fleeing the lonely regime which fastened her into backboards, corsets and stays to improve her posture. The same friendless regime which advertised her as an ambassadress of grace. Almost thirty. Too old to be secretly stifling her misery into lace handkerchiefs. The ship was ready to sail" (4).

29 Haggis (1998: 51) notes the substantial increase during the last three decades of the nineteenth century in the recruitment of single British women as missionaries to the "foreign field," due partially to the large number of British middle-class women lacking the financial or social support of husband, father or brother (54). Haggis's point is that this avenue for independence, as well as the carving out by missionary women of a separate sphere of activity within the institutional framework, marked the beginning of the incorporation and professionalization of women's work, achieved through invest-ment in the colonial system, and to a great extent, facilitated by the colonized subjects to whom these women "ministered" (55).

30 Where I have been able to find information, I include a brief biographical sketch of the writers discussed. Most accounts are partial, given my own lack of ongoing access to the relevant archives and the fact that information about nineteenth-century women was largely appended, if at all, to biographies of the men to whom they were in some way attached; it is for the new generation of scholars to harness technology and fill the gaps I have left. I include in my bibliography of primary texts all the published and manuscript writing I discovered, accessed and read, omitting only those "dead ends" which proved to have no West Indian content at all. In the body of this book, however, I have concentrated on narratives that fall within my specified time period and are by women who, as far as I can determine, actually spent some time in the region; thus works by women who never even visited the West Indies – such as the novel *Far Enough* (1928) by Helen Ashton – are mentioned only in passing.

1 Defamiliarizing "the mistress": representations of white women in the West Indies

1 Ferguson (1992: 19) details self-perceptions by Englishwomen during the colonial period of "their own sense of subjection to a cross-class patriarchal order within British society. Throughout the entire period of colonialist protest, for instance, in references to themselves as pawns of white men, denied education as well as access to law and allied deprivations, feminists of all classes were prone to refer loosely to themselves as slaves."

2 See Edward Long (1774), particularly vol. 2 (278–9 and 412–13) where white women are depicted eating and dressing like their "sable hand-maids," an observation reiterated in women's narratives such as Nugent's. Working-class white women in Barbados after indentureship found more "respectable" employment in towns within government agencies such as the Parish Vestries, as well as in stores and increasingly rarely, as domestics, although Beckles (1989: 73) also mentions huckstering, noting the way these women operated within the network of predominantly black women hucksters, and the amount of creolization they evinced in their practices.

3 Mary Prince's narrative suggests an ironic hierarchy of powerlessness in the vignette where a young white woman cannot legally prevent her father appropriating "*her* property" (1987: 189, emphasis in original); this property refers to black slave women like Mary.

4 I wish to acknowledge Professor Beckles for bringing the Fenwick material to my attention, and for much valuable discussion relating to issues discussed here. I analyze Fenwick's narrative more fully in the following chapter.

5 Elsewhere, Beckles (1998a: 14) observes of "middling" white women like Fenwick that, "[w]hile they subscribed to elements of patriarchal moral ideology, such as notions of 'virtue', 'decency' and 'honour', the thrust of their autonomous accumulationist activity violated and transgressed representations in patriarchal ideology of the woman as domestic capital." He concludes that although "their actual experiences were confined in large measure to small niches, or to the margins of areas of large-scale accumulation . . . it is important to know [their history] since it has relevance to an understanding of the social relations of gender within colonialism as a violent male-managed enterprise."

6 Maria Nugent (1771–1834) was born in New Jersey to American parents of European ancestry. After the war of Independence, the family moved to Britain; Maria married George Nugent (also of Irish descent) in Belfast in 1797 and accompanied him to Jamaica on his appointment to the highly prized governorship of the island. Her residence there to 1805 is the subject of her journal. General Nugent was appointed Commander-in-Chief of the army in India in 1811, where again Maria followed. The Nugents retired to England in 1813. For a fuller biographical account, see Philip Wright's edition of her journal (1966: xi–xvii).

7 As noted, Ferguson (1992) argues that white British women, in campaigning for emancipation of slaves, saw their own oppression as a form of bondage, and in organizing and consolidating power in the service of the anti-slavery cause, did achieve a measure of liberation. Like Brathwaite, Ferguson is quick to point out that this was not accompanied by any conception of social equality for black women.

8 Weiner (1996: 285) contends that many white women in the antebellum South, expected to minister to the plantation family (including "childlike" slaves), did ameliorate slave conditions in so far as their (moral) authority allowed, but were ultimately subject to male decisions; she cites cases where women who tried to intervene in the master's/husband's cruelty to, or rape of slave women, were themselves beaten for the attempt. Morton (1996: 7) too refers to the "softening influence" of the plantation mistress in the American south.

9 Quite a few narratives in my survey do articulate anti-slavery sentiments: examples include Harriet Martineau's "Demerara: A Tale"; *The System: A Tale of the West Indies* by Mrs C. Tonna ("Charlotte Elizabeth"); and Mrs Henry Lynch's *Years Ago*.

10 Brereton (1993) uses "Mrs Flannagin" to identify the reputed author of *Antigua and the Antiguans* (1844); the work is in fact anonymous, although the text is catalogued in the University of the West Indies (Cave Hill) library under "Flannigan, Mrs" and bibliographies of Caribbean writers, such as that of Herdeck (1979: 253), use this spelling. Ferguson (1993) refers to "Frances Lanaghan" as does Brereton (1994), and this is the name used for the Macmillan reprint of the text.

11 Brereton also deals with the narratives of Nugent, Fenwick, Mary Prince, Carmichael, Lanaghan, Seacole and Bridges, as well as others that are not strictly germane, by virtue of date or subject matter, to my study. Her essay was subsequently published, with some changes, in 1994.

12 An active and competent female plantation owner/manager features in Kevyn Arthur's novel, *View from Belmont* (1997), which is set in nineteenth century Trinidad. See also Linda Sturtz (1999) on Anne Elletson, a white widow who managed a plantation in Jamaica in the late eighteenth century, but as an absentee owner.

13 According to Paravisini-Gebert and Torres-Seda (1993: 268), Ada Quayle was born in Jamaica in 1927. Canton (1957: 23) describes her as "the daughter of a banana planter, [who] left Jamaica early in the war." She served in Egypt and East Africa with the Women's Royal Air Force, worked with the BBC and then moved to Kenya.

14 I am grateful to Kevyn Arthur for sharing his research on West Indian writing published in the regional press in the eighteenth and nineteenth centuries.

15 Wilcox's travel narrative (1909: 120) is equally caustic about some fellow Americans in the tropics, notably "Mr and Mrs Sudden Rich" whose ostentatious dress and possessions, vulgarity and lack of deportment are incongruous in the exclusive resorts they frequent, where "they may be seen walking out of the dining rooms of the best hotels and parading the verandas violently brandishing the toothpick." Just as bad are young women from small American hometowns, who assume a "haughty and exclusive air" in the West Indies. "It never occurs to them or to their parents and guardians," she chastises, "that a higher type of womanhood and a better phase of Christianity would be shown by a gracious word, a pleasant look and a kindly act toward humanity" (121–2).

16 An example is the evocation of a creole childbirth (Marks 1938: 175), which is clearly taken from Nugent's journal.

2 "With the utmost familiarity": black and white women

1 (1922, vol. 1: 43). Quoted in Brian Moore (1998: 104).

2 This is a complaint with a long shelf-life. For example, some seventy-seven years after Carmichael's text an Englishwoman, Isabel Maclean, published *Children of Jamaica* (1910), a potted ethnographic history with a strongly moral tone aimed at young people in Britain. The text is largely drawn from second-hand sources such as publications of the Jamaican "Folk Lore Society" acknowledged in her introduction. These were often the product of European expatriates like Walter Jekyll and "Wona" (Una Jeffery-Smith), both cited in *Children of Jamaica*. The title refers to "black children, cousins of the little African negroes over the sea" (8) whose ancestors were "ignorant, untaught savages from a heathen land" (21). In the process of civilizing these savages "to our shame, the British nation became slave-owners" (17), and slavery is blamed for moral backwardness among the present generation of young people. For although Jamaica's free black youth are now much more "confident and merry," yet "these terrible slavery days have left deep marks on their characters. Sweet and lovable as the children are, many, very many of them are what the negroes call 'trickified,' that is to say, not quite straightforward" (94). In other words, she clarifies coyly, they help themselves to "this and that" and lie if apprehended. Luckily, "there are some brave black boys and girls who can walk straight on" (95) in spite of such bad examples.

Interestingly, Maclean also indicts slavery for the exploitation of black women in Jamaica. Their burdensome workload is explained by the fact "that it is not so very long since the Jamaican negroes were a heathen people, a savage race, over in Africa. Now, in all savage races there is an idea that women are intended to be the slaves of men" (48). Maclean's claim that oppression of women is confined to the "savage" races ignores the fact that her choice of the marginal genre of didactic juvenile literature suggests her own exclusion as a woman writer from "serious" fiction, and her anxiety to claim allegiance to the feminine ideal by assuming the good mistress's role of "moral housekeeper". Maclean's privileging of the imperial gaze avoids acknowledging her own secondary status as woman in the colonial project, and blithely ignores centuries of feminist discourse – from Mary Wollstonecraft on – which made explicit links between the oppression of women under patriarchy and that of black people under slavery.

3 The other side is provided by Mary Prince (1987: 204), whose description of laundering a household's linen by hand mitigate any sympathy for such complaints: "Every week I had to wash two large bundles of clothes, as much as a boy could help me to lift; but I could give no satisfaction. My mistress was always abusing and fretting after me." In England, despite her rheumatism, Mary has to do the "great washing . . . every two months" which consisted of "a great many heavy things, such as bed-ticks, bed-coverlets, &c."(210).

4 Lynch's novel *Years Ago* (1865: 7–8) indicates that in the early nineteenth-century household of a family of means, there was no shortage of women servants. Eight are deployed for one hour just for one daily task: rubbing the mahogany floor of the plantation house with orange juice, and burnishing it with coconut husks.

5 A novelist and writer of educational works for children, Hays (1770s–1840s) moved in "radical" circles in England, according to Blain (1990: 365). Among her friends were William Godwin and Mary Wollstonecraft. *Secresy* (1795), a remarkable novel which advocates women's access to rational education, is Hays' only work for adults.

6 Bush (1990: 58) cites evidence from Punishment Lists, particularly in the late period of slavery, claiming that domestic "women slaves were frequently accused of insolence, shamming sickness, excessive laziness, disorderly conduct, disobedience and quarreling." This indicates that although the house slaves' supposedly had an "easier" lot, the women were seldom contented and obedient. The work of Brathwaite (1984) and Beckles (1998b) amply supports this interpretation.

7 A modern-day reconstruction of plantation society in the pre-emancipation West Indies, Phillips's novel *Cambridge* draws on sources of the kind I have been discussing and explicitly teases out some of the contradictions to which I have been alluding. As I have discussed (O'Callaghan 1993b: 4), Emily comes to question the significance of her role and of the very term, "mistress," which after all means mistress *of* someone, with the necessary authority conferred by the appellation. While Emily has written herself within the stereotype of the mistress, her narrative destabilizes the term as she learns how little she knows of the plantation dynamic, and how little power she actually has over anyone.

   See also Long's *The Golden Violet* (1936), set at the end of the slavery period, which delineates the clash between an ideal and actual role as mistress of an estate.

8 Slavery thus institutionalized the right of white men to multiple sexual partners, and black men followed suit. In Nugent's journal (1966: 87) a Member of the Assembly, "and a profligate character," advises one of his male slaves to marry, only to be told: "Hi, Massa, you telly me marry one wife, which is no good! You no tinky I see you buckra no content wid one, two, tree, or four wifes; no more poor negro." In time, black men were represented as suspicious of the institution of marriage itself: "Married man! What you know bout married? Married hab teet an it bitin me. You eber hear de saying, 'when poverty come, lobe jump trew de winda.' Me, ah go down ah Memie yard. Ashes cole dag sleep dah." The source is Elspeth Fielding's *Romance in Jamaica* (1957: 262; according to the author, the novel was written much earlier). The promiscuity of black and white West Indian men to the present day has been uncritically attributed to this precedent.

9 See, for example, Douglas Hall (1989) on Thomas Thistlewood, an overseer-turned-smallholder who lived in western Jamaica from 1750 until his death in 1786. Thistlewood kept a detailed journal of daily life and, isolated from social contact with other whites, records countless sexual (and other) relations with slave women.

10 Moving into the twentieth century, it is worth noting that women writers – from Alice Durie to Jamaica Kincaid – represent West Indian women turning to obeah as a means of dealing with a rival. Clementina in Durie's *One Jamaica Gal* (1939), who has been supplanted in her employer's affections, pays an obeah woman to work a spell that will (and does) terminate her successor's pregnancy. Equally, the mother in Kincaid's *Annie John* (1985) engages in "witchlike" consultations with obeah women and utilizes non-Christian rituals to protect her daughter and herself from the malign intentions of her husband's "outside women." Ironically, Annie prefers this aspect of her mother's role modeling to her normal manifestation as a paragon of domestic management and feminine respectability.

11 Like Zabette, Mary Prince recalls being raised with a white girl like a sister: "I was made quite a pet of by Miss Betsey, and loved her very much" (1987: 187). When only a little older, she is entrusted with near total care of a white infant "and I grew so fond of my nursling that it was my greatest delight to walk out with him by the sea-shore, accompanied by his brother and sister, Miss Fanny and Master James. – Dear Miss Fanny! She was a sweet, kind young lady, and so fond of me that she wished me to learn all that she knew herself . . . and in a few months I was able not only to say my letters but to spell many small words" (188–9). Mary's obvious skill with and warmth for her white charges must have been observed, as Mrs I – has enough confidence in her to straightaway "put a child in my arms, and, tired as I was, I was forced instantly to take up my old occupation as a nurse" (193).

12 According to Nicholas Guppy's forward to *Child of the Tropics* (1988: 9–11), his aunt Yseult Alice Lechmere Guppy was born in Trinidad in 1888, of an English father and a French Creole mother. After her first marriage, she contributed a weekly article on social events to the *Trinidad Guardian*, and during her second marriage, published two novels, *Questing Heart* (1934) and *Red Fruit* (later changed to *Creole Enchantment*, 1936). As the wife of a colonial official, she lived in Nigeria and South Africa; retired in England, she wrote several studies of famous crimes. She died in 1971.

13 Eliot [Eileen] Bliss was born in Jamaica in 1903 to Eva Lees and Captain John Plomer Bliss of the West India Regiment. She spent her childhood in the island, and then was sent to England to be educated. Like her character Em in *Luminous Isle*, she returned to Jamaica in 1923 for two years before settling permanently in England where she died in 1990. She apparently worked in a number of publishing jobs, and established friendships and correspondences with other literary women such as Jean Rhys, Dorothy Richardson and Vita Sackville-West.

3 "This is another world": travel narratives, women and the construction of tropical landscape

1 An anonymous novel, *The Koromantyn Slaves* (1823) – ostensibly by a woman – claims that its aim is a "dispassionate view of the subject" of slavery (viii), but acknowledges from the outset that its findings "have been principally derived from the voluminous 'History of the West Indies' by Bryan Edwards, Esq. The writer has also freely resorted to two or three well-known works, for the illustrations of her subject" (vii). Similarly, Minna Caroline Smith, in an author's note to her romance *Mary Paget* (1900), claims seventeenth-century historical documents as the primary resources for her construction of the West Indies. Her romance is apparently drawn from *Memorials of the Discovery and Early Settlement of the Bermudas or Somers Island, 1515–1685* by General Sir J. H. Lefroy (1817–90), a former governor of the island. Lefroy's sources, in turn, include a manuscript thought to be the inspiration for Shakespeare's *Tempest*.

2 Margaret Lenta (1991: 68) quotes Lady Anne Barnard, writing from South Africa in the early nineteenth century, that "publishing was for men." Keen to have her views taken into account, but only with appropriate decorum, her choice is the appropriately

feminine vehicle of the epistle, and like Nugent's journal her letters were circulated only to family and friends before her death.

3 James's self-conscious tone is perhaps also due to what Hooper (2001: 58) reminds us was increasingly sensed among travel writers, from the late nineteenth century onwards: that "travel can be no more than a derivative experience, a hand-me-down, slightly ironic, somewhat knowing expression of romantic desire" (59).

4 See Donaldson (1992: 6), Pratt (1992: 163) and Blake (1992 : 56).

5 One instance is the parallel James draws between Nugent's account of employing a nightcap for daytime wear on board ship, and James's similar discovery "one hundred and eleven years after that," of the superior comfort on deck of "boudoir caps" to bonnets (1913: 119).

6 Mary Eliza Bakewell Gaunt (1861–1942), novelist, short-story and travel writer, was born in Australia where her father worked as a magistrate in the gold fields of Victoria. One of the first women to enrol in the University of Melbourne, she left after a year to pursue a career in writing, and produced several romances set in Australia. After the death of her husband in 1900, she moved to England to make her living from fiction. She visited West Africa in 1908 and again in 1911, and produced both novels and travel books based on her research. Gaunt continued to travel, and to write about her travels, with trips to China, Russia, the West Indies and continental Europe, where she settled, drawing on her experiences of exotic lands in her fiction. War forced her to leave Italy in 1940, and she died in France. For analysis of her travel writing, see Whitlock (2000: 96–111).

7 May Crommelin, also known as Maria Henrietta de la Cherois Crommelin (c.1850–1930), was an Irish novelist and travel writer. She spent time in North and South America, the West Indies, Syria, Palestine and Japan, publishing travel narratives and some forty novels.

8 Gertrude Franklin Horn Atherton (1857–1948) was an American feminist and writer of social and historical fiction, mostly set in California. After the death of her husband, she traveled to New York and on to Europe, using these locales as settings for her books. As part of her research for a novelized account of the life of Alexander Hamilton (*The Conqueror* 1902), she visited the West Indies, spending time in St Kitts and Nevis; her impressions are recorded in *Adventures of a Novelist* (1932) and the visit also provided material for *The Gorgeous Isle* (1908), which relates a romance between a West Indian poet – based on Swinburne, according to Blain et al. (1990: 36) – and an Englishwoman. She published more than forty novels, as well as non-fiction and autobiographical works.

9 Although Ragatz (1932) claims that "the authoress was herself a native of the island" of Jamaica, Mrs Henry Lynch [nee Theodora Elizabeth Foulkes], 1812–1885, was the English-born daughter of Arthur Foulkes, a sugar planter of Jamaica. She apparently grew up in Jamaica where she married Henry Lynch, a Jamaican-born barrister of Kingston, and must have spent her married life here as Mr Lynch died in Jamaica in 1845. Mrs Lynch died in England some forty years later, and it is during these forty years that her writing was published.

Ethel Maude Symmonett, according to the frontispiece of her text, is "of Kingston, Jamaica, BWI," and her book was published in Kingston and delivered to the Colonial Secretary's Office on February 23, 1895, under the provisions of a law for the registration of all books printed in the island.

10 Of course the misnomer by which the region came to be known, itself encapsulates its indeterminacy. "The Indies" signified riches, oriental luxury and sensuality; but Columbus was wrong, and the Caribbean is *not* part of India. "West" signifies a corrective of this exotic excess, indicating the region's connection (annexation) to the West, to civilization, the ostensible goal of the imperial project; but the Caribbean remains stubbornly *other* than the West.

11 Letter from Jane B. Kerby from Antigua dated August 2, 1805 (Kevyn Arthur, forthcoming).

12 For example, see pp.109, 115, 117, 137, 232.

13 Detailing the dangers of earthquakes and hurricanes in the West Indies, Maclean (1910: 85) supplies an interesting derivation which further supports this anthropomorphic mind set: "That very word has been left to us by the Arawaks, who thought they were sent by Hurrica the Devil."

14 Clarine Stephenson, a Jamaican writer, describes Kingston in an equally unflattering light in her romance *Undine: An Experience* (1911). From her attic room in Upper Duke Street, the protagonist looks out on "an expanse of dust laden roofs" (11) and rails against the "dust and heat"of the city (13).

15 Ann Marsh-Caldwell (1791–1874) was born in Staffordshire, England and married Arthur Marsh in 1817, moving with him to his extensive estate near London. She obviously began writing at a young age but not until Harriet Martineau encouraged her did she publish her first book, anonymously, in 1834, and thereafter produced one or two almost every year. After the death of her husband and son, she returned to her childhood home and remained there for the rest of her life.

16 Wilcox is, however, an unreliable authority for this sounds far more like the "chigger" than the common tick; elsewhere she misnames certain birds, and misspells the names of certain places and species of flora.

17 See, for example, Nugent (1966: 11, 13, 16, 15, 72).

18 In *Sailing Sunny Seas* (1909: 61), Wilcox seems to borrow Nugent's simile in describing a mountain retreat in Jamaica: "The evening was radiant with a spectacular sunset, and the night soft with a full moon. Winds sighed, and birds twittered, and the whole world seemed ours. We were Adam and Eve in a new corner of Paradise."

19 Sheller (2001: 8) cites Bishop Francis Goodwin's *The Man in the Moon* (1638), set on the Atlantic island of St Helena, as the first narrative to configure the tropical island as Eden.

20 The newly arrived protagonist of Long's *The Golden Violet* (1936: 126) is "almost nauseated by the brilliant flowers, the lustrous leaves, all the strange shaped plants that were, to her thinking, so large that they threw the whole landscape out of focus." Similarly the English husband in Rhys's *Wide Sargasso Sea* (1968: 59) is overwhelmed by the tropical excess of the landscape: "Everything is too much, I felt as I rode wearily after her. Too much blue, too much purple, too much green. The flowers too red, the mountains too high, the hills too near."

21 The same formula is used by Symmonett (1895: 17), Lanaghan (1844, vol. 2: 155–6) and Newton (1897: 168).

22 See also Wilcox (1909: 194–6) whose initial view of Charlotte Amalie as a "beautiful prospect," proves deceptive. Again, it is the local population ("[m]obs of children in varied colors" and "sailors who had freely sampled Santa Cruz rum") that spoil the inviting picture.

23 In this context, see Laura Chrisman (1990: 53) who discusses the self-representation of "the imperial unconscious" in the work of Rider Haggard, noting how he constructs a "good" and a "bad" Africa and suggesting that this bifurcation signals the conflicted self-knowledge of colonial writers regarding the nature of the imperial enterprise, a concept I will revisit in Chapter 5.

24 See also Crowninshield's *Latitude 19°* (1898b), a rather far-fetched adventure tale of American sailors shipwrecked in Haiti, who witness the horrors of "vodaux" mysteries and the cruelties of Henri Christophe's regime. The novel opens with a letter from the narrator, now safely at home in the United States, passionately warning of the dangers of a savage country so near American shores. "We send missionaries to Africa," he complains, "In God's name, let's send them nearer home, where iniquity of the vilest flourishes, and at our very doors" (256).

25 Lynch (1865: 40), Nugent (1966: 46), and James (1913: 156) note the rapid and frequent exchange of people and news between Haiti and Jamaica, and Gaunt's historical romance (1933) of early nineteenth-century Jamaica describes the planters' perception

of their island "on the verge of a volcano," as the example of nearby Haiti is compounded by growing anti-slavery agitation, giving rise to widespread unrest among
blacks at home (112). For the planters, Haiti is conceived as "inhabited by black savages
ravening for the blood of a white man" (72).

4 A female "El Dorado"

1 In Richard Hakluyt, *The Principal Navigations, Voyages, Traffiques, & Discoveries of the English
Nation 1598–1600*, 12 vols (Glasgow, 1903–5), vol. 10: 428.

2 Hence, Moore-Gilbert discusses Spivak's reading of *Jane Eyre* in which Jane's triumph
as a proto-feminist and autonomous individual(ist) is seen to ignore the role forced on
the "native" female in *enabling* the metropolitan woman's new identity. "For example,"
he elaborates (1997: 94), "the construction of the 'degraded' native woman as a subject
to be 'redeemed' creates a role for the benevolent western woman (as missionary, for
instance), which provides a new public space or role in citizenship into which she can
emerge." Catherine Hall (1992) makes a similar point, arguing that missionaries
derived authority from their ability to speak *for* and protest *on behalf of* powerless slaves.
Ferguson (1992) also demonstrates the empowerment of English middle-class women
via their organization within the anti-slavery cause.

3 Henrietta Camilla Jenkin, nee Jackson (1807–85) was the only daughter of Colonel
Robert Jackson of Mahogany Vale, St. Thomas, Jamaica, a local planter and Custos
Rotulorum of Kingston. She married Charles Jenkin, a naval officer, who fell in love
with her while traveling through the West Indies. They moved to his family's estate in
England, and subsequently lived in Europe until the French Revolution obliged the
family to flee. Described by Munro (2002) as "a woman of strong and energetic character," she played the harp, sang, wrote novels "which, however, failed to make their
mark," studied piano and, in her sixties, began to master Hebrew. Very close to her
only son, Henry Charles Fleeming Jenkin, she moved to Edinburgh after he married,
and died there.

4 Ashton's novel *Far Enough* (1928) utilizes a similar plot: a young English woman voyages
to Jamaica to become nanny to the children of a pen-keeper, and ends up his wife.
Helen (Rosaline) Ashton, later Mrs Jordan (1891–1958) was an English novelist and
biographer; for details, see Blain et al. (1990: 32).

5 Nancy Prince (née Gardener) was born in the United States in 1799 and, according to
Blain et al. (1990: 873), was of African-Indian ancestry. She went into service, but
always aspired to writing and teaching. In 1824 she met and married Mr Prince, the
servant of a Russian princess in the Czar's court. They lived in Russia for nine years
before returning to America, where her husband died. Having become religious long
before, Prince now involved herself in the abolitionist movement and determined after
emancipation to travel to the West Indies with a view to improving conditions among
the black population. She arrived in Jamaica in 1840 to teach and work with a missionary association, but had differences of opinion with them and decided to venture out
on her own, setting up a school for destitute girls. After a fund-raising trip to the United
States, unsettled conditions on her return to the island and financial disasters put paid
to the school, and indeed to her next project: a "Manual Labour School." Disillusioned, she returned home where she wrote *A Narrative of the Life and Travels of Mrs.
Nancy Prince*, published in 1850.

6 *Undine; An Experience* recounts the story of a wealthy daughter of "a Kingston
Croesus," who returns from school in England at 18 to take her place in society and
enjoy the luxury of her widowed father's home. After a few years of the gay life, she
becomes engaged to an English government official and goes to England to meet his
family, only to rush home again at the news of her father's illness. He dies, she is left
with nothing and her intended defects "like a golden sun ray before the storm
clouds" (Stephenson 1911: 16). Living in reduced circumstances in an attic room and

working as a governess, life holds little promise, so she agrees to a proposal of marriage from a man she does not love. But on a visit to the country with an aunt, Undine meets a handsome stranger, is smitten and disillusioned, all in quick succession, for the stranger has a wife in England, a wife "void of every moral or noble principle" (64) whom he is trying to cast off, but a wife none the less. Unable to ask Undine to live in "forbidden love," and knowing that should she discover him flawed her "soul would die" (51), Colin leaves and returns to England a broken man. His tragic face inspires a painter who captures his likeness in a picture of Christ. The now-married Undine sees the scandalous portrait some years later in Jamaica when her husband buys it for his private chapel. Undine dies on the altar steps, gazing at the painting, having "found her God" (93). Most of the action takes place in Jamaica with many local references and descriptions, and a good ear for Jamaican Creole, but the main focus is on the overheated passions of the heroine and the far-fetched plot of thwarted love.

An "undine," according to the Swiss physician Paracelsus, is a water sprite, a nymph able to assume human form; if she bears a child by a mortal, she gains a human soul. Friedrich Heinrich Karl de la Motte Fouqué's *Undine* (1811), inspired by the writings of Paracelsus, was published in English in 1882. Stephenson may have been alluding to the myth in her novel of spiritual rebirth through love.

7 Napier's *A Flying Fish Whispered* (1938: 34) testifies to the resilience of this self-indulgent immersion in romantic fantasy among women, even her level-headed heroine. Teresa is well aware of the "foolishness" in her heart even as she lets

> this tide sweep her beyond the breakers. Sweep her to—what? But that night she would not consider 'what.' There might be calm water ahead, or rocks, or dangerous currents, but to-night she would think only of the intoxicating look on a man's face, of the whisper of his voice. To-night he and she would be alone together in a world of her own dreams.

8 Gabrielle Margaret Vere Campbell (1885–1952) was born in Hampshire, England, and had a difficult childhood. According to Salmonson (1998), the family lived in poverty after being abandoned by her alcoholic father. Still in her teens, Margaret – as she was known – began her first novel and soon after was supporting the family by her writing. In 1912, she married a Sicilian engineer and moved to Italy, where they lived narrowly on her earnings after he became ill. She nursed her demanding husband through his final months and in 1916, returned to England. A year later she married Arthur Long, who proved yet another bad-tempered dependent. Undoubtedly, her fiction's cynical view of marriage reflected her own experience. With three children to support, she worked tirelessly on her writing, producing some ninety works, mostly sensational historical dramas.

Francis Sypher (1999) suggests *The Golden Violet*, in which the heroine poisons her husband, was inspired by the history of Letitia Elizabeth Landon, an English poet prominent in the 1820s, who died suddenly and suspiciously in Africa (her husband was governor at Cape Coast) from an overdose of "medicine." One of her collections of poetry is entitled *The Golden Violet* (1827).

9 This pattern fits some modern fictional treatments of the West Indies by metropolitan women writers: the tropics as utopia/escape fantasy gives way to experiences of fear, violence and alienation. Margaret Atwood's *Bodily Harm* (1999) is a case in point. Even more interestingly, the pattern survives in reverse in contemporary fictions by West Indian women who seek escape/fortune/liberation in England or North America, only to find themselves equally intimidated and marginalized. The work of Joan Riley is apposite.

10 Kim Robinson-Walcott (2001) has culled a fascinating selection of media testimonials by modern-day "white" Jamaicans which reveal a very similar sense of cultural exclusion and unbelonging within their own country, the result of an apparent promotion of black nationalism since the 1970s as "official" ideology.

11 Joyce Walker Johnson (1994: 18) notes that in popular English novels of the nineteenth century, "[a]n important indicator of Negro blood for many writers was the appearance of the eyes."

12 A variant meaning, of course, is *"[a]lmost the same but not white"*; see Bhabha's essay "Of Mimicry and Man" (1994: 86–9).

13 According to Allsopp (1996: 176), the term "creole" (from the Spanish "criollo": someone born in the New World) was originally used with pride in the seventeenth century "by European colonists (esp the Fr) to refer to themselves as born and bred in the 'New World' . . . It was then extended to distinguish 'local' from imported breeds esp of horses and livestock, then slaves locally born as different from original African importees." The creation and expansion of the term signifies, perhaps, a perceived need to name this indeterminate group.

14 This generalization applies not just to the writing of white creoles, but also to that of "complicatedly colonial" black and brown women too: Seacole's text is a case in point, as I will discuss in Chapter 6.

15 I have been unable to find details of the author, born in Barbados in 1867, beyond what she tells us in the typescript manuscript, which was presented to the Rhodes House Library in Oxford by her daughter Miss D. Burslem.

16 Elma Napier (nee Gordon-Cumming) was born in Scotland in 1892 (Blain et al. 1990: 786). She married M. Gibbs in 1912 and accompanied him to Australia where they spent nine years, and where she began to write. Having divorced him, she married Lennox Napier and the couple traveled extensively. Honeychurch (forthcoming) records them settling finally in Dominica in 1932, where they spent the rest of their lives. Active in local politics, Napier was the first woman elected to a West Indian Legislative Council in 1940. She also pioneered cooperative efforts, encouraged the formation of village boards and self-help programs, and campaigned for a road to link north and south Dominica. Napier wrote several novels – some under the pseudonym Elizabeth Garner, possibly because of their frank sexual content – as well as travel sketches, and a two-part autobiography, and contributed to the local press and to the regional literary journal *Bim* in the 1950s and 1960s. She died in 1973.

According to her grandson, the well-known Dominican historian Lennox Honeychurch, Lennox Napier was elected representative for the Eastern District and fought a notable battle for boat-landing and sea shore rights for villagers, thus establishing the right of Dominicans to have access to their beaches. The incident is fictionalized in *A Flying Fish Whispered* (1938).

17 And indeed it is Liris who most forcefully asserts her race: "[w]e have to learn that we are not ashamed of our own birth . . . that if we have been handicapped by it hitherto, we can and will surmount it; that we shall become respected not by trying to be white . . . not by pretense, but by showing what we can do, what we can be" (Fraser 1896a: 304). As Joyce Walker Johnson observes (1994: 16), the novel is unusual in stressing the potential role of the "educated brown minority . . . in the future development of West Indian societies."

18 Em's "strong instinctive sympathy felt since childhood for the black people" (Bliss 1984: 88), and her admiration for "black and brown women" is complex. Her attraction to the peasant Rebekkah, for example, has lesbian overtones: she is referred to as "a magnificent creature" (203) who responds to Em's friendliness with "a lover-like glow" (205). However, Em's feelings have more to do with an attraction to what (essentialized) blacks represent for her: they are "natural," "less civilized," "rhythmical," and sensual (131). In comparison with her own restricted life, black women's freedom seems enviable. As noted, James (1913: 103–4) similarly asserts that "the Jamaican negress" has far more sensible attitudes to sexual relationships than white Englishwomen, for whom respectable marriages often mean lifelong imprisonment. Teresa in Napier's *A Flying Fish Whispered* is more explicit about the double sexual standards for black and white women. Her maid Tilly is quite forthright about her desires: "I must have a man every fortnight . . .

else I am ill" (1938: 13). Again, black women are portrayed as more in tune with nature and their own natures: while white bodies look out of place in the tropics (163), sex "for servants and livestock" is "an ever-recurring feature of existence" (14). None the less, for all this admiration and genuine affection, the difference between them is inviolable. "Tilly was among her own people and their ways were not hers," acknowledges Teresa (120), just as Em admits that "too many things" divide her world from Rebekkah's. On black women's subversion of English gender roles, see Maria Olaussen (1993).

5 Narratives of tainted empire

1 See Moore-Gilbert (1997: 19–20) for a review of similar critical positions, such as that of Aijaz Ahmad.

2 Gikandi (1996: 122). Pouchet Paquet (1994: 4) further observes that in respect of "the ambivalent location of women in the colonial economy of representation . . . these issues are further complicated when the women identify themselves as creoles," a complication I will explore further.

3 Charlotte Elizabeth Browne (1790–1846) was an English-born evangelical writer and editor, who married an army captain stationed in Nova Scotia. Separated from him, she married another officer, L.H.J. Tonna. They lived in Ireland for many years, where she wrote numerous anti-Catholic tracts and some verse. On her husband's death in 1837, she returned to England and published poetry and fiction (including a novel on the condition of women factory workers) as well as a collection of essays and sketches, *The Wrongs of Women* (1844). There is no evidence that she visited the West Indies. See Blain et al. (1990: 1087); also Ferguson (1992: 372–3, note 55) for biographical references; for a brief discussion of *The System* (270–1); and for an anti-slavery poem by Tonna (371).

4 When young British soldiers hear of planters shooting blacks for sport, Sir William is prompted to mutter, "Thus early are the noblest feelings of the British bosom stifled by your influence, and cruelty linked with that courage whose proper handmaid is mercy!" (1827: 194). But condemnation is also voiced by non-whites. The colored Caesar acidly suggests to a missionary preaching submission to the slaves that he "set before your white brethren the error of *their* ways; bid them meditate on the crimes of rapine [*sic*], murder, torturing murder, the murder of souls, to use your own manner of speaking. Tell *them* to repent, to repent of these, of their thefts, their adulteries, their revellings in the blood of their fellow men" (142; emphasis in original).

5 There is something disquieting about the absolute power Louis has over Stella, by law – he is her guardian and trustee – and by the rules of popular romance, in which Stella is steeped: she who equates him with "the light of heaven" (Jenkin 1859, vol. 2: 289). This adoration is posited on and valorizes unequal power relations, such as obtain between black and white under slavery, and which inform exaggerated portrayals in the text of the obsequious behavior of "good" women and slaves.

For example, when greeted delightedly by his old retainers, Louis remarks that "these blacks have the memory and instincts of spaniels" (vol. 1: 241); Stella's maid Rebecca, sorry for causing trouble, begs "me young missus, put your foot on my head – trample me into the dust; do, me missus, it do me good" (vol. 2: 283). But if the narrator observes that "negroes in general have a tendency to worship" (vol. 2: 293), the story demonstrates that young white women do too! Implicit in Louis's mastery over blacks and women (he rules the hearts of his mother, Stella and a female book-keeper, all of whom live under his roof), is the assertion of the natural superiority of men and a vindication of the policy of firm rule that Louis embodies. One is reminded of Catherine Hall's comment (1992: 257) on the "appalling relations of men and women under slavery" and the extent to which "the system" naturalized inferiority in certain groups.

6 Quoted in Brereton (1995: 74).

7   Ragatz (1928: 5).

8   Chapman, who was born in Sussex in 1904 but lived in Jamaica for much of her life, is included in Paravisini-Gebert and Torres-Seda's bibliography of Caribbean women writers (1993: 56). She founded and edited the *West India Review* and also edited the *Jamaica Annual* for many years.

9   The *Anthenaeum* (July 1896: 155–6).

10 The association of beauty and decay is also a strong symbolic construct in Allfrey's *The Orchid House* (first published 1953), and evokes a similar atmosphere of doom pervading the white population: "Beauty and disease, beauty and sickness, beauty and horror: that was the island" (1982: 75). Similarly, Rhys's *Wide Sargasso Sea* (1968: 17) describes the paradisal garden of Antoinette's post-emancipation Jamaican childhood as having "gone wild. The paths were overgrown and a smell of dead flowers mixed with the fresh living smell." The implication of something nasty just under the surface speaks to the anxiety of post-slavery white society about the recent past.

11 A Jamaican word meaning a white overseer on an estate. According to Cassidy and LePage (1980: 84), and supported by Lalla and D'Costa (1990: 224), the term dates from 1790 and derives from the Jamaican Creole "obisha" (overseer). The word is omitted from Allsopp's dictionary (1996), but in correspondence he confirms its Jamaican derivation and usage, and cites a folk-song published in 1787 where the word is spelt "Obeshay"; other specifically Jamaican Creole terms, such as the exclamation "Chaw" (cho!) occur in the same verses.

12 The novel was printed, presumably for the author, by "G.A. Uphill, Printer and Bookbinder, St. John's, Antigua." It is undated, but, according to Nicholson's "Record of Persons in Antigua and Barbuda's History," it was published in 1890. This supports Farquhar's contention, in her review of the novel, that "references made in it to the celebration of the Queen's birthday and an oblique reference to the Negro Education Act suggests a date between 1831 and 1901" (1981: 31). Set "on one of the smaller West Indian islands," Farquhar observes that the novel's use of "dialect, place names such as Fig Tree Hill, and All Saints, and a description of the island's jetty all serve to identify the imaginary place as Antigua"; indeed, she goes on to praise the novel for the "excellent view it gives of Antiguan society of that period" (31). Cassin's biographical details are incomplete, but it is very likely she was a member of the island's creole elite (of English descent).

   Cassins are mentioned in Nevis and Antigua since the eighteenth century, and the records of the Museum of Antigua and Barbuda (a chronological history, 1632–1998, researched by D.V. Nicholson) cites a Mr F. S. Cassin advertising in Antigua in 1871 as a commission agent and ship owner. There is also mention of Mr and Miss Cassin in the *Antigua Standard* of December 20, 1890, and of Frieda Cassin as the author of the first known Antiguan novel and editor of Antigua's earliest literary journal, the *Carib* in the late nineteenth century. See also O'Callaghan (2002).

13 Mrs William Wilkins, an American, rails against such bias toward colored people of "good class" in American and British colonies, in her text *The Slave Son* (1854). Indeed, she feels, "slavery can never be said to be abolished where prejudice of caste keeps the people degraded."

14 The phrase is from Carmichael (1969 vol.1: 59).

15 See also McClintock (1995: 52–4) on the depiction of the Irish in the late nineteenth century "as an inferior race – as a kind of white negroe."

16 Iremonger was born in Jamaica in 1921 of English-French descent, and educated there and later in England where she met her husband. After living for many years in the Pacific where he worked in the Colonial Service, she wrote a travel book, *It's A Bigger Life*, which was well received. After travels to the West Indies, Australia, new Zealand, India and Europe, she finally settled in London, working as a writer and BBC broadcaster.

17 Ada Quayle – real name, Kathleen Woods – was born in 1927 in Jamaica, the daughter of a local planter. During World War II, she joined the Women's Auxiliary Air Force

and was posted to Egypt and East Africa, where she married an English journalist. After the war they moved from Kenya to London.

18 Mary Lockett's novel *Christopher* (1902), though set in Virginia and thus of only comparative interest to my study, does contain a strange take on the origins of this climate of materialism and greed in the colonies. The Italian-born hero, Christopher Columbus, reflecting on his famous ancestor of the same name, constructs him as a good man with worthy intentions: his motive for seeking a new route to India is given as "that of a missionary" as much as for the desire for trade (175). However, the narrative concedes that greed has corrupted the spiritual goals of the colonial enterprise and now "the continent to which he had been first to open a pathway, was teeming with speculators, whose ambition was only to gather treasures and attain great names, thereby trampling down the religious movements he had established" (175). The "pure" quest has been subverted by uncontrolled mercantilism.

19 Parham was the first English settlement in Antigua, and the island's first port.

20 As in Mary Prince's narrative, the very landscape is polluted. This is suggested in Wilkins' *The Slave Son* (1854), which closes with the escape from Trinidad of a noble mulatto slave and his beloved. In his farewell to the island paradise, the colored hero mourns: "God might have chosen you for Eden when he first created man; angels might have lived among your gardens . . . – all spoiled, corrupted, poisoned by the white man!" (347). Napier's fiction of a traumatized tropical paradise is hardly more positive, so long as the exploitative ethos of colonial rule continues to dominate relationships with land and people.

6 Colonial discourse and the subaltern's voice

1 For example, Ferguson (1992: 363) observes abolitionist British women writers' comparison of strategies for subjugating women, with those for keeping blacks in their place. She suggests that in the portrayal of the slave Yarico, in eighteenth-century discussions of the Countess of Hertford's legend of *Inkle and Yarico*, the reader's sympathies were wholly with Yarico whose "problems intersect with those of white women," while "Inkle epitomizes dual exploitation, both sexual and commercial" (88–9). Here, anti-slavery sentiments were informed by anti-patriarchal ones. Generally, however, involvement in the abolitionist cause became a way of mobilizing for the liberation of *white* women, while still consigning black women to homogeneous Otherness. Ferguson acknowledges a few anomalies – like Mary Wollstonecraft – whose "radical anti-slavery discursive practices in the late eighteenth century . . . specifically treated Africans, like Europeans, as subjects in and for themselves" (186). Such radical women "were much more keenly aware of their commonality with slaves" and drew "parallels based on experiential analogies between what they called white female slavery and colonial slavery" (197).

2 These are fictional names for Jamaica, just as "Alice Spinner" of "Santa Anna, West Indies," is the *nom-de-plume* of Augusta Fraser. Such elaborate disguises intend the distancing of the author's own experience of the West Indies from that of her narrators.

3 May Harvey Drummond was the daughter of Octavius Charles Harvey, listed as a Member of the Royal College of Surgeons, Jamaica, and "Justice" of a country town, Savannah-la-Mar. She married William Drummond, an Irish poet who had emigrated to Canada, where he practiced as a doctor. She may also have spent some time in the southern United States too, producing *Scenes in Georgia* (date uncertain) before *Quamin*.

4 Allsopp (1996: 29) explains that Anancy is "[t]he cunning rascal and hero of a countless number of Car[ibbean] folk-tales (originating in W[est] Afr[ican], esp Ashanti, folklore) in wh[ich] he is a mythical spider in human form, usu[ally] outwitting opponents of superior strength, or barely escaping being caught, but always amusing in his greed and selfishness."

5 Alice Chase Durie (*née* Hopkins) was born in Port Antonio, Jamaica on February 17, 1886, of American parents. Her father, Elisha Hopkins, helped start the banana export business in the island. After graduating from Wellesley College in 1908 with a degree in English literature, she returned to Jamaica and in 1916 married Alexander Durie, the founder of Times Store. His family also owned the *Jamaica Times*, which published *One Jamaica Gal*. Alice Durie died in Mexico City in 1970; her ashes were scattered at sea off Port Royal, Jamaica.

According to her son, Alec Durie (chairman of Times Stores, Kingston, Jamaica) – whose help with these biographical details I gratefully acknowledge, and whom I quote below – her parents were wealthy "WASP" Americans and, until she was 16, Alice "thought that all men had unlimited money in their pockets." Sensitized to social conditions in the island, she based *One Jamaica Gal* "on her knowledge of the experiences of her mother's servants and their relations." The Governor's wife was asked for her imprimatur for the novel, as the proceeds from its sale were donated to a war charity, "but refused on the grounds that she did not want to be associated with such a 'disgusting tale.' " In several ways, the text prefigures Roger Mais's gritty novels of urban squalor and violence in the 1950s. However, Durie represented the "old order" in Jamaica, dependant on the limited ballot, and found distasteful the literary intellectual circle led by Edna Manley, which represented the "new order" gaining ground in the island. Another manuscript remains published.

6 According to Allsopp (1996: 75), the balm-yard is a Jamaican word referring to an "enclosed yard where faith-healing ceremonies are performed (including devotional fasting, sacrifices, bush-baths, drumming, dancing, speaking in tongues, ritual feasting, etc.) supervised by a recognized balm-man or shepherd or sometimes a woman in the same role."

7 As noted previously, JanMohamed's "colonising subject" is unitary: "the European," "he." Further, although his specific focus is on literary productions in the "dominant phase" of colonialism – the nineteenth century – he ignores the West Indies of the period. Therefore he neglects the fact that *creole* culture was a major influence on locally born or resident whites, and distinguished them from the (generic) "European." Again, it seems to me that JanMohamed elides distinctions between narrator and author when he asserts that "a 'native' writer, such as V. S. Naipaul, can also be inducted, under the right circumstances, to fulfil the author-function of the colonialist writer" (82). At the same time, he *also* allows for exceptions to the essentialized "colonialist" writer, citing the case of Kipling: "in the context of colonial fiction, [*Kim* is] a novel that proceeds from emotional identification with the Other [and thus] offers the most thorough vision of the syncretic possibility" (97). Surely then, creolization – a "vision of the syncretic possibility" – impacts on the inherent nature of the "colonising subject"?

8 That such unions end badly underscores the narrative censure of miscegenation: all the colored characters in Fraser's novel are rotten (Mrs Gordon, Malcolm). "I like black people, I like de white Buckra, but I hate de colored ladies," says little Angelina (Fraser 1894: 108). JanMohamed (1986: 98) maintains that the mixed-race native was a frightening anomaly for the colonialist writer, since as previously discussed, the syncretic, manifestly *creolized* nature of such a product complicates the manichean dichotomy.

9 See also Mary Seacole (1984: 55–6): "Many people have also traced to my good Scotch blood that energy and activity which are not always found in the Creole [mulatto] race, and which have carried me to so many varied scenes: and perhaps they are right. I have often heard the term 'lazy Creole' applied to my country people; but I am sure I do not know what it is to be indolent." Importantly, Seacole puts the racial-moral proposition into the mouths of other people, and suspends her own endorsement of their truth: "*perhaps* they are right" (my emphasis).

10 See Moore-Gilbert (1997: 149–50) on the "lack of attention to gender in Bhabha's work ... This might help explain why the role and position of white women in

imperialism is almost completely ignored in Bhabha's work (to an even greater extent than in [Said's] *Orientalism*)."

11 However, Moore-Gilbert (1997: 134) suggests that if, as Bhabha seems to suggest, the process is largely unconscious, then neither mimicry nor the refusal to return the colonizer's gaze, however unsettling, can destabilize relations of power resident in colonial authority in any meaningful way. This is one of the observations, as Moore-Gilbert points out, used by Bhabha's critics to impugn what they see as his inflation of theory at the expense of the more crucial (materialist) role played by armed resistance and political solidarity (138). None the less, I find more persuasive, for my purposes, Moore-Gilbert's insistence that Bhabha's work does politicize textuality.

12 Watson's fascinating study (2000) is a case in point. He chronicles a history of resistance by the women of "Old Doll's" Barbados slave family in the late eighteenth and early nineteenth centuries, based on official documents and records which include *their* letters, petitions and interviews with the slaves themselves.

13 Mario Cesareo (2001: 124), observing correspondences between the slave narrative and the picaresque tale, comments that Pringle's annotation, intended to counter charges of Mary's untruthfulness, "underscores what it seeks to dispel, confirming the subaltern status of the narrator's voice within the political and rhetorical economy of the slave narrative." Attempting to legitimize the text, the multiplicity of voices within the *History* "makes difficult the identification of *a* narrator, problematizing the source(s) of textual authority."

14 Allsopp (1996: 123) defines this as a synonym of "busing," that is: "Loud (and often prolonged) personal attack in vulgar terms and/or obscene language" usually conducted publicly, and most often by women.

15 In fact, *outside* of her medical practice – and people paid, some handsomely, for her nursing services in Central America (79) and in the Crimea (166) – everything Seacole undertakes is for gain.

Afterword

1 Gregg's study of Rhys observes that "through quotations, allusions and other forms of intertextuality, Rhys rewrites many of the topoi and texts of European discourse on the West Indies . . . In order to write her self, she has to write through the constructions of selfhood assigned to her within prior and dominant discourses, to read her way through them" (1995: 51).

2 Just one example is the recurrent withdrawal on the part of threatened female characters into a safe, protective camouflage that can also become a prison, as explored by Brodber in the image of the kumbla in *Jane and Louisa Will Soon Come Home* (1980: 123): "A kumbla is like a beach ball . . . the kumbla is an egg shell . . . It is a round seamless calabash that protects you without caring. Your kumbla is a parachute . . . Safe, protective time capsule." Napier seems to be groping for a similar construct when she describes her grieving protagonist seeking a similar internal refuge: "she likened herself to a sausage, to a chrysalis, to anything sheathed" (1938: 125).

3 Both Cobham (1990) and Brodber (1982) have noted the enduring narrative dichotomy in contemporary Caribbean women's writing between black women (constructed in terms of African cultural values) and brown women (constructed in terms of approximation to European ideals). This is also a feature, as previously noted, in the writing of Fraser, Carmichael and Lanaghan, in which colored women are represented as courting "respectability" and imitative acculturation while black women defiantly refuse such mimicry. The interrogation of this polarization is an important focus in later texts such as Hodge's *Crick Crack Monkey* and Brodber's *Myal*.

4 The fiction of Olive Senior is a good example, but there are ealier examples such as Sylvia Wynter's *The Hills of Hebron* (1962) and Paule Marshall's *The Chosen Place, The Timeless People* (1969).

Bibliography

Primary sources

Allfrey, P. S. (1982) *The Orchid House*, London: Virago [1953].

Anon (1823) *The Koromantyn Slaves; Or, West Indian Sketches.* London: J. Hatchard and Sons.

—— (1881) *The Babes in the Basket; or, Daph and Her Charge*, London: Frederick Warne and Co. (attributed to Sarah Schoonmaker Baker or Charlotte Elizabeth Browne).

Ashton, H. [Mrs Jordan] (1928) *Far Enough*, London: Ernest Benn.

Atherton, G. F. H. (1902) *The Conqueror: A Dramatized Biography of Alexander Hamilton*, New York: Frederick Stokes Co.

—— (1908) *The Gorgeous Isle, a Romance: Scene, Nevis, B.W.I.,1842*, London: J. Murray.

—— (1932) *Adventures of a Novelist*, New York: Liveright.

Barker, Lady M. A. (1873) *Stories About:-*, London: Macmillan.

Bliss, E. (1984) *Luminous Isle*, London: Virago [1934].

—— (1986) *Saraband*, London: Virago [1931].

Bridges, Y. (1988) *Child of the Tropics: Victorian Memoirs*, N. Guppy (ed.), Port of Spain: Aquarela Galleries [1980].

Burslem, M. [18–?] "A West Indian Childhood." Ts. Rhodes House Library, Oxford.

Carmichael, A.C. Mrs. (1969) *Domestic Manners and Social Condition of the White, Coloured, and Negro Population of the West Indies*, 3 vols., London: Whittaker, Treacher and Co.; New York: Negro Universities Press [1833].

Cassin, F. (1890) *With Silent Tread*, St. John's, Antigua: G. A. Uphill.

Chapman, E. (1928) *Study In Bronze*, London: Constable.

—— (1953) *Too Much Summer*, London: Chantry Publishers.

Creole, A. (1755) *Fortunate Transport; or The Secret History of the Life and Adventures of the Celebrated Polly Haycock*, London: F. Taylor.

Crommelin, M. de la C. (1898) "The Mountain-Heart of Jamaica," *The Ludgate*, VI (October): 525–532.

—— (1902) *A Daughter of England*, London: John Long.

Crowninshield, S. Mrs. (1898a) *Where the Trade Wind Blows: West Indian Tales*, New York: Macmillan.

—— (1898b) *Latitude 19°: A Romance of the West Indies in the Year of Our Lord Eighteen Hundred and Twenty*, New York: D. Appleton and Co.

deLisser, H. G. (1914) *Jane's Career: A Story of Jamaica*, London: Methuen.

—— (1958) *The White Witch of Rosehall*, London: Ernest Benn [1929].

Drummond, M. H. (1911) *The Story of Quamin: A Tale of the Tropics*, New York: Knicker-bocker Press.

Duff, W. Mrs (1925) *His Promise*, London: Arthur Stockwell (published under the pseudonym Freda Granville).

Durie, A. (1939) *One Jamaica Gal*, Kingston: Jamaica Times.

E. J. W. (A Woman) (1862) *Constance Mordaunt; or, Life in the Western Archipelago*, 2 vols., London: Saunders Otley and Co.

Fenwick, E. (1927) *The Fate of the Fenwicks: Letters to Mary Hays (1798–1828)*, A. F. Wedd (ed.), London: Methuen.

Fielding, E. (1915) *Short Stories of Jamaica and The War*, Kingston: P. A. Benjamin Manufacturing Co. Press.

—— (1957) *Romance in Jamaica*, London: Arthur Stockwell.

Fraser, A. Z. (1894) *A Study in Colour*, London: T. Fisher (published under the pseudonym Alice Spinner).

—— (1896a) *Lucilla, An Experiment*, 2 vols., London: Kegan Paul (published under the pseudonym Alice Spinner).

—— (1896b) "Margaret: A Sketch in Black and White." In A. Z. Fraser, *The Reluctant Evangelist and Other Stories*, London: Edward Arnold (published under the pseudonym Alice Spinner): 288–309.

Gaunt, M. (1922) *Where the Twain Meet*, London: John Murray.

—— (1932) *Reflection – in Jamaica*, London: Ernest Benn.

—— (1933) *Harmony, a Tale of the Old Slave Days in Jamaica*, London: Ernest Benn.

Hart Gilbert, A. (1993) "History of Methodism." *The Hart Sisters: Early African Caribbean Writers, Evangelicals, and Radicals*, M. Ferguson (ed.), Lincoln and London: University of Nebraska Press [1804].

Hart Thwaites, E. (1993) "History of Methodism." *The Hart Sisters: Early African Caribbean Writers, Evangelicals, and Radicals*, M. Ferguson (ed.), Lincoln and London: University of Nebraska Press [1804].

Hart, Miss (1948) *Letters from the Bahama Islands, written in 1823–4*, London: John Culmer [1827].

Hofland, B. H. (1831) *The Barbadoes Girl: A Tale for Young People*, New York: William Burgess.

Hutchins, M. A. (1839) *The Youthful Female Missionary: A Memoir of Mary Ann Hutchins*, London: G. Wightman, Hamilton, Adams and Co.

Iremonger, L. (1950) *Creole*, London: Hutchinson.

James, W. (1913) *The Mulberry Tree*, London: Chapman and Hall.

Jeffrey Smith, U. (1899) *A Selection of Anancy Stories*, Kingston: Author (published under the pseudonym Wona).

Jenkin, H. C. (1859) *Cousin Stella; or, Conflict*, 3 vols., London: Smith and Elder.

Lanaghan, F. (1844) *Antigua and the Antiguans: A Full Account of the Colony and its Inhabitants from the Time of the Caribs to the Present Day*, 2 vols., London: Saunders and Otley.

Layard, G. Mrs. (1887) *Through the West Indies*, London: Sampson Low, Marston, Searle and Rivington.

Lockett, M. (1902) *Christopher, a Novel*, New York: Abbey Press.

Long, G. M. V. C. J. [better known as "Marjorie Bowen"] (1936) *The Golden Violet; The Story of a Lady Novelist*, London: Heinemann (published under the pseudonym Joseph Shearing).

Lynch, H. Mrs. (1847) *The Cotton Tree: Or Emily, the Little West Indian, a Tale for Young People*, London: John Hatchard and Son.

—— (1848) *The Family Sepulchre: A Tale of Jamaica*, London: Seeley, Jackson and Halliday.

—— (1852) *The Mountain Pastor*, London: Seeley, Jackson and Halliday.

—— (186-) *Rose, and Her Mission*, London: n.p.

—— (1861) *The Wonders of the West Indies*, London: Seeley, Jackson and Halliday.

—— (1865) *Years Ago: A Tale of West Indian Domestic Life of the Nineteenth Century*, London: Jarrold and Sons.

Maclean, I. C. (1910) *Children of Jamaica*, Edinburgh: Oliphant, Anderson and Ferrier.

Marks, J. (1938) *The Family of the Barrett: A Colonial Romance*, New York: Macmillan.

Marsh-Caldwell, A. (1850, 1852) *Adelaide Lindsay; a Novel*, 3 vols., London: Cox and Wyman.

Marson, U. (1931) "Sojourn." *The Cosmopolitan* (February):8+.

Martineau, H. (1832) "Demerara: A Tale," in H. Martineau, *Illustrations of Political Economy*, vol. 2, 2nd edn., London: Charles Fox.

Maxwell, K. (1757) *The History of Miss Katty N——*, London: F. Noble.

Milne-Home, M. P. (1890) *Mama's Black Nurse Stories*, Edinburgh: n.p.

Moore, R. W. (1867) *Journal of Rachel Wilson Moore, During a Tour to the West Indies and South America in 1863–64*, Philadelphia: T. Ellwood Zell.

Napier, E.(1936) *Duet in Discord*, London: Arthur Baker (published under the pseudonym Elizabeth Garner).

—— (1938) *A Flying Fish Whispered*, London: Arthur Baker (published under the pseudonym Elizabeth Garner).

—— (1949) *Winter is in July*, London: Jonathan Cape.

Newton, M. (1897) *Glimpses of Life in Bermuda and the Tropics* London: Digby, Long and Co.

Nugent, Lady M. (1966) *Lady Nugent's Journal of her Residence in Jamaica from 1801 to 1805*, P. Wright (ed.), Kingston: Institute of Jamaica [1907].

Osborne, F. (1854) *Black Sam and His Master: A Tale of the West Indies*, London: Darton and Co.

Prince, M. (1987) *History of Mary Prince, a West Indian Slave: Related by herself*, Thomas Pringle (ed.) in *The Classic Slave Narratives*, Henry Louis Gates Jr. (ed.), New York: New American Library [1831].

Prince, N. (1850) *A Narrative of the Life and Times of Mrs. Nancy Prince*, Boston: The Author.

Quayle, A. (1957) *The Mistress*, London: MacGibbon and Kee.

Rhys, J. (1968) *Wide Sargasso Sea*, Harmondsworth: Penguin [1966]

Sargeant, J. (1843) *Scenes in the West Indies; and Other Poems*, London: John Mason.

—— (1855) *Stray Leaves: Poetry and Prose*, London: John Mason (published under the pseudonym Adeline).

Satchell, A. (1858) *Reminiscences of Missionary Life*, Loughborough: Thomas Danks.

Schaw, J. (1921) *Journal of a Lady of Quality, Being the Narrative of a Journey from Scotland to the West Indies, North Carolina and Portugal, in the Years 1774 to 1776*, E. W. Andrews and C. M. Andrews (eds.), New Haven, Conn.: Yale University Press.

Seacole, M. (1984) *The Wonderful Adventures of Mary Seacole in Many Lands*, Ziggi Alexander and Audrey Dewjee (eds.), London: Falling Wall Press [1857].

Smith, M. C. (1900) *Mary Paget, a Romance of Old Bermuda*, New York: Macmillan.

Smith, P. C. (1899) *Anancy Stories*, London: Robert Howard Russell.

Stephenson, C. (1911) *Undine: An Experience*, New York: Broadway Publishing.

Symonett, E. M. (1895) *Jamaica: Queen of the Carib Sea*, Kingston: Mortimer C. DeSouza.

Tonna, C. Mrs (1827) *The System; A Tale of the West Indies*, London: F. Westly and A. H. Davis (published under the pseudonym Charlotte Elizabeth).

Touzi, L. L M.A. [Mrs. Symonds] (1840) *Les Jumelles; or, The Twins*, London: J. Barfield.

Wilcox, E. W. (1909) *Sailing Sunny Seas: A Story of Travel*, Chicago: W. B. Conkey Co.

Wilkins, W. N. Mrs (1854) *The Slave Son*, London: Chapman and Hall.

Wogan, J. R. (1936) *Go Down Moses*, London: Hutchinson and Co. (published under the pseudonym Janet Cousins).

W.P. (1963) "The Jamaican Lady, or, The Life of Bavia," in *Four Before Richardson: Selected English Novels, 1720–1727*, William H. McBurney (ed.), Lincoln: University of Nebraska Press [1720].

Secondary sources

Abruna, L. N. de (1991) "Family Connections: Mother and Mother Country in the Fiction of Jean Rhys and Jamaica Kincaid," in S. Nasta (ed.) *Motherlands: Black Women's Writing from Africa, the Caribbean and South Asia*, London: The Women's Press.

Adams, P. (1983) *Travel Literature and the Evolution of the Novel*, Lexington: University Press of Kentucky.

Allen, W. (1954) *The English Novel: A Short Critical History*, London: Penguin.

Allibone, S. A. (1877) *A Critical Dictionary of English Literature and British and American Authors*, London: Trübner. 3 vols.

Allsopp, R. (ed.) (1996) *Dictionary of Caribbean English Usage*, Oxford: Oxford University Press.

Arthur, K. (1997) *View from Belmont*, Leeds: Peepal Tree Press.

—— (forthcoming) *Nineteenth Century Caribbean Literature*.

Asein, S.O. (1972) "West Indian Poetry in English, 1900–1970: A Selected Bibliography," *Black Images* 1, 2: 12–15.

Ashcroft, B. (1989) "Intersecting Marginalities: Post-Colonialism and Feminism," *Kunapipi* 11, 2: 23–35.

Ashcroft, B., G. Griffiths and H. Tiffin (1989) *The Empire Writes Back: Theory and Practice in Post-Colonial Literatures*, London: Routledge.

Bandara, S. B. (1980) "A Bibliography of Caribbean Novels in English," *Journal of Commonwealth Literature* 15, 1: 141–70.

Barker, F. et al. (eds.) (1985) *Europe and its Others: Proceedings of the Essex Conference on the Sociology of Literature, July 1984*, Colchester: University of Essex.

Baugh, E. (1981) "Edward Brathwaite as Critic," in E. Smilowitz and R. Knowles (eds.) *Proceedings of the First Annual Conference on West Indian Literature*, St Thomas, V.I.: College of the Virgin Islands.

Baym, N. (1980) *Women's Fiction: A Guide to Novels by and about Women in America, 1820–1870*, Ithaca, NY.: Cornell University Press.

Beauman, N. (1983) *A Very Great Profession: The Woman's Novel 1914–1939*, London: Virago.

Beckles, H. (1989) *Natural Rebels: A Social History of Enslaved Black Women in Barbados*, London: Zed Books.

—— (1993) "White women and Slavery in the Caribbean," *History Workshop Journal*, 36: 66–82.

—— (1995) "Sex and Gender in the Historiography of Carribean Slavery," in V. Shepherd et al. (eds.) *Engendering History: Carribean Women in the Historical Perspsective*, Kingston, Jamaica: Ian Randle; London: James Currey.

—— (1998a) "White Women and a West India Fortune: Gender and Wealth During Slavery," in H. Johnson and K. Watson (eds.) *The White Minority in the Caribbean*, Kingston, Jamaica: Ian Randle; London: James Currey.

—— (1998b) "Taking Liberties: Enslaved Women and Anti-slavery in the Caribbean," in C. Midgely (ed.) *Gender and Imperialism*, Manchester: Manchester University Press.

—— (1998c) "Historicizing Slavery in West Indian Feminisms," *Feminist Review* 59: 34–56.

Benson, R. (1992) "Columbus at the Abyss: The Genesis of New World Literature," *Jamaica Journal* 24, 3: 48–54.

Berrian, B. (1989) *Bibliography of Women Writers from the Caribbean (1831–1986)*, Washington: Three Continents Press.

Bhaba, H. (1984) "Representation and the Colonial Text: A Critical Exploration of Some Forms of Mimeticism," in F. Gloversmith (ed.) *The Theory of Reading*, New Jersey: Barnes and Noble.

—— (1985) "The Other Question: Difference, Discrimination and the Discourse of Colonialism," in F. Barker et al. (eds.) *Literature, Politics and Theory: Papers from the Essex Conferences, 1976–1984*, Colchester: University of Essex.

—— (1992) "The World and the Home," *Social Text* 31–2: 141–53.

—— (1994) *The Location of Culture*, London: Routledge.

Birbalsingh, F. (1989) "Esther Chapman and the Expatriate West Indian Novel," *Kyk-Over-Al* 40: 72–7.

Blain, V., P. Clements and I. Grundy (eds.) (1990) *The Feminist Companion to Literature in English: Women Writers from the Middle Ages to the Present*, London: B. T. Batsford.

Blake, S. L. (1992) "A Woman's Trek: What Difference Does Gender Make?" in N. Chaudhuri and M. Strobel (eds.) *Western Women and Imperialism: Complicity and Resistance*, Bloomington: Indiana University Press.

Boyce Davis, C. (1992) "Collaboration and the Ordering Imperative in Life Story Production," in S. Smith and J. Watson (eds.) *De/Colonizing the Subject: The Politics of Gender in Women's Autobiography*, Minneapolis: University of Minnesota Press.

—— (1994) *Black Women, Writing and Identity: Migrations of the Subject*, London: Routledge.

Boyce Davies, C. and E. Savory Fido (eds.) (1990) *Out of the Kumbla: Caribbean Women and Literature*, Trenton, New Jersey: Africa World Press.

Boxill, A, (1966) "The Novel in English in the West Indies 1900–1962," unpublished thesis, University of New Brunswick.

—— (1971) "Bibliography of West Indian Fiction 1900–1970," *World Literature Written in English* 19: 23–44.

—— (1979) "The Beginnings to 1929," in B. King (ed.) *West Indian Literature*, London: Macmillan.

Brantlinger, P. (1988) *Rule of Darkness: British Literature and Imperialism, 1830–1914*, Ithaca, NY.: Cornell University Press.

Brathwaite, E. K. (1963) "Roots: A Commentary on West Indian Writers," *Bim* 10: 10–21.

—— (1969) "Caribbean Critics," *Critical Quarterly* 11, 3: 268–76.

—— (1970) "Creative Literature During the Period of Slavery," *Savacou* 2/3: 46–73.

—— (1971) *The Development of Creole Society in Jamaica, 1770–1820*, Oxford: Oxford University Press.

—— (1974) *Contradictory Omens*, Kingston, Jamaica: Savacou.

—— (1978) "The Love Axe/l," Part 3, *Bim* 16, 63: 181–92.

—— (1984) "Caribbean Women During the Period of Slavery," *Caribbean Contact* 2: 13–14.

—— (1995) "A Post-Cautionary Tale of the Helen of Our Wars," *Wasafiri* 22: 69–78.

Breiner, L. (1993) "How to Behave on Paper: The *Savacou* Debate," *Journal of West Indian Literature* 6, 1: 1–10.

Brereton, B. (1993) "Text, Testimony and Gender: An Examination of Some Texts by Women on the English Speaking Caribbean, 1770s to 1920s," paper presented to Symposium on Engendering Caribbean History: Current Directions in the Study of Women and Gender in Caribbean History, University of the West Indies, Mona: Dept. of History.

—— (1994) *Gendered Testimony: Autobiographies, Diaries and Letters by Women as Sources for Caribbean History: The 1994 Elsa Goveia Memorial Lecture*, University of the West Indies, Mona: Dept. of History.

—— (1995) "Text, Testimony and Gender; An Examination of Some Texts by Women on the English Speaking Caribbean, 1770s to 1920s," in V. Shepherd, B. Brereton and B. Bailey (eds.) *Engendering History: Caribbean Women in the Historical Perspective*, Kingston: Ian Randle; London: James Currey.

—— (1998) "The White Elite of Trinidad, 1838–1950," in H. Johnson and K. Watson (eds.) *The White Minority in the Caribbean*, Kingston, Jamaica: Ian Randle; London: James Currey.

Brodber, E, (1980) *Jane and Louisa Will Soon Come Home*, London: New Beacon.

—— (1982) *Perceptions of Caribbean Women: Towards a Documentation of Stereotypes*, University of the West Indies, Cave Hill: Institute for Social and Economic Research.

—— (1988) *Myal*, London: New Beacon.

Brontë, C. (1987) *Jane Eyre*, New York: Norton [1847].

Brown University Women Writers Project: A Textbase of Women's Writing in English, 1330–1830, (1993) Providence, Rhode Island: Brown University, Online. Available HTTP <http://www.wwp.brown.edu/> (accessed September 8, 1998).

Brydon, D. and H. Tiffin (1993) *Decolonising Fictions*, Mundelstrup: Dangaroo Press.

Bush, B. (1981) "White 'Ladies,' Colored 'Favorites' and Black 'Wenches': Some Considerations on Sex, Race and Class factors in Social Relations in White Creole Society in the British Caribbean," *Slavery and Abolition: A Journal of Comparative Studies* 2, 3: 245–62.

—— (1990) *Slave Women in Caribbean Society 1650–1838*, Kingston: Heinemann; London: James Curry; Bloomington: Indiana University Press.

Butler, K. M. (1995) *The Economics of Emancipation: Jamaica and Barbados, 1823–1843*, Chapel Hill: University of North Carolina Press.

Bynum, V. (1992) *Unruly Women: The Politics of Social and Sexual Control in the Old South*, Chapel Hill: University of North Carolina Press.

Campbell, E. (1978) "Report from Dominica, B.W.I.," *World Literature Written in English* 17, 1: 305–16.

—— (1979) "Oroonoko's Heir: The West Indies in Late Eighteenth Century Novels by Woman [sic]," *Caribbean Quarterly* 25: 80–4.

—— (1982) "An Expatriate at Home: Dominica's Elma Napier," *Kunapipi* 4, 1: 82–93.

—— (1985) "Aphra Behn's Surinam Interlude," *Kunapipi*, 7, 2–3: 25–35.

Canny, N. and A. Pagden (eds.) (1987) *Colonial Identity in the Atlantic World, 1500–1800*, Princeton, N. J.: Princeton University Press.

Canton, E. B. (1957) "Bibliography of Caribbean Literature, 1900–1957," *Current Caribbean Bibliography*, vol. 7, Port of Spain: Caribbean Commission.

Carby, H. (1987) *Reconstructing Womanhood: The Emergence of the Afro-American Woman Novelist*, Oxford: Oxford University Press.

Cassidy, F. G. and R. B. LePage (eds.) (1980) *Dictionary of Jamaican English*, 2nd edn., Cambridge: Cambridge University Press [1967].

Cesareo, M. (2001) "When the Subaltern Travels: Slave Narratives and Testimonial Erasure in the Contact Zone," in L. Paravisini-Gebert and I. Romero-Cesareo (eds.) *Women at Sea: Travel Writing and the Margins of Caribbean Discourse*, New York: Palgrave.

Chaudhuri, N. and M. Strobel (eds.) (1992) *Western Women and Imperialism: Complicity and Resistance*, Bloomington: Indiana University Press.

Chrisman, L. (1990) "The Imperial Unconscious? Representations of Imperial Discourse," *Critical Quarterly* 32, 3: 38–58.

Christian, B. (1980) *Black Women Novelists: The Development of a Tradition, 1892–1976*, Westport, Conn.: Greenwood.

The Christian Remembrancer (1819–1834) 16 vols., London: British Museum.

Clark, S. (1999) *Travel Writing and Empire: Postcolonial Theory in Transit*, London: Zed Books.

Cliff, M. (1987) *No Telephone to Heaven*, New York: Dutton.

Cobham, R. (1990) "Women in Jamaican Literature 1900–1950," in C. Boyce Davies and E. Savory Fido (eds.) *Out of the Kumbla: Caribbean Women and Literature*, Trenton, New Jersey: Africa World Press.

Colby, V. (1970) *The Singular Anomaly: Women Novelists of the Nineteenth Century*, London: University of London Press; New York: New York University Press.

Commisong, B. and M. Thorpe (1978) "Select Bibliography of Women Writers in the Eastern Caribbean," *World Literature Written in English* 17, 1: 279–304.

Concise Dictionary of National Biography Part I: To 1900 (1953) London: Oxford University Press.

Concise Dictionary of National Biography Part II: 1901–1950 (1961) London: Oxford University Press.

Cooper, C. (1991) " 'Me Know No Law, Me Know No Sin': Transgressive Identities and the Voice of Innocence in Selected Female-centred Jamaican Oral Texts," paper presented to Tenth Annual Conference on West Indian Literature, University of the West Indies, St Augustine: Dept. of English.

Cooper, B. (1994) "Liberated Repressions: Escaped Thoughts of a White South African Critic," *Wasafiri* 19: 40–50.

Craig, C. (1984) "*Wonderful Adventures of Mrs. Seacole in Many Lands*: Autobiography as Literary Genre and Window to Character," *Caribbean Quarterly* 30, 2: 33–47.

Craton, M. J. (1974) *Sinews of Empire: A Short History of British Slavery*, Garden City, NY: Doubleday.

Cudjoe, S. (ed.) (1990) *Caribbean Women Writers: Essays from the First International Conference*, Wellesley, Mass: Calaloux.

Cundall, F. (1902) *Bibliographia Jamaicensis: A List of Jamaica Books and Pamphlets, Magazine Articles, Newspapers, and Maps*, Kingston: Institute of Jamaica.

—— (1920) *Jamaica in 1920; A Handbook of Information for Intending Settlers and Visitors*, Kingston: Institute of Jamaica.

Daiches, D. (ed.) (1971) *The Penguin Companion to Literature: Britain and the Commonwealth*, Harmondsworth: Penguin.

Daims, D. and J. Grimes (eds.) with editorial assistance of Doris Robinson (1982) *Toward a Feminist Tradition: An Annotated Bibliography of Novels in English by Women, 1891–1920*, New York: Garland.

Dance, D. (1986) *Fifty Caribbean Writers: A Bio-bibliographical Critical Sourcebook*, Westport, Conn.: Greenwood.

Davidoff, L. and C. Hall, (1987) *Family Fortunes: Men and Women of the English Middle Class, 1780–1850*, Chicago: University of Chicago Press.

Daymond, M. J. (1992) "A Woman's Narrative of Her Adventures in Southern Africa (1890–1900): The Case of Melina Rorke," paper presented to Ninth International ACLALS Conference, University of the West Indies, Mona: Department of English.

deCaires Narain, D. (1995) "Anglophone Caribbean Women Poets from 1940 to the Present: A Tradition in the Making?" unpublished thesis, University of Kent.

—— (2002) *Contemporary Caribbean Women's Poetry: Making Style*, London: Routledge.

—— and O'Callaghan, E. (1994) "Anglophone Women Writers," in Rutherford, A.. Jensen, L. and Chew, S. (eds.) *Into the Nineties: Post-colonial Women's Writing*, Mundlestrup: Dangaroo Press.

Dickson, W. (1789) *Letters on Slavery*, London: J. Phillips.

Dictionary of National Biography 1931–1940 (1950) London: Oxford University Press.

Dirks, N. B. (ed.) (1992) *Colonialism and Culture*, Ann Arbor: University of Michigan Press.

Donaldson, L. E. (1992) *Decolonising Feminisms: Race, Gender, and Empire Building*, Chapel Hill: University of North Carolina Press.

Donnell, A. (1995a) "She Ties Her Tongue: The Problems of Colonial Paralysis in Postcolonial Criticism,"*Ariel* 26, 1: 101–16.

—— (1995b) "Contradictory (W)omens? Gender Consciousness in the Poetry of Una Marson," *Kunapipi* 17: 43–58.

—— (1998) "Difficult Subjects: Women's Writing in the Caribbean pre-1970," paper presented to Sixth International Conference of Caribbean Women Writers and Scholars, Grande Anse, Grenada.

Drayton, A. (1970) "West Indian Consciousness in West Indian Verse: A Historical Perspective," *Journal of Commonwealth Literature* 9 (July): 60–88.

Edwards, B. (1793) *The History, Civil and Commercial, of the British Colonies in the West Indies*, 2 vols., London: J. Stockdale; Dublin: L. White.

Engber, M. (1970) *Caribbean Fiction and Poetry*, New York: Center for Inter-American Relations.

Esteves, C. C. and L. Paravisini-Gebert (eds.) (1991) *Green Cane and Juicy Flotsam: Short Stories by Caribbean Women*, New Brunswick, N.J.: Rutgers.

Farquhar, B. (1981) "Old and New Creative Writing in Antigua and Barbuda," *Bulletin of Eastern Caribbean Affairs* 7, 5: 29–34.

Ferguson, M. (1992) *Subject to Others: British Women Writers and Colonial Slavery 1670–1834*, London: Routledge.

—— (1993) *Colonialism and Gender Relations from Mary Wollstonecraft to Jamaica Kincaid: East Caribbean Connections*, New York: Colombia University Press.

Fox-Genovese, E. (1988) *Within the Plantation Household: Black and White Women of the Old South*, Chapel Hill: University of North Carolina Press.

Frankenberg, R. (1993) *White Women, Race Matters: The Social Construction of Whiteness*, London: Routledge.

Fuss, D. (1989) *Essentially Speaking: Feminism, Nature and Difference*, London: Routledge.

Gates, H. L. Jr. (ed.) (1985) *'Race,' Writing and Difference*, Chicago: University of Chicago Press.

—— (1991) "Critical Fanonism," *Critical Inquiry* 17: 457–70.

Gilbert, S. and S. Gubar (1970) *The Madwoman in the Attic: The Woman Writer and the Nineteenth Century Literary Imagination*, New Haven, Conn.: Yale University Press.

Gilderale, B. (1998) "Re-discovering a remarkable Victorian," *Quarterly Journal of the Royal Overseas League* (September–November): 7–8.

Gilkes, M. (1981) *The West Indian Novel*, Boston: Twayne.

Gilman, S. L. (1986) "Black Bodies, White Bodies: Toward an Iconography of Female Sexuality in Late Nineteenth-Century Art, Medicine, and Literature," in H. L. Gates, Jr. (ed.) *'Race,' Writing and Difference*, Chicago: University of Chicago Press.

Gilmour, R. (1986) *The Novel in the Victorian Age: A Modern Introduction*, London: Edward Arnold.

Gikandi, S. (1996) *Maps of Englishness: Writing Identity in the Culture of Colonialism*, New York: Columbia University Press.

Gilroy, P. (1993) *The Black Atlantic: Modernity and Double Consciousness*, Cambridge, Mass.: Harvard University Press.

Goveia, E. (1980) *A Study on the Historiography of the British West Indies to the End of the Nineteenth Century*, Washington: Howard University Press.

Greene, J. P. (1987) "Changing Identity in the British Caribbean: Barbados as a Case Study," in N. Canny and A. Pagden (eds.) *Colonial Identity in the Atlantic World, 1500–1800*, Princeton, N. J.: Princeton University Press.

Gregg, V. M. (1995) *Jean Rhys's Historical Imagination: Reading and Writing the Creole*, Chapel Hill: University of North Carolina Press.

Griffiths, G. (1987) "Imitation, Abrogation and Appropriation: The Production of the Post-Colonial Text," *Kunapipi* 9, 1: 13–20.

Grossberg, L., C. Nelson and P. Treichler (eds.) (1992) *Cultural Studies*, New York: Routledge.

Haggis, J. (1998) "White Women and Colonialism: Towards a Non-recuperative History," in C. Midgely (ed.) *Gender and Imperialism*, Manchester: Manchester University Press.

Hall, C. (1992) "Missionary Stories: Gender and Ethnicity in England in the 1830s and 1840s," in L. Grossberg et al. (eds.) *Cultural Studies*, New York: Routledge.

—— (1993) "Gender Politics and Imperial Politics: Re-thinking the Histories of Empire," paper presented to Symposium on Engendering Caribbean History: Current Directions in the Study of Women and Gender in Caribbean History, University of the West Indies, Mona: Dept. of History.

Hall, D. (1989) *In Miserable Slavery: Thomas Thistlewood in Jamaica, 1750–86*, London: Macmillan.

Hall, S. (1993) "Cultural identity and Diaspora," in P. Williams and L. Chrisman (eds.) *Colonial Discourse and Post-Colonial Theory: A Reader*, New York: Harvester Wheatsheaf.

Handler, J. (1971) *A Guide to Source Materials for the Study of Barbados History, 1627–1834*, Carbondale: South Illinois University Press.

—— (1974) *The Unappropriated People*, Baltimore, MD: Johns Hopkins University Press.

Hanna, W. J. (1989) "Tourist Travel to Jamaica in the 1890s," *Jamaica Journal* 22: 12–20.

Harris, W. (1967) "Tradition and the West Indian Novel," in W. Harris, *Tradition, the Writer and Society: Critical Essays*, London: New Beacon.

Harrison, J. F. C. (1971) *Early Victorian Britain, 1832–51*, London: Fontana.

Hawthorne, E. (1992) "Traditions and the Free(d) Subject: A Study of Mary Seacole in Post-Emancipation British Culture," paper presented to Ninth Triennial ACLALS Conference, University of the West Indies, Mona: Department of English.

Hearne, J. (1956) *Stranger at the Gate*, London: Faber.

Henry, P. (1985) *Peripheral Capitalism and Underdevelopment in Antigua*, New Brunswick, N.J.: Transaction.

Herdeck, D. E. (ed.) (1979) *Caribbean Writers: A Bio-bibliographical-Critical Encyclopedia*, Washington: Three Continents Press.

Hershatter, G. (1993) "The Subaltern Talks Back: Reflections on Subaltern Theory and Chinese History," *positions* 1,1: 112–29.

Hill, W. (1930) *The Overseas Empire in Fiction; An Annotated Bibliography*, Oxford: Oxford University Press.

Hippolyte, J. (1996) "Race in the Place: An Alternative Reading of *The Wonderful Adventures of Mrs Seacole in Many Lands*," paper presented to Fifteenth Annual Conference on West Indian Literature, University of the West Indies, St Augustine: Department of Literatures in English.

Hodge, M. (1970) *Crick Crack Monkey*, London: Andre Deutsch.

Holst Peterson, K. and A. Rutherford (eds.) (1986) *A Double Colonization: Colonial and Postcolonial Women's Writing*, Mundelstrup: Dangaroo Press.

Honeychurch, L. (forthcoming) *The A to Z of Dominica Heritage*. Excerpted Online. Available HTTP: <http://www.avirtualdominica.com/heritage2.htm#N> (accessed July 22, 2002).

Hooper, G. (2001) "Revisions and Transitions in the History of Travel Writing," *Wasafiri* 34: 56–9.

Houghton, W. (1957) *The Victorian Frame of Mind, 1830–1870*, New Haven, Conn.: Yale University Press.

Hoving, I. (2001) *In Praise of New Travelers: Reading Caribbean Migrant Women's Writing*, Stanford, Conn.: Stanford University Press.

Hulme, P. (1986). *Colonial Encounters*, London: Methuen.

—— (1994) "The Place of *Wide Sargasso Sea*," *Wasafiri* 20 (Autumn): 5–11.

Hutcheon, L. (1989) " 'Circling the Downspout of Empire:' Post-Colonialism and Post-Modernism." *Ariel* 22, 4: 17–27.

Hyam, R. (1991) *Empire and Sexuality: The British Experience*, Manchester: Manchester University Press.

Ingram, K. E. (1975) *Manuscripts Relating to Commonwealth Caribbean Countries in United States and Canadian Repositories*, St Lawrence, Barbados: Caribbean Universities Press in association with Bowker Publishing Company.

—— (1976) *Sources of Jamaican History 1655–1838*, Zug, Switzerland: Inter Documentation Co.

JanMohamed, A. (1986) "The Economy of Manichean Allegory: The Function of Racial Difference in Colonialist Literature," in H. L. Gates, Jr. (ed.) *'Race,' Writing and Difference*, Chicago: University of Chicago Press.

Jarrett-Macauley, D. (1998) *The Life of Una Marson, 1905–1965*, Manchester: Manchester University Press.

Johnson, H. and K. Watson (eds.) (1998) *The White Minority in the Caribbean*, Kingston, Jamaica: Ian Randle; London: James Currey.

Kincaid, J. (1985) *Annie John*, Farrar, Straus and Giroux.

—— (1988) *A Small Place*, London: Virago.

—— (1990) *Lucy*, New York: Farrar, Straus and Giroux.

King, B. (ed.) (1979) *West Indian Literature*, London: Macmillan.

King, W. (1996) "The Mistress and her Maids: White and Black Women in a Louisiana Household, 1858–1868," in P. Morton (ed.) *Discovering The Women in Slavery: Emancipating Perspectives on the American Past*, Athens: University of Georgia Press.

Kröller, E. (1990) "First Impressions: Rhetorical Strategies in Travel Writing by Victorian Women," *Ariel* 21, 4: 87–99.

Kunitz, S. and H. Haycraft (eds.) (1936) *British Authors of the Nineteenth Century*, New York: H. W. Wilson.

—— (1942) *Twentieth Century Authors: A Bibliographic Dictionary*, New York: H. W. Wilson.

—— (1952) *British Authors Before 1800: A Biographical Dictionary*, New York: H. W. Wilson.

Lalla, B. and J. D'Costa (eds.) (1990) *Language in Exile: Three Hundred Years of Jamaican Creole*, Tuscaloosa: University of Alabama Press.

Latimer, J. (1952) "An Historical and Comparative Study of the Foundations of Education in the British, Spanish and French West Indies (up to the end of slavery in the British Islands)," unpublished thesis, University of London.

Lenta, M. (1981) "Jane Fairfax and Jane Eyre: Educating Women," *Ariel*, 12, 4: 27–41.

—— (1991) "All the Lighter Parts: Lady Ann Barnard's Letters from Cape Town," *Ariel*, 22, 2: 57–71.

Leslie, S. (1984) "Education for Girls in Barbados in 1850," unpublished seminar paper, University of the West Indies, Cave Hill: Dept. of History.

Lindfors, B. and R. Sander (eds.) (1993) *Twentieth Century Caribbean and Black African Writers*, Dictionary of Literary Biography, vol. 125, Detroit: Gale Research.

Long, E. (1774) *The History of Jamaica, or General Survey of the Antient and Modern State of That Island*, 3 vols., London: T. Lowndes.

McClintock, A. (1995) *Imperial Leather: Race, Gender and Sexuality in the Colonial Context*, New York: Routledge.

McCormack, W. J. (1985) "On Gulliver's Travels," in J. Hawthorn (ed.) *Narrative: From Malory to Motion Pictures*, London: Edward Arnold.

McDowell, D. and A. Rampersad (eds.) (1989) *Slavery and the Literary Imagination*, Baltimore: Johns Hopkins University Press.

McFarlane, J. E. C. (1956) *A Literature in the Making*, Kingston, Jamaica: Pioneer Press.

Marsden, P. (1788) *An Account of the Island of Jamaica; With Reflections on the Treatment, Occupation, and Provisions of the Slaves*, Newcastle: Author.

Marshall, P. (1969) *The Chosen Place, The Timeless People*, New York: Random House.

Mathurin-Mair, L. (1975) *The Rebel Woman in the British West Indies During the Period of Slavery*, Kingston: Institute of Jamaica.

Matthews, B. (1986) "Australian Colonial Women and their Autobiographies," in K. Holst Peterson and A. Rutherford (eds.) *A Double Colonization: Colonial and Post-Colonial Women's Writing*, Mundlestrup: Dangaroo.

Maxwell, A. (1991) "The Debate on Current Theories of Colonial Discourse," *Kunapipi* 13, 3: 70–84.

Midgley, C. (ed.) (1998) *Gender and Imperialism*, Manchester: Manchester University Press.

Mills, S. (1991) *Discourses of Difference: An Analysis of Women's Travel Writing and Colonialism*, New York: Routledge.

Mohanty, C. (1988) "Under Western Eyes: Feminist Scholarship and Colonial Discourses." *Feminist Review* 30: 61–88.

Moi, T. (1985) *Sexual/Textual Politics: Feminist Literary Theory*, London: Routledge.

Moore, B. (1998) "The Colonial Elites of Nineteenth Century Guyana," in H. Johnson and K. Watson (eds.) *The White Minority in the Caribbean*, Kingston, Jamaica: Ian Randle; London: James Currey.

Moore-Gilbert, B. (1997) *Postcolonial Theory: Contexts, Practice, Politics*, New York: Verso.

Mordecai, P. and B. Wilson (eds.) (1989) *Her True-True Name: An Anthology of Women's Writing from the Caribbean*, London: Heinemann.

Morton, P. (ed.) (1996) *Discovering the Women in Slavery: Emancipating Perspectives on the American Past*, Athens: University of Georgia Press.

Munro, J. (2002) *Heroes of the Telegraph*, Online. Available HTTP: <http://www.bookrags.com/books/htgrf/PART7.htm#TOP> (accessed June 8, 2002).

Naipaul, V. S. (1962) *The Middle Passage*, London: Andre Deutsch.

Nasta, S (ed.) (1991) *Motherlands: Black Women's Writing from Africa, the Caribbean and South Asia*, London: Women's Press; Brunswick, N.J.: Rutgers (1992).

National Union Catalogue: Pre-1956 Imprints (1978) Los Altos, CA: Mansell.

Newton, J. (1962) *The Journal of a Slave Trader 1750–54*, B. Martin and M. Spurrell (eds). London: Epworth Press.

Nunez-Harrell, E. (1985) "The Paradoxes of Belonging: The White West Indian Woman in Fiction." *Modern Fiction Studies* 31, 2 (Summer): 281–93.

O'Callaghan, E. (1986) " 'The Outsider's Voice': White Creole Women Novelists in the Caribbean Literary Tradition." *Journal of West Indian Literature*, 1, 1: 74–88.

—— (1993a) *Woman Version: Theoretical Approaches to West Indian Fiction by Women*, London: Macmillan.

—— (1993b) "Historical Fiction and Fictional History: Caryl Phillips's *Cambridge*," *Journal of Commonwealth Literature* 29, 2: 34–47.

—— (2002) "Introduction" to Freida Cassin, *With Silent Tread*, Oxford: Macmillan Caribbean.

Oliphant, Mrs. et al. (1897) *Women Novelists of Queen Victoria's Reign: A Book of Appreciations*, London: Hurst and Blackett.

Olsaussen, M. (1993) "Jean Rhys's Construction of Blackness as Escape from White Femininity in *Wide Sargasso Sea*," *Ariel* 24, 2 (April): 65–82.

Paravisini-Gebert, L. (1996) *Phyllis Shand Allfrey: A Caribbean Life*, New Brunswick, N.J.: Rutgers University Press.

Paravisini-Gebert, L. and I. Romero-Cesareo, (eds.) (2001) *Women at Sea: Travel Writing and the Margins of Caribbean Discourse*, New York: Palgrave.

Paravisini-Gebert, L. and O. Torres-Seda. (1993) *Caribbean Women Novelists: An Annotated Critical Bibliography*, Westport, Conn.: Greenwood Press.

Parry, B. (1987) "Problems in Current Theories of Colonial Discourse," *Oxford Literary Review* 9, 31: 27–58.

Paxton, N. (1992) "Disembodied Subjects: English Women's Autobiography Under the Raj," in S. Smith and J. Watson (eds.) *De/Colonizing the Subject: The Politics of Gender in Women's Autobiography*, Minneapolis: University of Minnesota Press.

Philip, M. N. (1990) "The Absence of Writing or How I Almost Became a Spy," in C. Boyce Davies and E. Savory Fido (eds.) *Out of the Kumbla: Caribbean Women and Literature*, Trenton, N. J.: Africa World Press.

Phillips, C. (1991) *Cambridge*, London: Bloomsbury.

Pickles, J. D. (1977) *The New Cambridge Bibliography of English Literature*, 5 vols., Cambridge: Cambridge University Press.

Poovey, M. (1988) *Uneven Developments: The Ideological Work of Gender in Mid-Victorian England*, Chicago: University of Chicago Press.

Pouchet Paquet, S. (1992a) "The Enigma of Arrival: *The Wonderful Adventures of Mrs Seacole in Many Lands*," *African American Review* 26, 4: 651–663.

—— (1992b) "The Heartbeat of a West Indian Slave: *The History of Mary Prince*," *African American Review* 26, 1: 131–46.

—— (1994) "Surfacing: The Counterhegemonic Project of Representation, Identification, and Resistance in Nineteenth-century African-Caribbean Women's Texts," *Caribbean Studies* 27, 3–4: 278–97.

—— (1999) "Settlers and Creoles: Yseult Bridges' *Child of the Tropics* and Jean Rhys's *Smile Please*," paper presented to Eighteenth Annual Conference on West Indian Literature, University of Puerto Rico, Rio Piedras: Department of English.

Pratt, A. with B. White et al. (1981) *Archetypal Patterns in Women's Fiction*, Bloomington: Indiana University Press.

Pratt, M. L. (1992) *Imperial Eyes: Travel Writing and Transculturation*, London: Routledge.

Ragatz, L. J. (1928) *The Fall of the Planter Class in the British Caribbean, 1763–1833: A Study in Social and Economic History*, New York: Century.

—— (1932) *A Guide for the Study of British Caribbean History 1763–1834, including the Abolition and Emancipation Movements*, Washington: University S. Government Printing Office.

Raiskin, J. (1991) "Jean Rhys: Creole Writing and Strategies of Reading," *Ariel* 22, 4: 51–67.

Ramchand, K. (1972) *The West Indian Novel and its Background*, London: Faber.

—— (1988) "West Indian Literary History: Literariness, Orality and Periodization," *Callaloo* 11, 1: 95–110.

Reddock, R. (1990) "Feminism, Nationalism, and the Early Women's Movement in the English-speaking Caribbean (with special reference to Jamaica and Trinidad and Tobago)," in S. Cudjoe (ed.) *Caribbean Women Writers: Essays from the first International Conference*, Wellesley, Mass.: Calaloux.

Renk, K. J. (1999) *Caribbean Shadows and Victorian Ghosts: Women's Writing and Decolonization*, Charlottesville: University Press of Virginia.

Rhys, J. (1979) *Smile Please: An Unfinished Autobiography*, London: Andre Deutsch; New York: Harper and Row.

—— (1985) *Letters 1931–66*, Francis Wyndham and Diana Melly (eds.) Harmondsworth: Penguin.

Richards, J. E. (1972) *Literary Efforts in Jamaica, 1900–1950*, Kingston: Institute of Jamaica.

Robinson-Walcott, K. (2001) "Locating Anthony Winkler," unpublished thesis, University of the West Indies (Mona).

Ross, L. (1996) *All the Blood is Red*, London: Angela Royal Publishing.

Rutherford, A., L. Jensen and S. Chew (eds.) 1994. *Into the Nineties: Postcolonial Women's Writing*, Mundelstrup: Dangaroo Press.

Salmonson, J. A. (1998) "Rose Petals, Drops of Blood: The Life of Marjorie Bowen, Mistress of the Macabre." Online. Available HTTP: <http://www.violetbooks.com/bowen.html> (accessed May 21, 2002).

Sani, R. M. (1972) "A Bibliographical Survey of the West Indian Novel," unpublished thesis, Western Michigan University.

Schlueter, J. and P. Schlueter (1988) *An Encyclopedia of British Women Writers*, London: St James Press.

Sheller, M. (2001) "Natural Hedonism: The Invention of Caribbean Islands as Tropical Playgrounds," in S. Courtman (ed.) *The Society for Caribbean Studies Annual Conference Papers*, 2. Online. Available HTTP: <http://www.scsonline.freeserve.co.uk/olvo2.html> (accessed June 20, 2002).

Shepherd V., B. Brereton and B. Bailey (eds.) (1995) *Engendering History: Caribbean Women in the Historical Perspective*, Kingston, Jamaica: Ian Randle; London: James Currey.

Showalter, E. (1978) *A Literature of Their Own: British Women Novelists from Brontë to Lessing*, London: Virago.

Simmonds, L. (1987) "Slave Higglering in Jamaica 1780–1834," *Jamaica Journal* 20, 1: 3–38.

Smilowitz, E. (1984) " 'Weary of Life and All My Heart's Dull Pain': The Poetry of Una Marson," in E. Smilowitz and R. Knowles (eds.) *Critical Issues in West Indian Literature: Selected Papers From West Indian Literature Conferences 1981–1983*, Parkersburg, IA: Caribbean Books.

Smilowitz, E. and R. Knowles (eds.) (1984) *Critical Issues in West Indian Literature: Selected Papers from West Indian Literature Conferences 1981–1983*, Parkersburg, IA: Caribbean Books.

Smith, S. (1992) "The Other Woman and the Racial Politics of Gender: Isak Dinesen and Beryl Markham in Kenya," in S. Smith and J. Watson (eds.) *De/Colonizing the Subject: The Politics of Gender in Women's Autobiography*, Minneapolis: University of Minnesota Press.

Smith, S. and J. Watson (eds.) (1992) *De/Colonizing the Subject: The Politics of Gender in Women's Autobiography*, Minneapolis: University of Minnesota Press.

Sollors, W. (1997) *Neither Black Nor White Yet Both: Thematic Explorations of Interracial Literature*, Oxford: Oxford University Press.

Spivak, G. C. (1985) "Three Women's Texts and a Critique of Imperialism," *Critical Inquiry*, 12,1 (Autumn): 243–61.

—— (1987) "French Feminism in an International Frame," in G. Spivak, *In Other Worlds: Essays in Cultural Politics*, New York: Methuen.

—— (1988) "Can the Subaltern Speak?" in C. Nelson and A. L. Grossberg (eds.) *Marxism and the Interpretation of Culture*, Illinois: University of Illinois Press.

Stevens, H. (ed.) (1870) *Bibliotheca Historica; or, A Catalogue of 500 volumes of Books and Manuscripts Relating Chiefly to the History and Literature of North and South America*, Boston, Mass.: Houghton and Co.; Cambridge: Riverside Press.

Stoler, A. L. (1992) "Rethinking Colonial Categories: European Communities and the Boundaries of Rule," in N. B. Dirks (ed.) *Colonialism and Culture*, Ann Arbor: University of Michigan Press.

Stuart, B. C. C. (1979) *Women of the Caribbean: A Bibliography*, Leiden: Dept. of Caribbean Studies, Royal Institute of Linguistics and Anthropology.

Sturtz, L. (1999) "The 'Dimduke' and the Duchess of Chandos: Gender and Power in Jamaican Plantation Management – A Case Study or, A Different Story of 'A Man [and his wife] from a Place Called Hope,'" *Revista/Reiview Interamericana* 29, 1–4. Online. Available HTTP: <http://www.sg.inter.edu/revista-ciscla/volume29/sturtz.html> (accessed August 6, 2002).

Sypher, F.J. (1999) "The Occultation of Letitia Elizabeth Landon," Online. Available HTTP: <http://www.cosmos-club.org/journals/1999/sypher.html> (accessed February 3, 2002).

Tate, C. (1993) *Domestic Allegories of Political Desire: The Black Heroine's Text at the Turn of the Century*, Oxford: Oxford University Press.

Thomas, H. (1999) "Black on White: Textual Spaces in Black Britain," *Wasafiri*, 29 (spring): 5–7.

Thorpe, M. (1975) "Beyond the Sargasso: The Significance of the Presentation of the Woman in the West Indian Novel," unpublished thesis, Queens University.

Tidrick, K. (1992) *Empire and the English Character*, London: Tauris.

Tiffin, H. (1978) "Mirror and Mask: Colonial Motifs in the Novels of Jean Rhys," *World Literature Written in English*, 17: 328–41.

Townsend, L. C. (1825) *Scrap Book on Negro Slaves*, Oxford: Rhodes House Library. Ms. Brit Emp. s.4.

Trotter, D. (1990) "Colonial Subjects," *Critical Quarterly*, 32, 3 (Autumn): 3–20.

Underhill, E. B. (1862) *The West Indies: Their Social and Religious Condition*, New York: Negro Universities Press, 1970.

Visel, R. (1988) "A Half-Colonization: The Problem of the White Colonial Woman Writer," *Kunapipi*, 10, 3: 39–45.

Walker Johnson, J. (1994) " 'A Voyage at Anchor': Among the Sang Melées in the West Indies," paper presented to Eighteenth Annual Conference of the Society for Caribbean Studies, Oxford: University of Oxford.

Walne, P. (ed.) (1973) *Guide to Manuscript Sources for the History of Latin America and the Caribbean in the British Isles*, London: Oxford University Press.

Watson, K. (1979) *The Civilised Island Barbados: A Social History 1750–1816*, Bridgetown: The Author.

—— (1998) "Salmagundis *vs* Pumpkins: White Politics and Creole Consciousness in Barbadian Slave Society, 1800–34," in H. Johnson and K. Watson (eds.) *The White Minority in the Caribbean*, Kingston, Jamaica: Ian Randle; London: James Currey.

—— (2000) *A Kind of Right to Be Idle: Old Doll, Matriarch of Newton Plantation*, Bridgetown: Department of History, University of the West Indies, Cave Hill and the Barbados Museum and Historical Society (Rewriting History Series, 3).

Watt, G. (1984) *The Fallen Woman in the Nineteenth-century English Novel*, London: Croom Helm.

Weiner, M. F. (1996) "Mistresses, Morality, and the Dilemmas of Slaveholding: The Ideology and Behavior of Elite Antebellum Women," in P. Morton (ed.) *Discovering the Women in Slavery: Emancipating Perspectives on the American Past*, Athens: University of Georgia Press.

Wertz, D. C. (1984) "Women and Slavery: A Cross-cultural Perspective," *International Journal of Women's Studies*, 7, 4: 372–84.

Whitlock, G. (1994) " 'A Most Improper Desire': Mary Gaunt's Journey to Jamaica," *Kunapipi*, XV, 3: 86–95.

—— (2000) *The Intimate Empire: Reading Women's Autobiography*, London: Cassell.

Who Was Who, Vol. I (1897–1915): A Companion to "Who's Who" (1935) 3rd edn., London: A. and C. Black.

Who Was Who, Vol. III (1929–1940): A Companion to "Who's Who" (1960) 3rd edn., London: Adam and Charles Black.

Who Was Who, Vol. II (1916–1928): A Companion to "Who's Who" (1962) 3rd edn., London: Adam and Charles Black.

Who Was Who: Cumulative Index 1897–1980 (1992) New York: St Martins Press.

P. Williams and L. Chrisman (eds.) (1993) *Colonial Discourse and Postcolonial Theory: A Reader*, New York: Harvester Wheatsheaf.

Williams, R. (1970) *Caribbean Fiction, 1900–1960*, Kingston: Institute of Jamaica.

Willis, R. (1995) "Tropical Calm," *Vogue* 161, 2367 (October): 108–12.

Wilson, E. (1987) Introduction to M. Warner Viera *Juletane*, London: Heinemann.

Watt, I. (1972) *The Rise of the Novel; Studies in Defoe, Richardson and Fielding*, London: Pelican.

Wynter, S. (1962) *The Hills of Hebron*, London: Jonathan Cape; New York: Simon and Schuster.

—— (1990) "Beyond Miranda's Meanings: Un/silencing the 'Demonic Ground' of Caliban's 'Woman'," in C. Boyce Davies and E. Savory Fido (eds.) *Out of the Kumbla: Caribbean Women and Literature*, New Jersey: Africa World Press.

Young, R. (1990) *White Mythologies: Writing History and the West*, London: Routledge.

Index